Agricultural Productivity and Regional Imbalances

AGRICULTURAL PRODUCTIVITY AND REGIONAL IMBALANCES

Dr. Tanusree Chaudhuri

ABHIJEET PUBLICATIONS
NEW DELHI 110002

ABHIJEET PUBLICATIONS
4658-A, 21 Ansari Road, New Delhi 110002
Phone: 011-22960492, 65698474
E-mail: abhijeetpublication@gmail.com

AGRICULTURAL PRODUCTIVITY AND REGIONAL IMBALANCES

First Published 2012

ISBN 978-93-81136-60-7

PRINTED IN INDIA

Published by J.K. Singh for Abhijeet Publications, New Delhi-110002, Lasertypeset by Gaurav Graphics, Delhi and Printed at Himanshu Printers, Delhi.

Dedicated to my Father in Law

Late Dr. Tushar Kanti Chaudhuri

Acknowledgements

Since the beginning of the research work I have received valuable advice, comments, criticism and suggestions from a variety of people. In particular I would like to acknowledge the guidance I have received from my supervisor Prof. Pranab K. Chakravarti.

This research work required extensive data support form Govt. Sources. To make these data available I like to specially thank Mr. Pranab K. Poddar, Computor, Evaluation Wing Directorate of Agriculture, Govt. of West Bengal (Malda Office). His help was not only restricted to make the data available but also to provide valuable insight from his career.

The other key personnel and offices which helped me in collecting these informations are Mr. Ananta Hazra, DAIO, Principal Agricultural Office Malda, Mr. Manik Das Gupta, SAO, Sub-Divisional Agricultural Office Malda, the staff of District Planning and Rural Development Office, Bureau of Applied Economics and Statistics, Govt. of West Bengal, District Land and Land Reform Office, Malda, Govt. Records Room Staff, Zilla Parishad, Mango Development Office, to name a few.

I take this opportunity to thank the Library staff of North Bengal University for extending cooperation to use the library facilities extensively. A special thanks to Mrs. Vijaya Rajhansa, the Librarian of Mumbai University for permitting me to use the library for the research work.

On the personal front my sincere thanks to Mr. Anjan Chakravarti and Mrs. Prajana Paramita Sarkar Chakravarți for their support to make this study possible.

Thanks is too small a word to express my gratitude for my parents and my in-laws, whose continuous encouragements enabled me to face all odds.

Dr. Tanusree Chaudhuri

Preface

Agricultural productivity is an important concept that has been explored by geographers for various geographies. Through this thesis of mine I have attempted to analyse this concept and apply them for the development of a backward district of West Bengal, Malda. Along with agricultural productivity it has been observed that there is a regional imbalance in the district. An attempt is made to assess these imbalances and remedial measures have been suggested.

The study has been divided into the following nine chapters.

Chapter I Introduction: Presents the problem of varying agricultural productivity in the district and the regional imbalances present in the district. It also discusses the objective, scope and approach of the study alongwith the overview of related literature and models applied in the study.

Chapter II Physical Setting: Discusses the variability and similarity of a) Structure and relief b) Drainage c) Physical division-the terrain d) Soils e) Climate amongst the blocks and the regions of the district.

Chapter III Non-Physical Determinants: Discusses the various non-physical determinants viz. a) Technological factors – irrigation, other inputs, levels of agricultural modernization b) Population characteristics c) Cultural factors - ownership holding, tenural arrangement farm family characteristics and labour force d) Infrastructural services - marketing facilities, transport and accessibility and credit facilities. It shows the similarity and dissimilarity of the factors across regions and attempts to relate these determinants with overall productivity of the region.

Chapter IV Perspective of Regional Agriculture: Gives and overview of a) Land use profile b) Ground water potential c) Intensive cultivation programmes in the district.

Chapter V, Cropping Pattern, Crop Combination Region: Attempts to analyse the cropping pattern of the district and the direction in which the pattern is moving. It specifically analyses the growth trend of area under individual crops. Crop combination a major determinant of overall productivity is also discussed in this chapter. To enable comparison of crop combination pattern the analysis has been performed for two periods, Period I (1993-94 to 1996-97) and Period II (1997-98 to 2000-01).

Chapter VI, Concept of Agricultural Productivity: This chapter gives a conceptual overview of agricultural productivity. Herein the productivity of individual factors of production viz. land, labour, capital have been discussed alongwith the concept of total factor productivity.

Chapter VII, Measurement of Agricultural Productivity: Deals with the measurement techniques of agricultural productivity and analyses the pattern of productivity in the district. Herein productivity index of individual crops have been analysed and the significance of growth trend of yield rates examined.

Chapter VIII, Major Findings- Problems and Prospects: As the name suggests discusses the findings of the study, illustrates the problems the regions face and their prospects in terms of agricultural growth.

Chapter IX, Corrective Measures Suggested: Suggests the measures that need to adopted at micro and macro level for he improvement of overall productivity and bridging the productivity differential amongst the regions.

I expect this attempt of mine to analyse agricultural productivity and regional imbalance for the district of Malda will be useful to researchers and policy makers in stimulating further discussion and methodological development.

Dr. Tanusree Chaudhuri

Contents

Contents

Abbreviations

AMDP	Accelerated Maize Development Programme
ARDB	Agricultural Rural Development Bank
APO	Anchal Pradhan Office
BDO	Block Development Office
BSF	Block Seed Farm
CARG	Compounded Annual Rate of Growth
DTW	Deep Tube Well
GP	Gram Panchayat
GCA	Gross Cropped Area
HC	Health Centre
HYV	High Yielding Variety
IARI	Indian Agricultural Research Institute
ICDP	Integrated Cereal Development Programme
ISDS	Integrated Seed Development Scheme
JCI	Jute Corporation Of India
NPDP	National Pulse Development Programme
NSC	National Seed Corporation
NWDPRA	National Watershed Development Programme in Rain fed Areas
NSA	Net Sown Area

NPK	Nitrogen Phosphate Potash
OC	Organic Carbon
PRA	Participatory Resource Appraisal
PAO	Principal Agricultural Office
PWD	Public Works Department
RLI	River Lifting Irrigation
SMS	Seeds Multiplication Scheme
SHG	Self Help Group
STW	Shallow Tube Well
SJDP	Special Jute Development Programme
SSC	State Seed Corporation
SKU	Stock Keeping Unit
SAO	Sub-division Agricultural Office
SCDS	Sugar Cane Development Scheme
TFP	Total Factor Productivity
ZP	Zilla Parishad

1

Introduction

a) Presentation of the Problem

The district of Malda, located in the middle part of the West Bengal and drained by the Mahananda, the Kalindri and the Ganga is ideal for agricultural operation. The ecological setting viz. landscape, soil and climate, have made it more farming oriented. This apart, sericulture and the cultivation of mango have made the district famous. The physical variation along with the edaphic variation has controlled regional agricultural scene. With the motive of studying these variations in mind and as a researcher from this district, the agricultural pattern in Malda has been chosen for an in-depth study.

Malda district is one of the most under-developed districts of West-Bengal. Agriculture is the mainstay of the district's population. Majority of this population is dependent upon agriculture. One of the major objectives of the development of agriculture in Malda district is to improve the living standard of the people in the rural areas through effective agricultural operations.

This district is divided into two subdivisions, 15 administrative blocks, 11 police stations, 15 Panchayat samities and 147-gram panchayats. Physiographically, Malda district is divided into three regions 'Tal', 'Barind' and 'Diara'. The following table 1.1 shows the region wise distribution of blocks of the district.

Table 1.1: Natural Regions of Malda District

Physiographic Region	*TAL*	*BARIND*	*DIARA*
Blocks	Harischandrapur – I	Gazole	English bazar
	Harischandrapur – II	Bamangola	Manikchak
	Chanchal – I	Habibpur	Kalichak – I
	Chanchal – II	Old-Malda	Kalichak – II
	Ratua – I		Kalichak – III
	Ratua – II		
Nos of Blocks	6 (Six)	4 (Four)	5 (Five)
Total area in hectare	1,14,099	1,12,188	1,32,761

Source :- Agricultural Scenario – P.A.O. Malda (1999)

The low-lying area of the northwestern side of the district is known as **'Tal'**. Comparative highland on the east of Mahananda river is known as the **'Barind'** and the flat land on the western side of the Mahananda is known as the **'Diara'**. Map No-1.1 shows the different regions (with blocks) in this district.

There are certain areas in Malda district which are relatively affluent and the farmers are well to do, while there are other regions in which the rural population, in spite of their hard work, lives in poverty. So a unique feature of the district's agriculture is that production and productivity of various crops vary in different regions. Variation of the cropping pattern too is observed in district. The major determinants of these variations are a number of physical factors like relief, drainage, soil and climate. On the other hand non-physical determinants such as technological factors, population characteristics, cultural factors and infrastructural services also affect productivity.

In the district the farmers lack the knowledge about soil and water conservation, and land management practices are inefficient. Due to low quality of inputs, the farmers get a low return in the form of yield. Poor irrigation facilities, absence of farm building, agricultural machinery, market and lack of farmers' initiative, the district has lagged in respect of agricultural production and productivity.

In the first look these parameters are not likely to vary in any definite pattern within a district as 3,59,048 hectare area of the district is not enough to introduce wide variations. But the pattern of the agricultural production as well as productivity is not uniform in the district. The variations are found mainly due to variation with respect to physical and non-physical determinants.

Map No. 1.1

Blocks & Regions of Malda

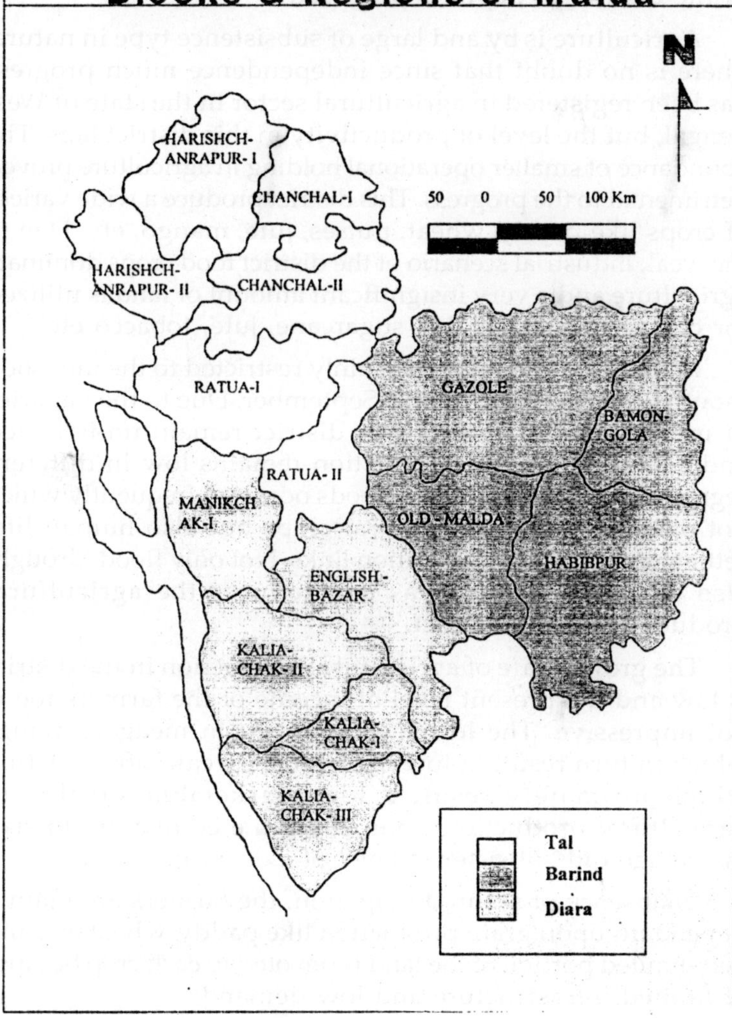

b) Scope, Approaches and Objectives

Agricultural productivity in any region is an outcome of the interaction of two main factors – natural and human. The district of Malda is characterised by environmental homogeneity but other physical factors like relief, drainage, soil are markedly different from region to region as well as from block to block. In this district some micro level spatial variations also are found, so studying the pattern of variation of the district in depth is proposed.

Agriculture is by and large of subsistence type in nature. There is no doubt that since independence much progress has been registered in agricultural sector in the state of West Bengal, but the level of productivity in this district lags. The abundance of smaller operational holding in agriculture proved detrimental to the progress. This district produce a wide variety of crops like paddy, wheat, pulses, jute, mango, etc. Due to the weak industrial scenario of the district food crops dominate agriculture and a very insignificant amount of land is utilized for commercial crops like sugarcane, jute, tobacco etc.

In this district rainfall is mainly restricted to the monsoon months, i.e. mid-June to mid-September. Due to the vagaries of monsoon vast areas of this district remain un-irrigated and as a consequence production remains low in different regions. In the last few years floods occurred frequently which not only damaged agricultural crops but also human life, settlements and communication links. Not only flood, drought also affect extensive areas and reduces the agricultural production in this district.

The growth rate of agricultural production in the district is low and the present level of income of the farmers too is not impressive. The low income result in meager savings which in turn result in low investment, weak infrastructure which ultimately result a low marketable surplus in agricultural production, compelling the cultivators to stay in the age-old subsistence level of existence.

In absence of secured irrigation, the farmers are mainly dependant upon grain production like paddy, wheat etc. and very limited portion of the land is devoted to each crop because of limited infrastructure and low demand.

Under the prevailing condition it is important to examine the productivity of individual crops and the spatial variation within the district. It is obvious that agricultural productivity along with cropping pattern varies from one region to another as well from block to block.

The scope of the present study is to determine the variation of productivity of crops within the district and find out the various causes for such variations and accordingly suggest remedial measures.

Such an analysis will help to increase the production as well as the productivity. In order to accelerate development, appropriate strategy based on the causes of backwardness, has to be identified. The planning of irrigation, transportation, communication, storage facilities, marketing and socio-economic changes have to be developed at the block level as well as at the district level.

The present agrarian situation in Malda district has to sustain not only its rural population particularly those directly dependent on agriculture but also has to make agriculture economically viable and attractive. The present study thus aims to indicate different physical and non-physical factors that are originally low in this district and so affect agricultural production as well as productivity. Therefore the main objectives of the study are:

Objectives:

1. To analyse the present status of geo-economic regions of Malda district on the basis of their Physiographic variations.
2. To analyse the present status of agricultural crops in terms of production and productivity as well as their regional variations.
3. To identify various physical and non-physical factors controlling agricultural productivity of different regions.
4. To identify the input-output relationship in the productivity region.

5. To assess the region wise potentialities of crop productivity.
6. To suggest the remedial measures for reducing the regional imbalance and maximizing the production and productivity

c) Methodology

With the objective of analyzing the agricultural productivity and its variation in the district of we propose to analyze secondary data along with the primary data. This section covers i) area of the study, ii) sampling design, iii) primary data collection and iv) primary data management v) analysis approaches of secondary data vi) data sources.

i) Area of the Study:

This study has been carried out in the rural areas of Malda district centrally located in West-Bengal, a state in eastern India. Map 1.2 provides the location map of Malda. This district is primarily a rural district with agriculture as the main source of income. Other than agricultural activities the district has *bidi* and silk industry. The district has an international boundary of 204 km. with Bangladesh and state boundary with Bihar. The other socio-economic profile of the district is provided in Table 1.2.

Table 1.2: Socio-Economic Profile of Malda District

Particulars	*Value*
Total Area (sq km)	3583
Population (1991)	26,37,032
Male	13,60,541
Female	12,76,491
Urban	24,50,495
Rural	1,86,537
Density (1991) (nos per sq km)	736
Religion (1991) (% of total population)	
Hindu	52.25
Muslim	47.49
Others	0.26

Urban Literacy Rate (1991) (%)	73.11
Rural Literacy Rate (1991) (%)	32.57
Number of female per 100 male	94
Number of Scheduled Caste	4,77,896
Number of Scheduled Tribe	1,71,326
Main Workers as % of Total Population (1991)	31.64

Map No 1.2

Location Map: Malda District

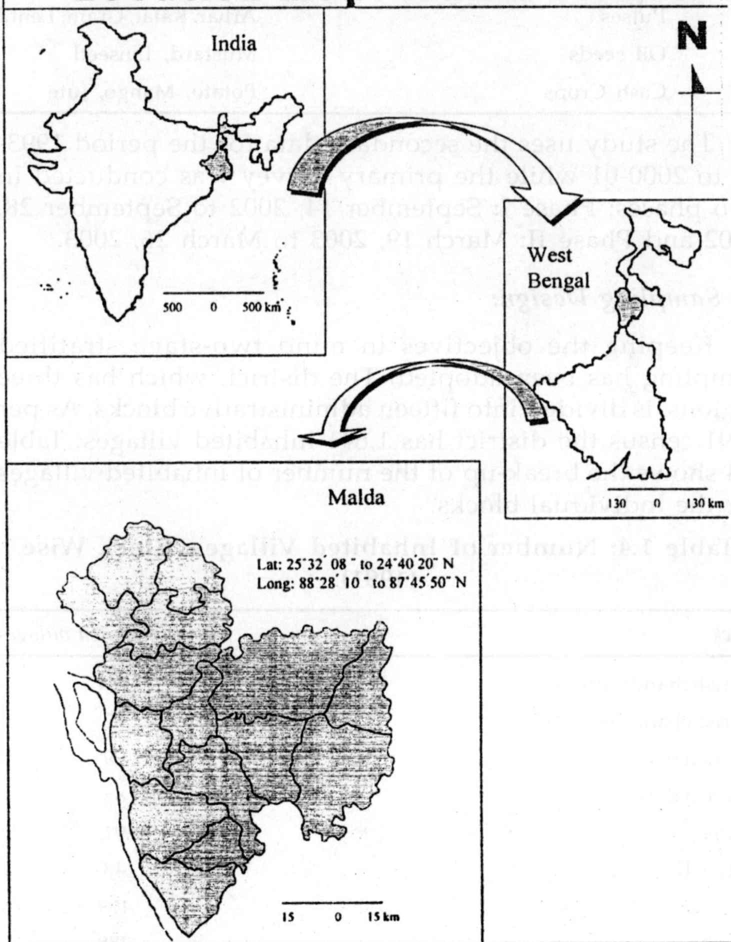

The district, which is primarily dependant on agriculture, cultivates various crops but in our analysis we will be considering thirteen major crops forming four crop groups. Table 1.3 provides the list of crops and their respective crop groups considered.

Table 1.3: Major crops Cultivated in Malda

Sl no.	*Crop Group*	*Crops*
1	Cereals	Aus, Aman, Boro, Wheat
2	Pulses	Arhar, Kalai, Gram, Lentil
3	Oil seeds	Mustard, Linseed
4	Cash Crops	Potato, Mango, Jute

The study uses the secondary data for the period 1993-94 to 2000-01 while the primary survey was conducted in two phases: Phase I: September 14, 2002 to September 28, 2002 and Phase II: March 19, 2003 to March 26, 2003.

ii) Sampling Design:

Keeping the objectives in mind two-stage stratified sampling has been adopted. The district, which has three regions, is divided into fifteen administrative blocks. As per 1991 census the district has 1,641 inhabited villages. Table 1.4 shows the break-up of the number of inhabited villages for the individual blocks.

Table 1.4: Number of Inhabited Villages: Block Wise (1991)

Block	*No. of inhabited villages*
Harishchandrapur I	104
Harishchandrapur II	72
Chanchal I	99
Chanchal II	85
Ratua I	91
Ratua II	48
Tal	499
Gazole	288

Bamongola	233
Habibpur	141
Old Malda	114
Barind	776
English Bazar	109
Manikchak	74
Kaliachak I	60
Kaliachak II	57
Kaliachak III	66
Diara	366
Malda	1641

Source: Government of India Census, 1991

In the study we have found that, the physical setting in terms of climate is same across the district while structure and relief, drainage and soils vary amongst the regions but these broad parameters are comparatively similar within a region. The blocks within each region vary in terms of socio-economic parameters. With the objective of understanding the variation amongst the blocks the first stage of sampling of villages has been designed.

The villages are sampled out of the strata defined by the blocks; and the desired sample is selected from the sample frame using simple random sampling approach. As regards the minimum number of sample villages to be covered under the study, among all the observations pertaining to a variable, lowest prevalence was anticipated as 40%. Accordingly taking into account 45% relative precision, required minimum sample size came to be 29 at 95% level of confidence. The formula used for this is

$$N = \left(\frac{\left(Z_{(1-\alpha)/2} \right)^2}{L^2} \right) * PQ$$

where $\left(Z_{1-\alpha/2}\right)$ = Normal deviate value at α level of significance

α = 5% level of significance

P = Anticipated lowest prevalence of 45%

Q = 1-P

L = 45% of P

All the blocks are to be covered in the district so no sampling of block was done. To distribute these 29 sample villages amongst the blocks we use the simplistic assumption of variation of village properties across blocks to be similar. We have calculated the N/n ratio for the district as a whole wherein N is total number of inhabited villages while n is total number of sample villages i.e. 1164/29 = 56.6. Using this relationship of 1 sample village for every 57 villages, sample size for individual blocks have been determined.

Using descrete random number generation mechanism (Microsoft Excel) the sample villages are identified. For this the villages were alphabetically arranged and assigned serial number for each block. Table1.5 shows the list of sample villages, block wise.

For the 2nd stage of sampling we have used simple random sampling of respondents. For the purpose of 2nd stage of sampling we have considered the total number of rural household. The desired sample size is selected using the random walk approach as regard the minimum sample size the approach adopted is similar to that of the 1st stage sampling wherein among all the observation pertaining to various variable lowest prevalence was anticipated at 50 percent, accordingly taking into account 10 percent relative precision, required minimum sample size came to be 384 at 95 percent level of confidence. The following formula has been used

$$N = \left(\frac{\left(Z_{(1-\alpha)/2} \right)^2}{L^2} \right) * PQ$$

Table 1.5: List of Sample Villages

Block	*No. of villages to be surveyed*	*Random Numbers*	*Sample Villages*		
Harishchandrapur I	2	43, 47	Ishadpur	Jhikadanga	
Harishchandrapur II	1	51	Msaldaha		
Chanchal I	2	31, 93	Gauri Pur	Sreepur	
Chanchal II	2	30,38	Damanbhiti	Gangadebi	
Ratua I	2	43	Gobindapur		
Ratua II	1	2	Ballabhpur		
Tal	10				
Gazole	4	28, 150, 183, 269	Baghi Pur Kutub Pur	Jibjalsar Sara Kandar	
Bamongola	3	98, 105, 124	Mirzapur	Nandinadaha	Salalpur
Habibpur	3	59, 86, 269	Dahar Langi	Gurila	SolaDanga
Old Malda	2	8, 67	Balia	Mabarakpur	
Barind	12				
English Bazar	2	4, 127	Arapur	Uttar Gobindapur	
Manikchak	2	10, 88	Bishanpur-Srirampara	Uttar Dharampur	
Kaliachak I	1	2	Alinagar		
Kaliachak II	1	35	Jotkasturi		
Kaliachak III	1	17	Chak Mailpur		
Diara	7				
Malda	29				

where $\left(Z_{1-\alpha/2}\right)$ = Normal deviate value at α level of significance

α = 5% level of significance

P = Anticipated lowest prevalence of 50%

11

Q = 1-P

L = 10% of P

In view of unavoidable no response rate of about 5 percent it is proposed to cover a sample of 400 instead of 384. This 400 samples gives a N/n ratio of 0.1 as N i.e. total number of rural households is estimated to be 4000 plus. So for individual village level 10 percent of total household were surveyed. The respondents were randomly chosen using the random walk principle.

iii) Data Collection Instrument:

The data collection instrument has been designed with the objective stated earlier in mind. Two instruments were designed a) Individual questionnaire and b)Village level questionnaire with the objective of collecting data at the village level and at individual level.

iv) Data Management Analysis:

After receiving the filled instrument from the field, they were reviewed and coded. The data was entered into data entry package. Data was then cleaned and checked for consistency and then analysis conducted using SPSS and Microsoft Excel.

Analysis is presented in the form of bi-variate cross tabulation and multivariate regression analysis.

v) Analysis Approaches of Secondary Data

For the purpose of secondary data analysis the methodology applied varied with the objective of the respective sections e.g. for the purpose of analysing the status of physical determinants in the district cross tabulation have been used. While finalizing the cropping pattern the share of top six crops is shown in the pie diagram. To analyse the change of cropping pattern with respect to individual crop groups viz. cereals, pulses, oil seeds and cash crops, radar diagram has been used. To analyse the significance of growth of area cultivatied of indidvidual crop the following exponential function $Y=AB_t$ was fitted to the data to compute the compound growth rates, to get Compound growth rate (r) =(Antilog b) 1* 100. The compound growth rates were tested for their significance by the students 't' test.

For the purpose of identifying crop combination for each block and region Doi's method of minimum sum of square deviations (Σd^2) of the actual crop share from the theoretical base has been applied.

For the purpose of measuring agricultural productivity, productivity index of individual crop at block / region level has been calculated using the following relationship. Productivity index has been calculated using the relation productivity

Index

$$\frac{Y}{Y_n} \div \frac{A}{A_n}$$

Where Y, is the total production of the selected crop/ region.

Y_n is the total production of the same crop on district level.

A is the total cropped area of the particular crop in the block/region area.

A_n total crop area for the same crop at district level

The yield growth trend has been analysed using exponential function $Y=AB_t$ was fitted to the data to compute the compound growth rates.

vi) Data Sources:

The relevant data for the district have been collected from the following sources

Principal Agricultural Office, Malda

Sub-Division Agricultural Office, Malda

Socio Economic Evaluation Office, Malda

Bureau of Applied Economics and Statistics, Malda

Government of India Census,1991

Carter's Gazetteer, 1928 to 1935

Office of Asst. Engineer, Agri Irrigation, Malda

P.W.D. (Roads), Malda

Zilla Parishad, Malda

District Agricultural Marketting Office, Malda

d. Survey of Literature

Geography has advanced from a more descriptive to an analytical stage where scientific techniques of regional analysis are applicable. The regional approach to present day analytical geography is not only practicable but also desirable and indispensable. Very recently interdisciplinary approach of agricultural geography of various regions at micro and macro levels have been attempted to evaluates and develop plans for regional planning and growth.

In India, particularly in West Bengal, the West Bengal State Planning Board in its various reports has made appraisal of physical resource. But they have not undertaken specific study at micro level. Academic institutions of higher education in their respective disciplines filled this gap. In most of the cases, land use and agricultural landscape were the main theme of researches and investigations. Notable among the pioneer geographers are studies of Dr. B. Banerjee, Dr. Md. Safi, Dr. P. Dayal, Dr. S. Sharma, Dr. D. P. Bharadwaj and Prof. S. P. Chatterjee (land utilization in the district of 24 Parganas W. Bengal, 1946). Work of Dr. M. Safi (1960, 1966, 1970, 1972,1974, 1979) on land use and nutrition and agricultural productivity are worthy of mention. His work is available in published form and is serving as useful guide in land use survey. He proposed a scheme based on sampling techniques suitable for vast country like India. His productivity analysis in respect of regional imbalances in Uttar Pradesh is useful for agricultural geographers. Encouraged by his pioneering studies many researches in this field have been undertaken by geographers both at a macro and micro level in their respective states. In agricultural geography Ali Mohammad has made a substantial contribution through his work (1972) 'Agricultural Efficiency Regions - case study of Kashmir valley'. The study aims to classify the Kashmir valley into agricultural efficiency regions on the basis of per hectare productivity.

It is important to mention the works of S.S. Bhatia (1965, 1967, 1970), B.N. Sinha (1975) H.S. Singh (1960) B.N. Ganguly (1964), B.K. Roy (1967, 1968,1973), V. R. Singh (1979), L.R.Singh (1964, 1975, 1976), M.F. Siddique (1967), A. Kumar (1993) Reddy N.R.S. and Reddy N. Bk (1993). Trends in spatial variation of H.Y.V. Rice in the Malda district has been done by Dr. C. Chattaraj in 1996 .

In agricultural geography Jasbir Singh has made a substantial contribution through his published books – 'Agricultural Atlas of India (1974)', Hussain Majid has analysed (1976), Agricultural productivity of India – An explanatory Analysis, R. S. Tripathi and R. P. Tiwari (1988) presented spatial inequalities in Agricultural profile of Vashishthi River Basin (Maharashtra). Another study, Regional disparities of Agricultural development in M.P. was carried out by C.K.Jain (1979).

A number of valuable studies have been made in the field of cropping pattern, agricultural production, and the problems of food and nutrition by the teachers, research scholars and students of department of geography of various universities like Aligarh, Banaras, Burdwan, Calcutta, Visva-Bharati, Madras, Patna etc. In various publications of the ICSSR, Survey of Research in geography and Journal of Abstract and Review, contributions in the field of productivity and agricultural geography are available. Other records of useful works on productivity are not mentioned here. Some of them have been published in various journals of India and a few notable works are mentioned in bibliography of the present work.

Survey of the relevant literature on agricultural productivity and regional imbalance reveals that very few work have been done on this aspect of agricultural geography. Most of the works have been confined to productivity aspect of agriculture at state, district and block levels. Moreover, it covers only one or two crops or four crops only, yet the regional imbalances in respect of physical and non-physical factors which affect agriculture productivity has been even less in number.

e) Models Applicable

India is a developing country. Most of her population and total workforce are engaged in primary occupation i.e. agriculture. Her economy totally depends upon rural sectors, which accounts for nearly about eighty percent of her total area. So the regional development in a developing country like India can be achieved by keeping attention to the development of the rural sectors.

Naturally the development of any region in India is based on the transformation of rural socio-economy. In early days the development programmes started by enriching the agricultural base of the rural economy. After developing the agriculture, attention was paid to the industrial activity (Millar and Parkins (1954).

Different geographers have studied the above-mentioned views of development from different angles. To eradicate the regional imbalances different views have been postulated to chalk out the right path on which the agricultural development as well as the rural transformation may be achieved. Different scholars built their models regarding the agricultural development, which are analysed in the present section.

Von-Thunen's Model

Von-Thunen tried to evaluate a theory of viable land use

pattern around town and villages situated in Germany. His model postulates how and why agricultural land use varies with the distance from a market centre. Regarding this model he developed two hypotheses:

(a) The intensity and productivity of crop decline with the distance from the market. He observed that if the non-physical determinants of agriculture like fertilizer, money, labour, irrigation etc. inputs are applied in a proper dosages then that may increase productivity and intensity of crop.

(b) The type of land use vary with the distance from the market.

Von-Tthunen's model is based on certain assumptions. These are

i. An isolated state, cut-off from out side influences.

ii. A single large city dominates as the sole urban market. The entire demand of crops for the people of the city should be met by the hinterland of that city only.

iii. All the farmers receives same price for a particular crop at anytime at any part of that agricultural region.

iv. The agricultural area should possess an uniform level land with equal fertility.

v. Farming is conducted rationally.

vi. There is only one form of transport that is horse drawn cart or boat.

vii. The town existed in the centre of the agricultural land, which had no counter magnets in its vicinity.

This model examines the location of different crops in different parts of the region in relation to the market. The location of crops is determined by the market price, transport cost, productivity per hectare. The transport cost varies with the bulk and the perishibility of the product. The remunerative and market oriented crops which have highest locational rent per unit of land should be preferred for cultivation because these crops give large amount of return. So the farmers can maximize their profit motive. If two crops have identical cost of production and productivity per hectare, but due to bulkiness or perishibility these may have different transport cost and market price in that case the crop with high transport cost market price should be cultivated near the market centre. On the basis of these assumptions he constructed a land use model, having a number of concentric belts around each town. His order of the developed belts are:

a) Market gardening
b) Wood products
c) Intensive crop cultivation
d) Pasture and dairying
e) Crop-rotation with three field system
f) Cattle rearing for meat.

Von–Thunen incorporated two examples in his modified model. One navigable river may flow through this region, where transport is speedier and cost is only 1/10th as much as on land and there may be smaller city or market centres, which can act as counter magnet to the main market centre.

Theoritical Criticism

His model is mainly based on a micro level study of the phenomena. His model is not always applicable in Indian situation. It is found in many cases that the cropping intensity decreases with increase of distance. On the other hand the alarming growth rate of population in India, dairy zone is practically absent. Moreover, uniform transport system, market prices are not available. Lastly, his model is neither diagnostic nor predictive. It is a descriptive model only.

Empirical Criticism

Though he considered the economic indicators to explain the cropping intensity but the other indicators like physical as well as ecological and also resource problems are neglected in his model. On the other hand, various socio-politico-administrative problems are not stressed in his model. Another drawback of his model is that he neglected, the problems of tenants and land inequality, which also affect the cropping, pattern, production etc.

Olaf Jonasson's Model

Jonasson modified the model of Von-Thunen relating to the economic rent of land in respect of the distance from market centre and means of transportation. He empirically studied that the hay and pasture regions are located at the developed regions where large number of industries produce different types of necessary items. Around this zone other regions produce different items, which spread in concentric zones where various grains grow, pasturing activities are performed and aforestation are made. His model also describes the potential land use pattern around an isolated city in Europe. He depicts different zones of production.

Zone – I	The city itself and immediate environs, green house floriculture.
Zone – II	Truck farming, fruits, potato and tobacco.
Zone – III	Dairy products and cattle
Zone – IV	General grain farming, hay, livestock
Zone – V	Bread cereal and flour for all
Zone – VI	Cattle, horses and sheep, salt, smoked, refrigerated and canned meats, bones, and hides.
Zone – VIII	The outermost peripheral area is forests.

Theoretical Criticism

Like Von–Thunen, Jonasson also adopted a descriptive model in the field of Agricultural productivity and land use pattern. But when the model is applied by his followers for the purpose of rural development and planning in the developing countries, it is found that the model can not be accepted in the under developed countries for the said purpose.

Empirical Criticism.

The above model is not applicable on the socio-economic structure of India because the land use pattern mentioned in his model is not found in this country. On the other hand he over looked the social forces, which influence the land use pattern in the country. Moreover social forces affect the distribution of holding, tenancy system and land use pattern also. For example in Malda district which comprises of fifteen blocks, the land of some of these blocks are fertile and can respond well if irrigation and other inputs are available but the drought, flood and land erosion degraded the land which is often converted into waste land. Among fifteen blocks some blocks are found where agricultural productivity is medium but cropping intensity is high. This may be due to the fact that farmers are not able to get production as per their expectation due to the vagaries of monsoon. So Jonasson's model cannot be of much help in an underdeveloped country like India.

The above discussion reveals the fact that different scientist realized that the agricultural development which depends upon the agricultural production and productivity can be achieved through viable land use pattern.

2

Physical Setting

Agriculture has always dominated the socioeconomic and cultural landscapes of the world and has claimed most of the man's working hours. Agriculture in India is not merely an occupation or business proposition for the people, it is a tradition a way of life, which for the centuries has shaped their thoughts, out-look and culture. An attempt therefore, needs to be made to identify, classify and describe the various forms of agricultural determinants and to assess regional and locational variations in agricultural activities. In this chapter these determinants are analysed for Malda district, which is one of the most underdeveloped district of West-Bengal, and is heavily dependent on agriculture.

The district lies between 25° 32′ 08″ and 24° 40′ 20″ north latitude and 88° 28′ 10″ and 87° 45′ 50″ east longitude. The district is bounded on the north by Purnea and Dinajpur districts, on the east by Dinajpur and Rajshashi districts, on the south by Murshidabad and the west by Murshidabad and Purnea districts. The physical setting of this district can be best identified with the help of the physical divisions, structure and relief, drainage, soils, climate, water bodies etc.

a) Structure and Relief

The district is situated on the western part of the alluvium filled gap between the Rajmahal hills on the west and the

Garo hills on the east. The entire area is covered by alluvium, which is of two different ages displaying different physical and physiographic characteristics.

The river Mahananda flowing north and south roughly divides the district into two equal parts – the Rarh and the Barind. The eastern part of Mahananda is called Barendra (the Barind) and western part of Mahananda is called the Rarh. West of the Mahananda, the Kalindri River flowing west and east from the Ganga again divides the district into two well-defined parts. North of the Kalindri the distinguishing natural feature is the 'Tal' land. The most striking natural feature is the continuous line of islands and accretion formed in the bed of Ganga, by its ever-changing course and known as the Diara.

In the north is the alluvial fan surface of the Himalayan foot – hills the Piedmont alluvial plain, formed by the streams descending from the mountains. The recent alluvium found in the western part of the district is typically dark loosely compacted and has a high water content and variable but appreciable quantities of organic material.

The pleistocene deposits can be readily distinguished from the recent alluvium. They generally stand above monsoon floods and are drained by relatively few streams, which have developed distinctive meandering courses. Local relief consists of well oxidized massive argillaceous beds typically reddish brown or tan and mottled and some times weathering yellowish. Kankar and Pisolitic ferruginous concretion are plentifully distributed throughout this formation.

There are no hills in the district other than a few elevated tracts with an elevation from 15.24 to 30.48 metre. Apart from these undulations the district is a low lying plain covered with a succession of settlement sites with their adjacent fields and swampy tracts.

The district slopes generally from the north to south. The highest elevation of this district is 39.7 meters and the elevations range between 30 and 39 meters above sea levels. In other places of the district the elevation varies between 23.54 meters and 38 meters.

b) Drainage

The main rivers of the district are all of Himalayan or sub-Himalayan origin and flow in southerly direction. Mahananda, the next most important river after the Ganga, flows north to south, through the middle of the district. The Kalindri, the Tangan and the Punarbhava are the tributaries of the Mahananda. Two other streams of the Kalindri are the Pagla and the Bhagirathi. Map 2.1 shows the drainage pattern of Malda district. A short account of the rivers of the district is given below.

i. *The Ganga:* The Ganga first touches the district as it sweeps south round the Rajmahal hills. At this point it is connected with the Kalindri, though at the present much of the Ganga water does not finds it's the connection having been silted up considerably as the Ganga has receded further to the west. About two miles below Rajmahal the Ganga sends off a small stream the Chota Bhagirathi. A little way further down near Gour the Ganga sends off, also to the last, a larger branch, the Pagla into which chota-Bhagirathi ultimately flows. During the rains they carry huge volume of water to rejoin the Ganga near the mouth of the Mahananda.

ii. *The Mahananda:* The Mahananda enters the district from the north. It acts as the boundary between the police station of Itahar in the district of North – Dinajpur and that of Chanchal in the district of Malda. The actual entry is made at the tri-junction point of the police stations of Chanchal, Ratua and Gazole. It acts as the boundary between the police station of Ratua and Gazole and flows along the towns of Englishbazar and Old-Malda keeping the town of Old Malda slightly to the north until it is joined by the Tangan at Aiho. The length of the river in this district is 55 miles (88.6 Kilometers).

iii. *The Kalindri:* The Kalindri is taken as an off-shoot the eastern branch of the Ganga but actually it is a branch of the Mahananda, which by the name of Fulahar

Map No 2.1
Drainage Pattern of Malda District

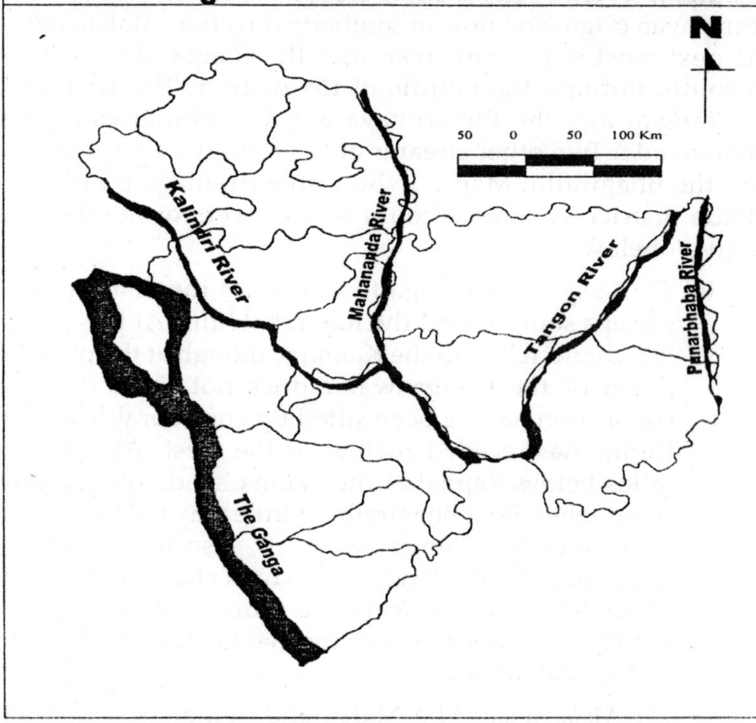

passes through the district of Purnea, enters the district of Malda near Mihaghat from where it is known as the Kalindri. It is flowing mainly in the south-eastern direction, to its junction with the Mahananda opposite the town of Old Malda.

iv. *The Tangan and Punarbhaba*: The Tangan and Punarbhaba on the left bank are the next important tributaries of the Mahananda. These rivers flow from Dinajpur into the north-eastern corner of the district, where there are connected. Both the Tangan and Punarbhava have steep banks, particularly where they pass through the Barind. Their average width is about 40 yards.

Table 2.1 shows the river system of Malda district.

Table 2.1: The River System of Malda District

Sr. No.	*Particulars*	*The Ganga*	*The Mahananda*	*Punarbhaba*	*Tangon*	*Kalindri*
1	Entry Point	Gadai of Bhutnichar (Manikchak Block)	Trijunction Point of Chanca–I Ratua–II and Gazale Block	North-East Bamongola	Junction of Bamongola and Gazole	Mihaghat of Harischand-rapur-II
2	Runs through	Manikchak, Kaliachak –II and III blocks	Gazale, Old-Malda, English – bazar, Habibpur blocks	Bamongola	Bamongola, Habibpur, Old-Malda and Gazole Blocks	Harischand-rapur II Ratua –I, Manikchak and English bazar block
3	Length of the river in the district	172 Kms. (including tributaries)	88.6 Km. (including tributaries)	64.4 Km. (including tributaries)	64.6 Kms. (including tributaries)	N. A.
4	Branches	Fulahar, Bhagirathi and Kalindri	Kalindri and Pagla	Haria	Hara Tangon and ChunaKhali Khal	Fulahar
5	End Point	Par – deonapur of Kaliachak III blocks	Aiho and Habibpur block	Eastern border of Bamogola Block	Mahananda	Mahananda at Bachamari of Old-Malda Block

v. Beels and Tanks: Beels are like lakes frequently brought into existence by a river abandoning its existing bed and flowing along new channel. The largest beell in the district is Ahora in Tangan valley covering an area of about 2 sq. miles. Other than Ahora there are some other beels located mainly in the marshy tract between the Mahananda river and the main road from English Bazar to Gour. Some beels are also found in the Diara tract caused by depressions left by the Ganga e.g. Gadai beel. In the district here are approximately thirty thousands tanks of different size out of which about eleven thousands are irrigation tanks.

c) Physical Division – The Terrian

On the basis of the physiography, Malda district can be divided into three regions i) Tal ii) Barind and iii) Diara. Map 2.2 shows the physiographic divisions of Malda district.

i. *Tal Region*: The northern portion of the Kalindri river is popularly known as 'Tal'. This is a low-lying area, subjected to inundation, by floodwaters of the rivers during the rainy season. The region reveals a gradual slope towards south and west. The total area of this tract is about 1,14,099 hectares and covers Ratua-I, Ratua-II, Chanchal-I, Chanchal-II, Harishchandrapur-I and Harishchandrapur-II blocks. Tal area is composed of mud and finer variety of sand. Retaining capacity of this type of soil is very poor. Wheat, paddy, jute, pulses and oil seeds are abundantly grown in this area. The physiographic aspects of this region are shown in Table 2.2. It shows the physical situation of cultivable land, categorized for the individual blocks of the region.

ii. *Barind Region*: Extending eastward from the Mahananda river is a relatively upland tract, the Barind, composed mostly of ferallitic materials. The Barind land is undulating in character and presenting a dissected appearance (Chakraborty 1970). The tract extends over a wide area east of the Mahananda and continues into the district of Dinajpur in West-Bengal and Rajsahi and Bogura in Bangladesh. The highest elevation of this tract, within the district, is 39.7 meters above mean sea level in Gazole police station. In Malda district Barind tract extends over an area of 1,32,761 hectares comprising the areas of Gazole, Bamongola Habibpur and Old-Malda blocks.

The Barind is composed of old alluvial soil of reddish colour with medium degree of acidity. Granite stone is occasionally found below this soil. In Barind region ground water level is very low, except in the rainy season. The complex geological evolution has given these tracts a distinct character in contrast to the most

Table 2.2: Physical Situation of Cultivation Land (Tal Region)

Block	*Geographical Area in hect.*	*% of the district*	*High land in hect.*	*% of the district*	*Medium land in hect.*	*% of the district*	*Low land in hect.*	*% of the district*	*Total area in hect.*
Harischandrapur-I	17202	4.82	2194	16.0	9598	70.0	1920	14.0	13712
Harischandrapur–II	21156	5.93	1855	11.0	11977	71.0	3036	18.0	16868
Chanchal - I	15855	3.79	1280	12.0	7793	73.0	1600	15.0	10673
Chanchal – II	20550	6.42	2550	14.0	12933	71.0	2735	15.0	18218
Ratua – I	22126	6.21	2655	15.1	12174	68.8	3850	16.1	17679
Ratua – II	17210	4.83	1915	14.0	9712	71.0	2055	15.0	13682
Total Tal	114099	32.02	12449	13.70	64187	70.66	14196	15.63	90832

Source: Annual Plan – Malda District (1998-99)

Map No. 2.2
Physiographic Division of Malda

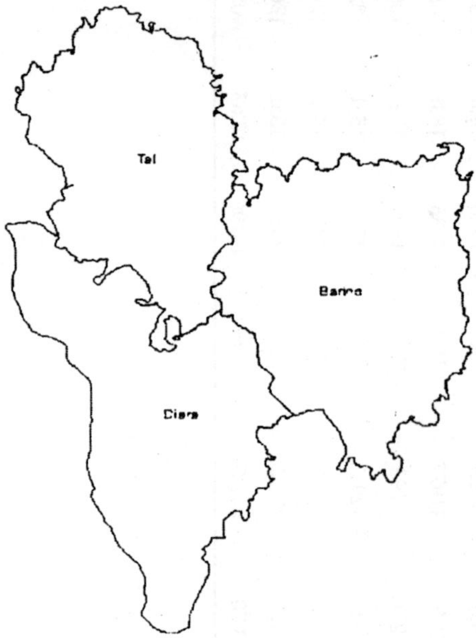

recent alluviums of north. The characteristic features of this 'Barind' region are its surface undulation with depression and wide valleys of small watercourses. Due to the presence of ferralitic materials, surface becomes hard during summer season and underground water levels fall. The physical situation of the cultivable land of Barind has been categorized as highland, medium land and low land in the Table 2.3.

iii. *Diara Region*: The flat land on the western side of Mahananda, is the result of the fluvial action of the river Ganga. The Ganga has shifted westward from its old-course and traces of its old channel are found in this area. This tract is known as the 'Diara' covering an area of 1,09,494 hectare and covers Englishbazar, Manikchak, Kaliachak-1, Kaliachak-II and Kaliachak-III blocks. The soil of this area is extremely fertile due to regular deposition of alluvium by the Ganga.

As a result the cropping pattern of this region is comparatively different from other parts of the district. A large 'area' of 'Diara' is covered with mango orchards while other crops are jute, aus, paddy, wheat, pulses etc. The water level of this region is very high. The physical situation of cultivable land has been categorized with the help of the following table 2.4.

d) Soil

Soil is the basic component of agriculture. Soil properties are determined by parent materials, climate, relief and living organisms. In Malda district there is the presence of different physical and physiographic characteristics. It is mainly covered by alluvium. Older alluvium dominates in Barind region. The red soil of old alluvium formation is composed of clay containing iron and lime which becomes extremely hard in the cold weather. The soil is mostly acidic and the PH of soil mainly varies from 4.6 to 5.9. Newer alluvium dominates both Tal and Diara tracts of this district. This soil consists of a mixture of sand and clay. The proportion of clay increases towards the east whereas proportion of sand increases towards the west. The PH ranges from 6 to 7 in 'Tal' areas; while in Diara region the PH value of soil ranges from 6.5 to 8 which means slightly alkaline soil is found in this region. In low lying areas of Malda district like beels, and river valleys dark loam soil with admixture of clay are also found which is also known as 'Matial.'

Soil Texture

Soil texture refers to the size and proportion of soil particles and is the measure of the average size of channel between the particles. The retaining capacity and moisture largely depend upon soil texture. Heavy clay becomes hard during hot dry period and under heavy rainfall become too heavy which restrict the intensity of cropping. Light sandy alluvium is too friable. Hot-rainless condition is best in wet season. Under monsoon rainfall heavy soil is able to store moisture for use during the ensuring dry period.

An attempt has been made by the soil survey branch of

Table 2.3: Physical Situation of Cultivation Land (Barind Region)

Block	*Geographical Area in hect.*	*% of the district*	*High land in hect.*	*% of the district*	*Medium land in hect.*	*% of the district*	*Low land in hect.*	*% of the district*	*Total area in hect.*
English bazar	25190	7.07	2613	14.0	13257	71.0	2795	15.0	18665
Manickchak	31654	8.90	3017	12.0	18358	73.0	3772	15.0	25147
Kalichak - I	10350	3.76	1015	10.0	7902	78.0	1215	12.0	10132
Kalichak – II	21377	5.34	1500	10.0	11752	78.0	1807	12.0	15059
Kalichak – III	23617	5.67	1430	9.0	12366	78.0	2065	13.0	15861
Total Diara	112188	30.72	9575	11.28	63635	75.00	11654	13.73	84864

Source: Annual Plan – Malda District (1998-99)

Table 2.4: Physical Situation of Cultivation Land (Diara Region)

Block	Geographical Area in hect.	% of the district	High land in hect.	% of the district	Medium land in hect.	% of the district	Low land in hect.	% of the district	Total area in hect.
English bazar	25190	7.07	2613	14.0	13257	71.0	2795	15.0	18665
Manickchak	31654	8.90	3017	12.0	18358	73.0	3772	15.0	25147
Kalichak - I	10350	3.76	1015	10.0	7902	78.0	1215	12.0	10132
Kalichak – II	21377	5.34	1500	10.0	11752	78.0	1807	12.0	15059
Kalichak – III	23617	5.67	1430	9.0	12366	78.0	2065	13.0	15861
Total Diara	112188	30.72	9575	11.28	63635	75.00	11654	13.73	84864

Source : Annual Plan – Malda District (1998-99)

soil conservation wing of Malda district to classify soils of cultivable areas of the blocks on the basis of their texture. The spatial variation of soil texture within the physiographic region of Malda district is shown in Table 2.5. It is revealed that 29.7 percent of agricultural area of the district has clay loam while soils of 28.8 percent and 25.5 percent of agricultural lands are dominated by loam and clay. Sandy loam and silt loam cover 7.6 and 5.2 percent of cultivable areas of the district.

Regional variation of soil texture is much obvious in Tal, Barind and Diara tracts. Clay soil covers 42.3 percent in Tal region followed by loam with 35.3 percent sandy laom with 8.7 percent.

In Barind region clay soils cover 57.4 percent of the cultivable lands followed by the clay loam with 32.1 percent area under it, loam occupies 10% cultivable areas of Barind region.

Table 2.5: Textural Classification of Soil (Malda District)

Region	*Block*	*Soil texture (hectare)*					
		Sandy	*Sandy Loam*	*Loam*	*Clay Loam*	*Silt Loam*	*Clay*
TAL	Harischandrapur-I	....	680	3427	8915	--	690
	Harischandrapur-II	60	790	4374	9964	--	1680
	Chanchal – I	100	436	3065	6937	--	1135
	Chanchal – II	150	761	5350	11042	--	915
	Ratua – I	1200	3270	8991	1168	2500	550
	Ratua – II	1000	1971	6893	1368	2000	450
BARIND	Gazole	--	500	4060	12647	--	23382
	Bamongola	--	50	1578	4565	--	10070
	Habibpur	--	--	3123	10246	--	17861
	Old-Malda	--	100	1607	6268	--	9097
DIARA	English Bazar	....	933	2800	9199	--	5733
	Manikchak	2257	4788	13102	500	4500	--
	Kaliachak-I	940	1500	5592	600	1500	--
	Kaliachak-II	1518	2500	8541	500	2000	--
	Kaliachak-III	2000	3151	8310	400	2000	--
District Total		9225	21430	80813	83319	14500	71563

Source: Annual Plan (2000-01), Soil Survey Branch of Soil conservation wing.

In Diara tract the dominant soil texture is loam which occupies 45.2 percent of cultivable land. Sandy loam and clay loam also occupy 15.2 and 13.2 percent of land respectively. Sandy soils also occupy 15.2 and 13.2 percent of land respectively. Sandy soils also cover 8.0 percent of cultivable land of the region. Fig. 2.5 shows the textural classification of soil of Malda district.

Soil Types

The soils of Malda district has been classified taxonomically into broad types by the soil survey branch of soil conservation wing in Malda District. Table 2.6 shows the classification of soil types in Malda district.

Entisol

Entisols are rich in mineral soil materials with absence of pedogenic horizon. It is associated with recent deposit of alluviam in which insert parent materials such as quartz, sand are present in abundance and lack of sufficient time has restricted the development of pedogenic horizons. Due to restrictions on their depth, clay content and water balance, the intensive use of this soil is limited. This is the dominant soil of Diara tract. Crops like aus, paddy, jute, maize, wheat, pulses, oilseeds, barley and sugarcane are grown in the soil with the help of adequate water supply and fertilizers.

Altisol

Altisols considers moderately active soil forming processes by accumulation of silicate clays and other five materials without much depletion of base. The soil has a thick dark coloured low base (ochric) on light coloured organic (umbic) surface horizon, water is available for more than ½ of the year or more than three months during warm season. Soil is naturally fertile. They generally occur in Barind and Diara tracts and it is intensively utilized for cultivation.

Table 2.6: Classification of Soil Types: Malda District

Region	*Block*	*Area Available for cultivation (ha.)*	*Soil Types*			
			Predominent Type	*% of Total areas*	*Other Types*	*% of Total area*
TAL	Harischandrapur-I	13712	Inceptisal	100%	Nil	Nil
	Harischandrapur-II	16868	Inceptisal	100%	Nil	Nil
	Chanchal – I	10673	Inceptisal	100%	Nil	Nil
	Chanchal – II	18218	Inceptisal	100%	Nil	Nil
	Ratua – I	17679	Inceptisal	100%	Nil	Nil
	Ratua – II	13682	Inceptisal	100%	Nil	Nil
DIARA	English Bazar	18665	Entisol	96%	Altisol	4%
	Manikchak	25147	Entisol	96%	Altisol	4%
	Kaliachak-I	10332	Entisol	96%	Altisol	4%
	Kaliachak-II	15059	Entisol	96%	Altisol	4%
	Kaliachak-III	15851	Entisol	96%	Altisol	4%
BARIND	Gazole	40589	Inceptisal	95%	Entisol Allisol	3%
	Bamongola	16263	Inceptisal	95%	Entisol Allisol	2%
	Habibpur	31230	Inceptisal	95%	Entisol Allisol	2%
	Old-Malda	17072	Inceptisal	95%	Entisol Allisol	2%
District Total		280850	Inceptisal Entisol	68% 29%	Entisol Allisol	1% 2%

Source: Annual Plan (2000-2001) Soil Survey Brand, Soil Conservation Wing, MALDA

Note: The classification is based on tentatine broad soil type (order) as per comprehensive

Inceptisols

This is the dominant soil type in Tal and Barind regions of the district. This is an advanced stage of entisal, where soil-forming process is active. In this type of soil one or more pedogenic horizon are found. Soil texture is finer than loamy sand. Retaining capacity of this soil is very high during the greater parts of the year. These type of soils are generally fertile and intensively used for cultivation. In northern parts of Malda district, jute and aman paddy is main Kharif crop and in some places wheat is grown during Rabi season. While in the doba areas summer paddy is extensively cultivated because these areas are subjected to water stagnation.

Soil Nutrient Status

The amount of nutrients in soil, to a considerable degree determines crop growth. These nutrients viz. organic carbon, potassium, and phosphorus account for soil fertility, have been rated as low, medium and high according to limit, laid down by the co-ordinating unit at the Indian Agricultural Research Institute (Ramamoorthy and Bajaj, 1969) to determine the nutrient level of the soil. On the basis of the survey conducted by the soil testing unit of Malda district the fertility status of soils of the various blocks have been determined and presented in the Table 2.7.

Table 2.7: Soil Fertility Status: Malda District

Region	*Block*	*Range of Nutrient Status and pH*				
		O.C.	*AV.P_2O_5*	*AV.K_2O*	*pH*	*Conductivity*
TAL	Harischandrapur-I	L to M	VL	L to H	SA to N	N
	Harischandrapur-II	ML to M	VL to L	VL toML	SA to N	N
	Chanchal – I	L to ML	VL to L	ML	SA to N	N
	Chanchal – II	L to ML	VL	L to M	SA to N	N
	Ratua – I	L to ML	VL	L to M	SA to N	N
	Ratua – II					
BARIND	Gazole	L to ML	VL	VL to ML	N	N
	Bamongola	L to ML	VL	VL to ML	VA to N	N
	Habibpur	L to ML	VL	ML to VH	SA to N	N
	Old-Malda	L to ML	VL	VL to M	SA to N	N
DIARA	English Bazar	L to ML	VL	ML to M	N	N
	Manikchak	L to ML	VL	ML to M	N to AL	N
	Kaliachak-I	L to ML	VL	VL to H	N	N
	Kaliachak-II	ML to M	VL	VL to H	N to AL	N
	Kaliachak-III	ML to M	VL	L to H	N to AL	N

INDEX

	O.C.	*AV. P_2O_5*	*AV. K_2O*	*pH*	
Very Low (VL)	Upto 0.20	Upto 22	Upto 120	Very Acidic (VA)	Less than 4.5
Low (L)	0.21 - 0.40	23-45	121-180	Slightly Acidic	4.6 to 5.9
MEDIUM LOW (ML)	0.41 – 0.60	46-72	181-240	Neutral (N)	6.0 to 8.0

MEDIUM (M)	0.61 - 0.82	73-92	241-300	Alkaine (AL) Above 8.0
HIGH (H)	0.83 – 1.00	93-115	301-360	
VERY HIGH (VH)	Above 1.00	Above-115	Above-360	

Source: Annual Plan (2000-2001), Soil Survey Branch, Soil Conservation wing, MALDA

Soil acidity and alkalinity confirm that proportion of neutral soil is more than acidic or alkaline soil in the district. Frequency of occurrence of slightly acidic and slightly akaline soils in different parts however, may be responsible for nutritional uptake of the crops.

As a whole the soils with PH value ranging from 4.6 to above 8.0 are not resistant to crop growth as crop like potatoes favour slightly acidic soils. Most of the crops are suited to neutral to slightly akaline soils. The PH value of soils in the district is suitable for paddy.

Organic matter is an important chemical constituent of productive soil. Its content in the soil increases with the rate at which plant residues are added. The organic status of soils in the district ranges between 0.20 to 0.82 percent, which reveals improper management of soils.

The organic matter content of soils plays a dominant part in crop production by interacting with other nutrients.

Soil potassium and phosphorus are macronutrients for crop production and are sufficiently low in the soil of the district.

It has been observed that in case of alluvial loamy and red soils the availability of Phosphorus decreases with increasing pH (Roy Chowdhury and Landay,1960). It is commonly low in alluvial soils and its proper application is required to maintain the status in the soil otherwise this excess of phosphate some times retards the crops yield.

Although potassium has no direct influence of the crop yield, it is considered essential for the photosynthesis process and plays an important role in plant metabolism. The table 2.7 indicates that soils of the district are low in phosphorus status compared to potash status.

Crop productivity such as paddy, wheat potatoes are positively related to the nutrient status of soils.

e) Climate

The climate of Malda district is more or less same in the three physiographic divisions of Tal, Barind and Diara. The climate of this district is characterized by hot and oppressive summer season, plentiful rain and moisture in the air through out the year. The year may be divided into four seasons. The winter season starts about the middle of November and continues till the end of February. The period from March to May is the summer season. The south-west monsoon season commences by about first week of June and continues till the end of the September. October and 1st half of the November constitute the post monsoon season.

The year which has been divided into various seasons following the temperature and rainfall are characterized by different agricultural operation. Table 2.8 shows the agricultural crop year for the district.

Table 2.8: Agricultural Crop Year: Malda District

Season	*Period*	*Crops*
Bhadoi season	1st Jul. to 15th Oct.	Aus, Maize, Jute, Kalai, Mesta and Sugarcane
Winter season	16th Oct. to 15th Jan. to 31st Mar.	Aman, Kalai Rabi season 16th Jan. Wheat, Job, Gram, Arhar, Lentil, Khesari, Mustard, Lineseed and Potato
Summer season	1st Apr. to 30th Jun.	Boro, Moong and Til

Note: Agriculture crop year has been determined based on the crop harvesting period

Source: Crop Harvesting Survey, Evaluation Brnch, Agriculture Office, Govt of West Bengal

Temperature:

The eight meteorological stations in this district record climatic data. From the month of March, temperature begins to rise rapidly. The day temperature reach the maximum in

May or June. The night temperature continues to rise even in the monsoon season. In April the mean (Avg. of 4 yrs.) maximum temperature is 34.2°C and minimum is 20.8°C (1994 to 1998) January is the coldest month, with the maximum average temperature 22.1°C and minimum average temperature 9.7°C (4 yrs. Aug. 1995 to 1998). Table 2.9 shows the monthly temperature variation in the district.

Table 2.9: Monthwise Average Temperature: Malda District (1995-98) (in°C)

Month	*Maximum*	*Minimum*	*Mean*
January	22.1	9.7	15.9
February	26.2	12.5	19.4
March	31.4	16.9	24.2
April	34.2	20.8	27.5
May	35.9	24.6	30.3
June	34.3	25.5	29.9
July	32.1	26	29
August	31.3	25.9	28.6
September	32.1	24.3	28.2
October	31	22.8	26.9
November	28	17.1	22.5
December	24.1	12.2	18.1
Average	30.2	19.9	25.0

Source: Annual Plan, APO (1999-2000).

Rainfall:

The average annual rainfall in the district is 1,655.9 mm for the period 1990 to 1999. The rainfall during the south-west monsoon season constitutes 78% of annual total; July to September are the months of the heavy rainfall. The variation in rainfall from year to year is significant (Fig 2.1).

Table 2.10: Month wise Rainfall: Malda District (in mm)

YEAR	*JAN.*	*FEB.*	*MAR.*	*APRIL*	*MAY*	*JUNE*	*JULY*	*AUG.*	*SEPT.*	*OCT.*	*NOV.*	*DEC.*	*Total*
1990	0.0	37.3	28.8	30.5	170.1	205.0	447.3	209.6	239.4	164.6	6.4	0.0	1539.0
1991	16.7	6.1	11.8	17.6	206.2	358.3	392.4	247.4	522.8	39.8	0.0	51.6	1870.7
1992	1.1	10.4	1.5	4.9	118.3	113.5	493.3	226.6	161.5	79.7	15.7	0.6	1227.1
1993	49.5	0.1	24.9	99.6	115.6	157.3	197.8	288.7	311.7	79.2	46.9	0.0	1371.3
1994	29.1	28.3	0.0	12.6	93.1	415.5	181.6	181.2	214.4	112.1	0.0	0.0	1267.8
1995	3.2	7.3	3.2	3.5	52.7	300.4	359.6	551.7	716.6	8.2	81.4	8.8	2096.6
1996	9.3	15.8	3.0	33.0	37.8	199.2	233.8	316.3	464.8	64.9	0.0	0.0	1376.9
1997	16.6	9.5	7.8	77.9	90.0	206.0	387.6	541.5	266.7	25.5	1.2	30.8	1661.1
1998	7.3	7.9	84.4	60.6	101.3	172.0	502.3	328.8	316.9	232.6	18.3	0.0	1832.4
1999	0.0	0.0	0.1	12.1	143.4	342.2	515.9	466.6	656.0	176.1	3.7	0.0	2316.1
2000	0.0	49.6	38.9	115.4	191.5	324.3	n.a.	n.a.	n.a.	n.a.	n.a.	n.a.	719.7
2001	0.0	26.3	33.3	84.4	93.1	232.7	72.2	144.7	493.5	34.7	0.0	0.0	1214.9

Source:- Annual Plan, Agriculture Principal Office, Malda – 2001-02

Table 2.10 shows the month wise average rainfall (mm) of the Malda district.

Fig 2.1: Total Rainfall in Malda District: Year wise

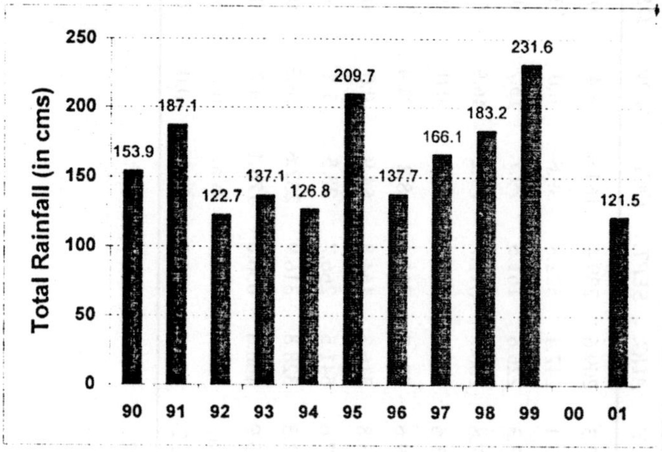

Source :- Annual Plan, Agriculture Principal Office – 1999-2000

Humidity

Relative humidity is high throughout the year, but during the early part of the summer they are relatively less. In March, April and May, minimum relative humidity are accordingly 36 %, 43% and 49% (Avg. of 4 yrs. 1995 to 1998). In the month of the July, August and September it is very high at 94%, 93% and 94% (Avg. of 4 yrs. 1995 to 1998) respectively.

Table 2.11 shows the level of humidity of Malda district.

Table 2.11: Monthwise Average Relative Humidity: Malda District (1995-98) (in %)

Month	*Maximum*	*Minimum*	*Mean*
January	98.0	51.0	74.5
February	95.0	43.0	69.0
March	87.0	36.0	61.5
April	83.0	43.0	63.0
May	87.0	49.0	68.0
June	92.0	68.0	80.0
July	94.0	81.0	87.5

August	93.0	80.0	86.5
September	94.0	79.0	86.5
October	89.0	64.0	76.5
November	94.0	57.0	75.5
December	92.0	55.0	73.5
Average	92.0	59.0	73.5

Source:- Annual Plan, Agriculture Principal Office, Malda – 1999-2000.

Winds:

Winds are generally moderate with some increase in speed in the late summer. In monsoon season winds blow mostly between south and east. In October winds are variable in direction. Southerlies and South westerlies appear in March and in the April winds are variable in direction.

Clouds:

Skies are moderately clouded in May and heavily clouded to overcast in southeast monsoon season. There is some moderate clouding in October. During rest of the year, skies are mainly clear on lightly clouded.

3

Non-Physical Determinants

In Chapter-II we have seen varying physical condition are indeed responsible for variations in regional patterns of agricultural phenomena. However, the differential degree of combinations in institutional, biotechnological, operational, demographic, cultural and infrastructural factors influencing agricultural patterns must be considered useful. This is because the combination of these circumstances furnish the basic material need for explaining the modification brought about in agricultural activities which otherwise are the primary creation of natural forces. Therefore, their discussion is unavoidable to comprehend the varying levels of agricultural development within Malda.

This chapter discusses the various non-physical determinants viz. a) Technological factors –irrigation, other inputs, levels of agricultural modernization b) Population characteristics c) Cultural factors - ownership holding, tenural arrangement farm family characteristics and labour force d) Infrastructural services - marketing facilities, transport and accessibility and credit facilities. It shows the similarity and dissimilarity of the factors across regions and attempts to relate these determinants with overall productivity of the region.

a. Technological Factors

It has been established that various technological variables are important towards supporting agricultural activities and for the improvement of productivity. In any part of the world land surface is fixed and only a certain proportion of land is available for cultivation. So to increase production, improvement of productivity is the norm, which in turn implies intense use of inputs by adopting modern methods of production through use of improved technology. Thus agricultural production and its efficiency largely depend upon inputs applied and the methods adopted. Among the technological factors irrigation, machines for farming, improved quality of seeds, fertilizers, pesticides etc are the important ones which needs to considered individually for analysis and this section attempts to do so.

Irrigation

It has been concluded time and again that agriculture in India is exposed to the vagaries of monsoon. So without assured irrigation agricultural production is a risky venture. But the Sub-Himalayan West Bengal and Terai region is comparatively less affected by the irregularities of rainfall as this area regularly receives normal or above normal rainfall. Malda, which happens to be a part of this geographical region, too receives normal rainfall but to enable multiple cropping irrigation is important and also to facilitate continuous and timely water supply irrigation assumes a great importance.

Irrigation plays significant role in the efficient use of arable land. By artificial application of water, deficiencies and variabilities of rainfall can be compensated to improve crop yield and cropping pattern through substantial exploitation of soil potential. Since most of the traditional sources of irrigation depend on collected amount of run off, enough water is rarely available for irrigational purposes all the year round. According to the farmers of the district with the introduction of tube-wells remarkable progress in irrigation has been achieved in the district. Presently the agricultural stability and development in the district depend upon the availability of irrigational water by various sources.

Table 3.1. Provides the area irrigated block wise.

Table :3.1 Irrigation Potentials of Malda District (2000-2001)

	Net Irrigated Area (ha)	*Net Sown area (ha)*	*Area irrigated as % of Net Sown Area*
Harishchandrapur I	9,616	13,757	69.9
Harishchandrapur II	11,250	12,415	90.6
Chanchal I	9,330	13,042	71.5
Chanchal II	7,640	14,599	52.3
Ratua I	9,530	13,137	72.5
Ratua II	8,943	13,413	66.7
Tal	56,309	80,363	70.1
Gazole	10,997	40,024	27.5
Bamongola	5,585	15,511	36.0
Habibpur	9,404	30,920	30.4
Old Malda	5,202	16,084	32.3
Barind	31,188	102,539	30.4
English Bazar	6,230	17,952	34.7
Manikchak	6,719	24,590	27.3
Kaliachak I	2,760	6,583	41.9
Kaliachak II	2,538	7,030	36.1
Kaliachak III	5,853	16,167	36.2
Diara	24,100	72,322	33.3
Malda	111,597	255,224	43.7

Regionally the sources of irrigation are utilized in Tal region more extensively and 70.1 percent of net sown area is irrigated, while in Barind and Diara region only 30.4 and 33.3 percent of net sown area is irrigated. Table 3.2 substantiates the difference in level of irrigation with the help of primary data.

Table 3.2: Availability of Irrigation in Malda: Region Wise

	Avails Irrigation	*Do not Avail Irrigation*
Tal	98%	2%
Barind	47%	53%
Diara	73%	27%
Malda	73%	27%

Derived from Primary Survey result of 368 respondents.

The principal cause of low irrigation in these two regions is different. In Barind region it can be attributed to the physiographic factors, while in Diara it is the cropping pattern. It has been found that the water level depth in Barind region is high, so to enable irrigation DTW is required. Table 3.3 shows the result from the primary survey that the water level depth affects the availability of water in Barind region.

Table 3.3: Water Depth Level: Region-wise

	5-10mts	*10-15mts*	*15-20mts*	*>20mts*
Tal	1%	3%	17%	79%
Barind	4%	0%	4%	92%
Diara	0%	0%	66%	34%
Malda	1%	2%	27%	70%

Derived from Primary Survey result of 184 respondents.

In Diara region the low irrigation percentage is mainly because a high percentage of area is under Mango cultivation wherein the irrigation facility is not required.

As seen earlier, physiography of the district has profound influence on sources of irrigation and each source has its potentials to provide irrigation. Therefore it is necessary to study the distribution of source wise irrigation areas in the study region. The study indicates that the entire district is irrigated by D.T.W., S.T.W., R.L.I. and Other sources (Canal, Tank, Bodo-Bunds) etc. Map 3.1 illustrates the sources of irrigation in Malda.

The age-old practice of irrigation through various means and from various sources reflects the awareness of farmers who not only perceived but developed sources to collect run-off and utilize it for irrigation. With the introduction of various seasonal crops irrigation has acquired significant place in agriculture, because many of these crops are not possible to grow economically in areas of periodic and erratic rainfall in the district. Table 3.4 ahead provides the number of units, area irrigated and share of each type of irrigation to total irrigated area in Malda district.

Table 3.4: Type of Irrigation in Malda: Blockwise (2000-01)

	D.T.W			S.T.W			R.L.I			OTHERS		
	No. of Units	*Area (ha)*	*%*	*No. of Units*	*Area (ha)*	*%*	*No. of Units*	*Area (ha)*	*%*	*No. of Units*	*Area (ha)*	*%*
Harishchandrapur I	25	300	3.1	3,074	7,705	80.1	9	142	1.5	362	1,469	15.3
Harishchandrapur II	10	105	0.9	4,474	10,000	88.9	31	435	3.9	175	710	6.3
Chanchal I	21	500	5.4	2,111	6,800	72.9	22	180	1.9	761	1,850	19.8
Chanchal II	32	525	6.9	2,194	4,600	60.2	22	290	3.8	445	2,225	29.1
Ratua I	33	590	6.2	2,616	6,995	73.4	32	975	10.2	110	970	10.2
Ratua II	71	1,045	11.7	1,405	3,590	40.1	60	1,358	15.2	290	2,950	33.0
Tal	192	3,065	5.4	15,874	39,690	70.5	176	3,380	6.0	2,143	10,174	18.1
Gazole	62	415	3.8	4,000	6,000	54.6	45	1,022	9.3	2,122	3,560	32.4
Bamongola			0.0	1,850	4,285	76.7	28	450	8.1	966	850	15.2
Habibpur	13	80	0.9	1,800	3,009	32.0	39	740	7.9	1,051	5,575	59.3
Old Malda	47	715	13.7	1,150	1,925	37.0	37	1,062	20.4	230	1,500	28.8
Barind	122	1,210	3.9	8,800	15,219	48.8	149	3,274	10.5	4,369	11,485	36.8
English Bazar	46	970	15.6	1,043	2,760	44.3	20	500	8.0	137	2,000	32.1
Manikchak	17	434	6.5	2,387	5,084	75.7	21	651	9.7	26	550	8.2
Kaliachak I	13	160	5.8	1,295	2,330	84.4	4		0.0	23	270	9.8
Kaliachak II	24	336	13.2	768	1,652	65.1	11	350	13.8	18	200	7.9
Kaliachak III	38	293	5.0	2,670	5,300	90.6	3	60	1.0	14	200	3.4
Diara	138	2,193	9.1	8,163	17,126	71.1	59	1,561	6.5	218	3,220	13.4
Malda	452	6,468	5.8	32,837	72,035	64.5	384	8,215	7.4	6,730	24,879	22.3

Source: Annual Plan Malda district, PAO, 2000-01.

Map No: 3.1

SOURCES OF IRRIGATION IN MALDA: BLOCK WISE (2000-01)

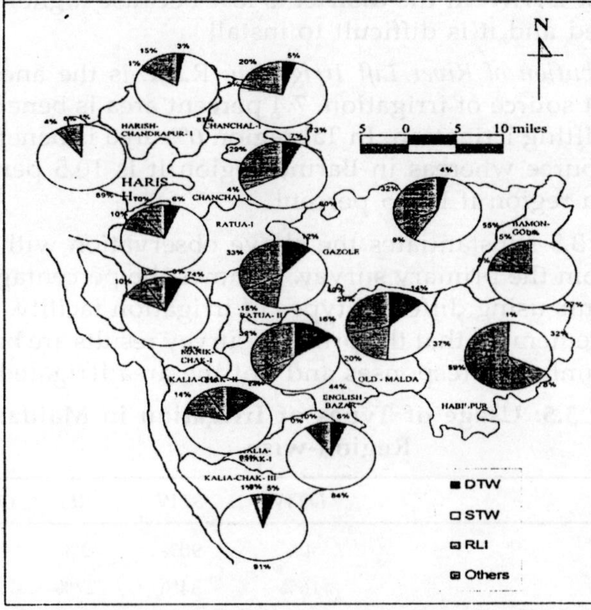

Distribution of Shallow Tube-Well Irrigation: Tube wells are an important source of irrigation in this district. Shallow tube-wells are technically feasible in most of the places in Tal and Diara Region because these areas are rich in sub-soil water resources. But in Barind region only 'doba' area offers opportunity for S.T.W. Tube well irrigation can be summerized by the fact that the number of S.T.W. in the district was 32,837 in 2000-01. In Malda district the percentage of irrigated area is mainly benefited by S.T.W., because it is easy to install. Wherever ground water level is not at depth and the farmers can afford to invest for S.T.W., this is the preferred mode. In Tal region, area benefited by S.T.W. is 70.5 percent, while in Barind it is only 48.8 percent and Diara is 71.1 percent. Of the 15 blocks S.T.W. is most important source of irrigation in Kaliachak III (90.6%) in Diara region followed by Harishchandrapur II (88.9%) in Tal region and Kaliachak I (84.4%) in Diara region. While in Barind region Bamongola is the only block where percentage of S.T.W. irrigation is high (76.7 %).

Distribution of Deep Tube-Well Irrigation: The total number of D.T.W. in Malda district for the year of 2000-01 is 452. The number of D.T.W. in the district is low because higher cost is involved and it is difficult to install.

Distribution of River Lift Irrigation: R.L.I. is the another important source of irrigation. 7.4 percent area is benefited by river lifting irrigation. In Tal region 6% area is benefited by this source whereas in Barind region it is 10.5 percent and Diara region it is 6.5 percent.

Table 3.5 substantiates the above observation with the results from the primary survey. It shows the percentage of respondents using different types of irrigation facility. One needs to remember that the primary survey results are based on the number of responses and not the area irrigated.

Table 3.5: Usage of Types of Irrigation in Malda: Region-wise

	DTW	*STW*	*RLI*	*Others*
Tal	4%	90%	2%	4%
Barind	16%	34%	27%	23%
Diara	28%	49%	20%	3%
Malda	14%	65%	13%	8%

Derived from Primary Survey result of 265 respondents

Other Inputs

Fertiliser:

For proper growth of plants and higher yield of crops fertilizer plays an important role. Fertilizer usage should be according to the crop and quality of the soil. For this proper soil testing and consultation is required. Here, we try to take stock of this important ingredient in the district.

Table 3.6 provides an understanding of the level of awareness in the district and its regional variation. It shows that the awareness is spread from low to high.

Table 3.6: Fertiliser Awareness Level: Region Wise

	Very High	*High*	*Medium*	*Low*	*Very low*
Tal	2.4%	16.5%	42.5%	36.2%	2.4%
Barind	0.7%	29.1%	46.3%	21.6%	2.2%
Diara	2.0%	30.6%	54.1%	11.2%	2.0%
Malda	1.7%	25.1%	47.1%	24.0%	2.2%

Derived from Primary Survey result of 359 respondents.

We find that the level of awareness is comparatively poor in Tal region. People are comparatively more aware of fertilizer facility in Diara region. The awareness was measured in the survey based on the responses to the investigator's query on name of fertilizers to be used crop wise, the ratio of NPK to be used etc.

In many cases we find that even the farmers are aware of the fertiliser usage pattern but they are unable to use the same because of low capital and accessibility problems. Table 3.7 provides an overview of the number of fertiliser outlets in the different blocks of the district. It shows that the number of outlets is comparatively more in Gazole, Habibpur and Kaliachak-III. This does not provide much insight, as we are unable to comment on the outlet density. So, we calculated the outlet density for each block shown in the same table.

Table 3.7: Number of Fertilizer Depots in Malda: Block Wise (2000-01)

	Number of Fertiliser Depots	*Fetilizer depot per 1000 ha*
Harishchandrapur I	45	2.62
Harishchandrapur II	46	2.17
Chanchal I	45	2.84
Chanchal II	24	1.17
Ratua I	54	2.44
Ratua II	77	4.47
Tal	291	2.55
Gazole	180	3.55
Bamongola	83	4.07

Habibpur	113	2.88
Old Malda	61	2.73
Barind	437	3.29
English Bazar	68	2.70
Manikchak	30	0.95
Kaliachak I	69	6.67
Kaliachak II	42	1.96
Kaliachak III	131	5.55
Diara	777	6.93
Malda	1505	4.19

Source: District Statistical Handbook, Malda, Bureau of Applied Economics & Statistics, Government of West Bengal, 2001.

It shows the outlet density is comparatively high in Kaliachak-I, Kaliachak-III, Ratua-II and Bamongola. But this analysis is again unable to provide an insight regarding the accessibility of outlets by the farmers, as these outlets can be concentrated at a particular place. Table 3.8 provides an overview of the accessibility of region wise.

Table 3.8: Accessibility of Fertiliser Outlets in Malda: Region Wise

	Very easy	*Easy*	*Medium*	*Difficult*	*Very Difficult*
Tal	0.8%	56.7%	17.3%	4.7%	20.5%
Barind	1.5%	41.8%	30.6%	17.9%	8.2%
Diara	0.0%	27.6%	5.1%	56.1%	11.2%
Malda	0.8%	43.2%	18.9%	23.7%	13.4%

Derived from Primary Survey result of 359 respondents

It shows that though in Tal region density of fertiliser outlets is comparatively low (56.7 percent) but farmers can easily access the outlets. But a considerable number of farmers (20.5 percent) from Tal also find extremely difficult to access the outlets.

Another important aspect of fertiliser usage is the right usage and maintenance of the NPK ratio. The Table 3.9 provides the consumption of fertiliser in terms of NPK for the years 1994 to 2000-01.

Table 3.9: Consumption of Fertilizer in Malda (in MT)

Year	*N*	*P*	*K*	*Total*
1993-94	28,500	17,100	12,000	57,600
1994-95	28,600	17,200	12,500	58,300
1995-96	24,400	12,000	9,500	45,900
1996-97	34,918	21,947	18,315	75,180
1997-98	29,700	14,300	12,870	56,870
1998-99	29,870	15,200	13,050	58,120
1999-00	29,899	15,197	13,986	59,082
2000-01	26,901	11,862	11,142	49,905

Source: Agricultural Scenario, PAOMalda, 2001.

We find that the ratio of fertiliser usage is gradually shifting towards nitrogen and potash. This is seen from the Fig 3.1 which shows the NPK ratio over the same period.

Fig. 3.1: NPK Ratio of Fertilizer Consumption in Malda

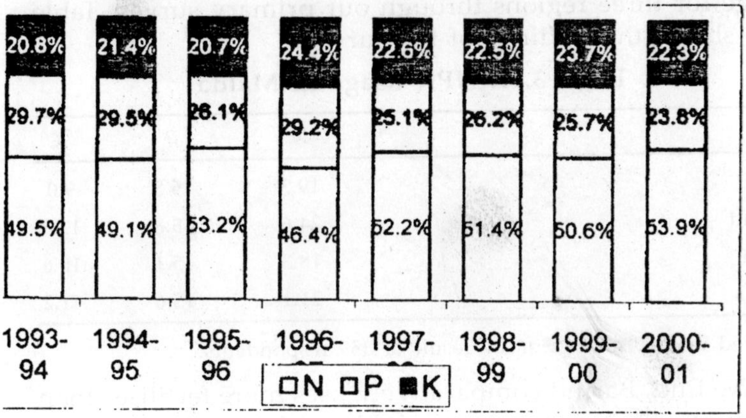

Derived from Table 3.9.

Table 3.10 provides the right composition of NPK for various crops.

Table 3.10: Correct Dosage of NPK: Crop Wise (kg Per Hectare)

CROP	*N*	*P*	*K*
Aus	50	25	25
Aman	60	30	30
Boro	125	60	60
Wheat	10	50	50
Mustard	80	40	40
Jute	40	20	20
Potato	125	100	100
Kalai	4	16	
Arhar	40	20	20
Gram	4	16	
Lentil	4	16	

Source: Sub-Division Agriculture Office, Chanchal.

Against this right composition, as no secondary data is available at region level, we have collected the data of NPK usage for three regions through our primary survey. Table 3.11 shows the findings of the survey.

Table 3.11: NPK usage in Malda

	N	*P*	*K*
Tal	19.3	15.8	9.0
Barind	24.6	15.8	13.3
Diara	18.3	15.1	10.6
Malda	21.1	15.6	11.2

Derived from Primary Survey result of 359 respondents.

We find, Barind comparatively uses more fertiliser than its counterparts and the usage is biased for nitrogenous and potash fertilizers. Usage pattern of Tal and Diara is almost similar. Thus we find fertiliser, which happens to be an important, an important factor to support HYV seeds and thereby increase production faces the problem of awareness accessibility and right composition.

Pesticide:

In progressive farming pesticides play an important role and in Malda's agriculture scenario where pests have played havoc and affected the yield substantially in certain years, pesticide assumes further importance.

Awareness of pesticide in Malda is normally spread with farmers' awareness level being medium (70.0 percent). Table 3.12 shows the awareness level for individual regions. No significant variance is observed among the regions.

Table 3.12: Pesticide Awareness Level: Region Wise

	Very High	*High*	*Medium*	*Low*	*Very low*
Tal	0.0%	10.1%	67.9%	22.0%	0.0%
Barind	1.6%	13.9%	63.9%	19.7%	0.8%
Diara	0.0%	13.1%	79.8%	7.1%	0.0%
Malda	0.6%	12.4%	70.0%	16.7%	0.3%

Derived from Primary Survey result of 330 respondents

Table 3.13 shows the accessibility of pesticide outlets in the various regions of Malda.

Table 3.13: Accessibility of Pesticide Outlets in Malda: Region Wise

	Very easy	*Easy*	*Medium*	*Difficult*	*Very Difficult*
Tal	0.9%	58.9%	22.3%	5.4%	12.5%
Barind	2.5%	41.8%	32.0%	17.2%	6.6%
Diara	0.0%	26.3%	8.1%	53.5%	12.1%
Malda	1.2%	42.9%	21.6%	24.0%	10.2%

Derived from Primary Survey result of 333 respondents.

We find that accessibility of pesticide outlets is an issue in Diara region which needs to be addressed for improving the usage of pesticide.

Table 3.14 shows the type of pesticide used in the regions of Malda. It shows that liquid pesticide is comparatively applied more in Diara. It is observed that half the farmers use both liquid and dust form of pesticide in the district.

Table 3.14: Type of Pesticide Used in Malda: Region Wise

	Liquid	*Dust*	*Both*
Tal	34.8%	14.3%	50.9%
Barind	25.4%	23.8%	50.8%
Diara	43.9%	16.3%	39.8%
Malda	34.0%	18.4%	47.6%

Derived from Primary Survey result of 332 respondents.

Agricultural productivity is impacted by the quality of the seed used. Green Revolution in the country brought in better quality of seeds and today HYV seeds are the norm of the day.

Seeds:

Towards higher productivity seed is an important non-physical determinant. The quality, preservation, availability, proper culture are important tenets that requires attention. We discuss these aspects with a regional perspective in Malda.

Table 3.15 shows the number of seed depots and the density of the same in the Blocks of Malda. It shows that the availability is a problem in Barind region. Tal region has the maximum number of seed depots. This gives an indication that farmers tend to use their own harvest as seed for the next year in Barind.

Table 3.15: Number of Seed Depots in Malda: Block Wise (2000-01)

	Number of Seed Depots	*Seed depot per 1000 ha*
Harishchandrapur I	9	0.52
Harishchandrapur II	7	0.33
Chanchal I	12	0.76
Chanchal II	3	0.15
Ratua I	16	0.72
Ratua II	7	0.41

Tal	54	0.47
Gazole	n.a.	n.a.
Bamongola	3	0.15
Habibpur	2	0.05
Old Malda	1	0.04
Barind	6	0.05
English Bazar	5	0.20
Manikchak	2	0.06
Kaliachak I	6	0.58
Kaliachak II	3	0.14
Kaliachak III	5	0.21
Diara	21	0.19
Malda	81	0.23

Source: District Statistical Handbook, Malda, Bureau of Applied Economics & Statistics, Government of West Bengal, 2001.

The other important aspect of seed is the farmers' awareness of seed treatment, proper preservation techniques and amount of seed to be used per acre of land. To understand the level of awareness of these parameters the farmers' awareness were categorised and the findings are presented in Table 3.16.

Table 3.16: Seed Awareness Level: Region Wise

	Very High	*High*	*Medium*	*Low*
Tal	1.6%	28.3%	70.1%	0.0%
Barind	3.0%	35.6%	54.1%	7.4%
Diara	4.7%	22.1%	70.9%	2.3%
Malda	2.9%	29.6%	64.1%	3.4%

Derived from Primary Survey result of 348 respondents.

Table 3.17 show the accessibility problems faced by the farmers in the different regions of Malda. It is seen that farmers in Diara region find it difficult to access the seed outlets while farmers in Barind find it easy to access. This is in contrast to the secondary data shown in Table 3.15.

Table 3.17: Accessibility of Seed Outlets in Malda: Region Wise

	Very easy	*Easy*	*Medium*	*Difficult*	*Very Difficult*
Tal	1.5%	51.5%	20.8%	13.1%	13.1%
Barind	0.0%	46.7%	27.4%	19.3%	6.7%
Diara	0.0%	17.4%	5.8%	65.1%	11.6%
Malda	0.6%	41.3%	19.7%	28.2%	10.3%

Derived from Primary Survey result of 351 respondents.

Point of purchase is an important determinant for seed as proper storage facility is not adhered to by local shops and vendors in the hats. Table 3.18 shows the point of purchase.

Table 3.18: Seed Purchasing Centre in Malda: Region Wise

	Own	*Agricultural co-operative shop*	*Open market*	*Certified Vendor*	*Others*
Tal	37.7%	2.3%	56.9%	3.1%	0.0%
Barind	47.8%	8.2%	29.1%	14.2%	0.7%
Diara	20.9%	3.5%	58.1%	17.4%	0.0%
Malda	37.4%	4.9%	46.6%	10.9%	0.3%

Derived from Primary Survey result of 350 respondents

It shows that 37.4 percent of the farmers in Malda use their own harvest as seed for the next year. Using the harvest is not suggested as the quality of the seed detoriates if applied on the same soil. It is therefore suggested to rotate the seeds amongst the farmers of the village. The farmers are aware of the practice and its benefits but do not practice it. The findings show that the practice of using own seed is more prevalent in Barind region (47.8 percent).

Level of Modernization:

Technology usage improves productivity and towards this objective policies are framed but the desired result is not observed in actuality as in the district traditional farming is still practiced. Table 3.19 shows the technology awareness level in the regions of the district. The findings are against our perception that the awareness level is low. In contrast it is seen that the awareness is moderate but due to non-availability of capital they are unable to use it.

Table 3.19: Technology Awareness Level: Region Wise

	Very High	*High*	*Medium*	*Low*	*Very low*
Tal	0.0%	57.3%	27.1%	6.3%	9.4%
Barind	2.1%	45.8%	31.3%	8.3%	12.5%
Diara	0.0%	28.3%	41.5%	24.5%	5.7%
Malda	0.8%	46.5%	31.8%	11.0%	9.8%

Derived from Primary Survey result of 245 respondents.

Table-3.20 shows the level of usage of technology understanding the nature of farming practiced in Malda. We do not expect high level of technology usage. We do not expect harvester, thresher and winnower, to be used in the marginal and small operational holding of the district. So we tested the level of technology usage with in form of tractor, power tiller, pumps etc. Depending on the level of usage of these we have categorized the responded into 5 categories of technology usage.

Table 3.20: Technology Usage Level: Region Wise

	Very High	*High*	*Medium*	*Low*	*Very low*
Tal	0.8%	30.8%	27.7%	3.1%	37.7%
Barind	10.4%	28.1%	10.4%	12.6%	38.5%
Diara	0.0%	19.4%	8.7%	12.6%	59.2%
Malda	4.1%	26.6%	16.0%	9.2%	44.0%

Derived from Primary Survey result of 206 respondents.

We find there is a wide disparity in the usage. While 53.2 percent of the respondents are found to be low and very low usage of technology 30.7 percent respondents use it considerable. Among the regions Diara region usage is less amount of technology. To understand the causes of low usage of technology, the low users were further probe and it it is lack of capital as the only cause. The Table 3.21 shows the results of causes of low usage.

Table 3.21: Causes of Low Technology Usage: Region Wise

	Hybrid	*Local*	*Both*
Tal	100.0%	0.0%	0.0%
Barind	96.8%	0.0%	3.2%
Diara	95.5%	4.5%	0.0%
Malda	97.8%	1.1%	1.1%

Derived from Primary Survey result of 93 respondents.

b. Population Characteristics

Geographers have shown time and again that population and its characteristics play important role in determining the overall productivity of land as in a agricultural dependent area, population pressure results in fragmentation of land and thereby operational holding is not economical. In this section we take a look at this non-physical determinant for the district of Malda and its regions.

Table 3.22 shows the population and sex ratio over the last six decade. It is seen that the population pressure on the land in the district has more than tripled. Another worrying feature is the declining sex ratio over the years. Only during the 90's it has improved to 947.5 female/thousand male.

Table 3.22: Population and Sex Ratio of Malda

	Total Population	*Male*	*Female*	*Sex Ratio*
1951	937,580	476,794	460,786	966.4
1961	1,221,923	621,990	599,933	964.5
1971	1,612,657	827,706	784,951	948.3
1981	2,031,871	1,042,498	989,373	949.0
1991	2,637,032	1,360,541	1,276,491	938.2
2001	3,290,160	1,689,409	1,600,751	947.5

Source: District Statistical Handbook, Malda, Bureau of Applied Economics & Statistics, Government of West Bengal, 2001.

It is to be noted that the population growth has marginally decline from 2.68 percent (CARG 1951-61) to 2.24 percent

(1991-2001). Though it has declined but the decline is not sufficient. It is observed that the high growth rate is mainly because of high birth rate in the rural areas and immigration from across the international and state border.

After analysing the problem due to the rising population we find the problem is further aggravated in the agriculture, as Malda is primarily a rural district with 92.7 percent population living in rural areas in 2001 (Table 3.23). This means there is no much industrial activity in the district and agriculture is the mainstay of the residents.

Table 3.23: Urbanisation in Malda

	Urban	*Rural*	*% of Rural Population*
1951	35161	902419	96.2
1961	50785	1171138	95.8
1971	68026	1544631	95.8
1981	97196	1934675	95.2
1991	186537	2450495	92.9
2001	240915	3049245	92.7

Source: District Statistical Handbook, Malda, Bureau of Applied Economics & Statistics, Government of West Bengal, 2001.

Analysing Table 3.24, which shows the block wise population distribution for 1991 we find the density at 736 person/Km2, is really high with only two blocks having urban centres viz. Old Malda and English Bazar.

Table 3.24: Population Density in Malda: Block-wise (1991)

Block/Region	*Population*	*Density*
Harishchandrapur I	129,829	757.5
Harishchandrapur II	157,077	723.1
Chanchal I	143,288	884.1
Chanchal II	132,697	646.6
Ratua I	173,655	771.2
Ratua II	125,762	1,241.6
Tal	862,308	796.7
Gazole	233,139	453.8
Bamongola	107,579	521.7
Habibpur	168,397	424.1
Old Malda	146,020	631.5

Barind	655,135	485.9
English Bazar	319,638	1,204.0
Manikchak	177,572	561.2
Kaliachak I	243,787	2,286.9
Kaliachak II	163,871	783.4
Kaliachak III	214,721	842.9
Diara	1,119,589	971.5
Malda	2,637,032	736.0

Source: District Statistical Handbook, Malda, Bureau of Applied Economics & Statistics, Government of West Bengal, 2001

It is seen that the central blocks of Ratua-II, English Bazar and Kaliachak-I have high density while eastern blocks of Gazole, Bamongola and Habibpur, and Manikchak from the west have low population density.

Table 3.25 shows the region wise population distribution of Malda. It is seen that Malda has primarily two religion Hindu and Muslim.

Table 3.25: Population by Religion in Malda (1991)

Religion	*Number*	*% to Total Population*
Hindu	1,377,844	52.25
Muslim	1,252,292	47.49
Christian	5,118	0.19
Sikhs	183	0.01
Buddhists	64	0.00
Jains	224	0.01
Others	1,307	0.05
Total	2,637,032	100

Source: District Statistical Handbook, Malda, Bureau of Applied Economics & Statistics, Government of West Bengal, 2001.

From the primary survey we found the religion wise population composition for the regions, as shown in Table 3.26. We find that the Muslim population is more concentrated in the Tal region.

Table 3.26: Population by Religion: Region-wise

	Hindu	*Muslim*	*Christian*
Tal	59.2%	40.8%	0.0%
Barind	68.9%	27.4%	3.7%
Diara	76.7%	23.3%	0.0%
Malda	67.7%	31.0%	1.4%

Derived from Primary Survey result of 368 respondents.

Table 3.27 shows the distribution of population by scheduled categories. It is observed that the share of scheduled caste and scheduled tribe is comparatively more in Barind region.

Table 3.27: Distribution of Population by SC and ST (1991)

Blocks	*Scheduled Caste*	*Scheduled Tribe*	*Total*
Harishchandrapur I	32737	2840	35577
Harishchandrapur II	19060	3424	22484
Chanchal I	21177	586	21763
Chanchal II	13573	10353	23926
Ratua I	15567	3990	19557
Ratua II	11028	1598	12626
Tal	113142	22791	135933
Gazole	78507	50153	128660
Bamongola	54493	22637	77130
Habibpur	78608	52789	131397
Old Malda	42858	17759	60617
Barind	254466	143338	397804
English Bazar	47129	4914	52043
Manikchak	21468	147	21615
Kaliachak I	7484	16	7500
Kaliachak II	15008	6	15014
Kaliachak III	19199	114	19313
Diara	110288	5197	115485
Malda	477896	171326	649222

Source: District Statistical Handbook, Malda, Bureau of Applied Economics & Statistics. Government of West Bengal, 2001.

When we analyse the above information with the help of the primary survey results for individual regions, it ratifies the results as 46.2 percent of Barind's population is found to be of scheduled caste type. (Table 3.28)

Table 3.28: Distribution of Population in Malda: Region Wise

	General	*SC*	*ST*	*OBC*
Tal	92.2%	7.8%	0.0%	0.0%
Barind	23.7%	46.2%	3.2%	26.9%
Diara	32.9%	17.7%	0.0%	49.4%
Malda	47.8%	25.3%	1.2%	25.7%

Derived from Primary Survey result of 249 Hindu respondent.

Another important population characteristic is the family size. Analysing the same for Malda district (Table 3.29) we find that family size is almost same across regions but there is a disparity among the blocks. While Kaliachak-III has the highest family size, it is lowest for English Bazar.

Table 3.29: Average Family Size in Malda: Block Wise (1991)

	Population	*No. of Household*	*Average Family Size*
Harishchandrapur I	129,829	26310	4.93
Harishchandrapur II	157,077	26331	5.97
Chanchal I	143,288	29337	4.88
Chanchal II	132,697	24354	5.45
Ratua I	173,655	29930	5.80
Ratua II	125,762	23354	5.39
Tal	862,308	159616	5.40
Gazole	233,139	44677	5.22
Bamongola	107,579	20911	5.14
Habibpur	168,397	33997	4.95
Old Malda	146,020	25261	5.78
Barind	655,135	124846	5.25
English Bazar	319,638	69870	4.57
Manikchak	177,572	31357	5.66
Kaliachak I	243,787	41429	5.88

Kaliachak II	163,871	28820	5.69
Kaliachak III	214,721	34997	6.14
Diara	1,119,589	206473	5.42
Malda	2,637,032	490935	5.37

Source: District Statistical Handbook, Malda, Bureau of Applied Economics. & Statistics, Government of West Bengal, 2001.

We have also analysed the average family size by religion for the regions of Malda through our primary survey. We find that the overall average family size is comparatively high in Diara region but in all three region the family size for Muslims is higher than the Hindu families. (Table 3.30)

Table 3.30: Average Family Size: Region Wise

	Hindu	*Muslim*	*Christian*	*Overall*
Tal	5.4	6.5		5.8
Barind	6.7	9.2	5.4	7.3
Diara	5.8	8.4		6.4
Malda	6.0	7.8	5.4	6.5

Derived from Primary Survey result of 368 respondents.

Table 3.31 shows the literacy rate for the individual blocks of Rural Malda. It is seen that the overall literacy rate in the district varies between 27.49 percent (Kaliachak-III) and 37.52 percent (Bamongola). The majority of the Blocks' literacy rate lie around 31 percent.

Table 3.31: Literacy Rate in Malda (Rural)

	Male	*Female*	*Total*
Harishchandrapur I	39.53	19.99	30.10
Harishchandrapur II	39.37	18.86	29.46
Chanchal I	48.82	29.93	39.76
Chanchal II	40.75	21.93	31.62
Ratua I	41.94	20.78	31.77
Ratua II	39.56	20.92	30.54
Gazole	41.59	19.98	31.07
Bamongola	49.27	25.07	37.52

Habibpur	45.29	25.07	33.43
Old Malda	43.80	21.72	33.30
English Bazar	45.24	25.73	35.85
Manikchak	44.33	18.23	31.70
Kaliachak I	44.97	24.55	35.09
Kaliachak II	41.52	21.57	31.92
Kaliachak III	37.77	16.21	27.49
Malda	42.80	21.60	32.57

Source: District Statistical Handbook, Malda, Bureau of Applied Economics & Statistics, Government of West Bengal, 2001.

After observing the regional variation in the literacy rate of Rural Malda we here analyse the education level for the regions. It is seen in Table 3.32 that the number of illiterates and primary educated respondents are comparatively more in Barind region (63 percent). It is lowest in the Tal region (35.9 percent).

Table 3.32: Education Level in Malda: Region Wise

	Illiterate	*Primary education*	*Secondary education*	*Higher secondary Education*	*Graduate and above*
Tal	23.4%	12.5%	44.5%	6.3%	13.3%
Barind	34.1%	28.9%	28.1%	5.9%	3.0%
Diara	18.4%	24.3%	51.5%	2.9%	2.9%
Malda	26.0%	21.9%	40.4%	5.2%	6.6%

Derived from Primary Survey result of 366 respondents.

Table 3.33 shows the distribution of population by sex and age group.

Table 3.33: Distribution of Population by Sex and Age Group in Malda (1991)

	Absolutes ('000)			*Share (%)*		
Age Group	*Male*	*Female*	*Total*	*Male*	*Female*	*Total*
0-4	191.5	187	378.5	14.1	14.6	14.4
5-9	198.9	188.5	387.4	14.6	14.8	14.7
10-14	166.1	154	320.1	12.2	12.1	12.1
15-19	122.5	111.9	234.4	9.0	8.8	8.9
20-24	112.1	112.7	224.8	8.2	8.8	8.5
25-29	106.3	113.8	220.1	7.8	8.9	8.3
30-39	187.3	164.3	351.6	13.8	12.9	13.3
40-49	116.8	101.7	218.5	8.6	8.0	8.3
50-59	71.8	64.5	136.3	5.3	5.1	5.2
60+	70.7	64	134.7	5.2	5.0	5.1
Age not stated	16.6	14.1	30.7	1.2	1.1	1.2
All Ages	1360.6	1276.5	2637.1	100.0	100.0	100.0

Source: District Statistical Handbook, Malda, Bureau of Applied Economics & Statistics, Government of West Bengal, 2001.

It is seen that 50 percent of the population in the district are in the age group below 19 years. If we include the number of people above 60 years then we find the ratio of mouth to feed to hands to work is 2.26: 1. This age composition has serious implication, as in near future the pressure on land is likely to increase in folds if no other job opportunity is created for the youth. But one positive indication is that the age composition by sex do not show any disparity.

After analysing the population parameter we find the pressure on land is increasing in the district and will be a serious problem in years to come.

c. Cultural Factors

Launching a direct attack on technical problems alone, i.e. extension work aimed at the use of improved technical methods and of modern agricultural requisites, will by itself be not sufficient to ensure agricultural development. Simultaneous attention must be given to other problems which at the moment are impediments to the rapid development of agricultural production. Among these problems some are sociological. The four most important sociological impediments in developing efficient agriculture are: i.Ownership holding, ii. Tenural arrangement, iii. Farm family characteristics iv. Labour force. These are important enough to be analysesd individually. In this section we analyse these factors for the district of Malda.

Ownership holding:

Considering the long period for which cultivation has been carried on in Malda the increase in population and the laws of succession, one can imagine their combined effect on land holdings. The laws of succession result in the sub-division and fragmentation of holdings. When the father dies, the land is divided equally among all his heirs. Each successor insists on having a share from each location and piece of land, resulting in further fragmentation of land. It is a wasteful method of land utilization and many improved agricultural practices cannot be adopted (Randhawa, 1974). The disadvantages of fragmentation and scattered holdings are well known: it puts a large proportion of land outside the possibility of effective cultivation or economic development; it wastes time in the need to supervise; it makes capital duplication necessary; the small plots are difficult to work with tractors; weed and pest control is made difficult, and it limits mechanization and experimentation. On the whole, it is a serious impediment to agricultural progress and acts as a deterrent to a full utilization of land and farmforce.

Table 3.34 and Table 3.35 shows the area and number of operational holdings in the district for individual blocks. The data used is from the Agricultural Census of 1995-96. These tables show that maximum farmers hold land less 0.5 hectare. Fig 3.2 shows the disparity of holding as 49.8 percent of farmers hold only 15.8 percent of the total cropped area and including the next 25.8 percentage of the holders the cumulative holding moves up to only 24.1 percent.

Thus we find that operational size in the district is not congenial for effective farm practices.

Fig 3.2: Lorenz curve: Area of Holdings vs No. of Holders

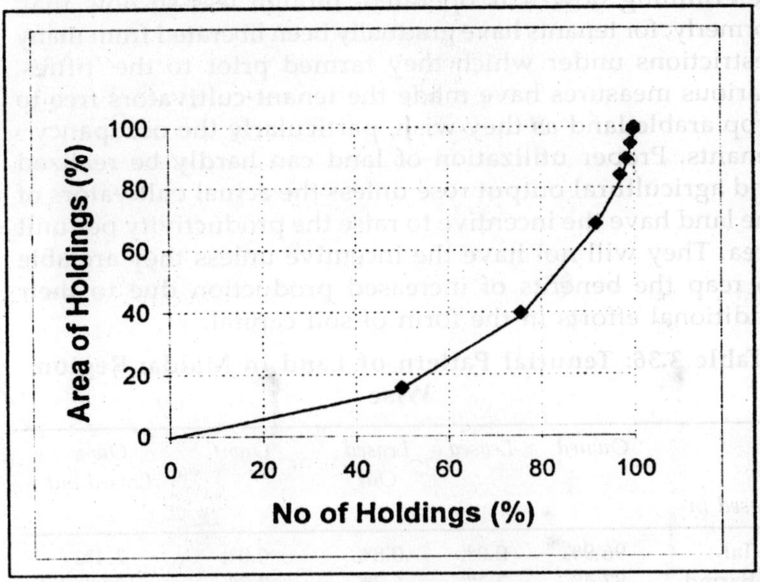

The situation is similar across the blocks and regions as in Tal lowest 51.5 percent peasants occupy 16.7 percent of the land and in Barind it is 43.9 percent holding 12.9 percent. The situation in Diara is no different as 54.8 percent of cultivators hold 18.9 percent of land.

Secured Land Tenure

While in the narrower sense land tenure may be described as the body of rules which govern the allocation and the apportionment of produce, in the wider sense it covers the whole relationship of man to the soil. This relationship, on the one hand, transforms the land and, on the other, causes human beings to live together in households and farming communities. A three-tiered structure characterizes the land tenure organization in the villages of Malda, comprising owner-cultivators, tenant-cultivators (with varying degree of security, but often with none) and lessee-cultivators.

The way in which the land is held is also a factor in determining how it is operated, though less so now than formerly; for tenants have gradually been liberated from many restrictions under which they farmed prior to the 'fifties. Various measures have made the tenant-cultivators free to crop arable land as they wish, particularly the occupancy-tenants. Proper utilization of land can hardly be realized and agricultural output rose unless the actual cultivators of the land have the incentive to raise the productivity per unit area. They will not have the incentive unless they are able to reap the benefits of increased production due to their additional efforts in the form of soil capital.

Table 3.36: Tenurial Pattern of Land in Malda: Region Wise

Leased in	*Owned*	*Leased*	*Leased Out*	*Own/*	*Own/ Leased out*
1. Tal	96.9%	0.0%	0.8%	0.0%	2.4%
2. Barind	87.4%	2.2%	6.7%	3.7%	0.0%
3. Diara	93.2%	1.9%	1.9%	1.0%	1.9%
Malda	92.3%	1.4%	3.3%	1.6%	1.4%

Derived from Primary Survey result of 365 respondents.

Table 3.36 shows the region wise tenurial pattern of land in the district. Its seen that the number of of landless agriculturist are minimal in the district. 92.3 percent of the respondents on their own land. But as regional level the situation in Barind is not so. Here only 87.4 percent of the respondents own their land. 6.7 percent of the respondents farm on leased land.

Farm Family Characteristics

The relationship between the size of operational holding and population characteristics is an interesting area to study. When we cross tab the religion with the average size of holding, (Table 3.37) we find the Hindus to have higher (8.9 bigha) farm size than those of Muslim (7.6 bigha). But the holding

Table 3.34: Area of Operational Holding in Malda: Block-wise (1995-96)

Area of Holdings	*Below 0.5*	*0.5-1.0*	*1.0-2.0*	*2.0-3.0*	*3.0-4.0*	*4.0-5.0*	*5.0-7.5*	*7.5-10.0*	*10.0-20.0*	*Total*
Harishchandrapur I	3392	5063	3176	2245	811	665	549	128	52	16081
Harishchandrapur II	3292	5029	8145	2902	1017	435	356	132	104	21412
Chanchal I	2601	3858	4894	2114	723	390	322	172		15074
Chanchal II	3674	5679	5098	2480	792	483	485	44		18735
Ratua I	2581	3908	3709	4128	1377	2231	1934	216	104	20188
Ratua II	1892	2838	4079	2177	758	597	550	44		12935
Tal	17432	26375	29101	16046	5478	4801	4196	736	260	104425
Gazole	5466	8685	15290	8522	2835	2277	1973	436	156	45640
Bamongola	2451	3813	5154	4030	1420	1205	1005	260	103	19441
Habibpur	4573	7311	12506	5735	1852	1633	1477	308	188	35583
Old Malda	2657	4152	5455	2228	759	938	744	216	52	17201
Barind	15147	23961	38405	20515	6866	6053	5199	1220	499	117865
English Bazar	3499	5183	6417	3280	1138	1678	1388	348		22931
Manikchak	5182	6192	4368	2069	706	967	871	88		20443
Kaliachak I	1414	5124	1594	1050	533	285	408	132	52	10592
Kaliachak II	2998	2948	2084	1400	310	660	430	44		10874
Kaliachak III	1872	2796	3703	2844	998	1105	903	132	104	14457
Diara	14965	22243	18166	10643	3685	4695	4000	744	156	79297
Malda	47544	72579	85672	47204	16029	15549	13395	2700	915	301587

Source: Agricultural Census, 1995-96.

Table 3.35: Number of Operational Holdings in Malda: Block-wise (1995-96)

No. of Holdings	*Below 0.5*	*0.5-1.0*	*1.0-2.0*	*2.0-3.0*	*3.0-4.0*	*4.0-5.0*	*5.0-7.5*	*7.5-10.0*	*10.0-20.0*	*Total*
Harishchandrapur I	12640	6340	2125	880	235	145	85	15	5	22470
Harishchandrapur II	12465	6295	5455	1130	295	95	55	15	10	25815
Chanchal I	9830	4825	3280	825	210	85	50	20		19125
Chanchal II	13900	7120	3405	965	230	105	75	5		25805
Tal	65905	33020	19485	6250	1590	1045	650	85	25	128055
Ratua I	9845	4890	2485	1605	400	485	300	25	10	20045
Ratua II	7225	3550	2735	845	220	130	85	5		14795
Gazole	19495	10940	10115	3340	820	500	305	50	15	45580
Bamongola	8540	4805	3410	1595	410	265	155	30	10	19220
Habibpur	15420	9240	8220	2262	534	360	228	36	18	36318
Old Malda	9675	5220	3625	875	220	205	115	25	5	19965
Barind	53130	30205	25370	8072	1984	1330	803	141	48	121083
English Bazar	13105	6485	4295	1280	330	365	215	40		26115
Manikchak	17125	7740	2930	805	205	210	135	10		29160
Kaliachak I	10625	6405	1070	407	155	64	65	15	5	18811
Kaliachak II	8855	3685	1400	543	90	141	65	5		14784
Kaliachak III	7145	3495	2485	1105	290	240	140	15	10	14925
Diara	56855	27810	12180	4140	1070	1020	620	85	15	103795
Malda	175890	91035	57035	18462	4644	3395	2073	311	88	352933

Source: Agricultural Census, 1995-96.

pattern has variation among regions. Barind has comparatively large average holding of 10.1 bigha while Diara has 9.6 bigha. Average holding of Tal rergion is of only 6.0 bigha. The disparity among Hindus and Muslims of Barind region is wide while in Diara it is the lowest.

Table 3.37: Average Land Holding by Religion in Malda: Region Wise

	Hindu	*Muslim*	*Christian*	*Total*
1.Tal	4.1	8.6		6.0
2.Barind	11.3	4.8	8.6	10.1
3.Diara	10.1	7.9		9.6
Malda	8.9	7.6	8.6	8.5

Derived from Primary Survey result of 365 respondents.

Table 3.38 shows the average holding of Hindus with the respect to caste. Against our perception that average ownership holding for general caste will be more, it is found to be the least. But when we analyse the regions individually we find in Barind region the size of the ST and OBC ownership holding is less than the general category, while in Tal and Diara the average holding of SC's are less than the general caste.

Table 3.38: Average Land Holding by Caste of Hindus in Malda: Region Wise

	General	*SC*	*ST*	*OBC*
1.Tal	4.2	2.5		
2.Barind	11.9	14.3	10.0	7.4
3.Diara	8.7	7.7		11.8
Malda	6.8	11.8	10.0	9.6

Derived from Primary Survey result of 249 respondents.

Labour:

To understand the labour situation of Malda we considered the Government of India data on workers. Using the census definition of main workers, marginal workers and non-workers i.e.

Main workers: Main workers are those who had workerd for the major part of the year preceding the date of enumeration, i.e those who were engaged in any economically productive activity for 183 days or more.

Marginal workers: Marginal workers are those who worked any time in the year preceding the date of enumeration but did not work for the major part of the year, i.e. those who worked for less than 183 days.

Non-workers: Non-workers are those who did not work ny time at all in the year prceding the date of enumeration.

Table 3.39: Distribution of Population as Workers, Non-workers in Malda: Block Wise (1991)

	Total Main Workers		*Marginal Workers*		*Non Workers*		*Population*
	Absolute	*(%)*	*Absolute*	*(%)*	*Absolute*	*(%)*	
Harishchandrapur I	41455	31.9	1450	1.1	86924	67.0	129829
Harishchandrapur II	47582	30.3	3321	2.1	106174	67.6	157077
Chanchal I	43295	30.2	2697	1.9	97296	67.9	143288
Chanchal II	42222	31.8	2951	2.2	87524	66.0	132697
Ratua I	48315	27.8	3727	2.1	121613	70.0	173655
Ratua II	36300	28.9	1327	1.1	88135	70.1	125762
Tal	259169	30.1	15473	1.8	587666	68.2	862308
Gazole	78713	33.8	6948	3.0	147478	63.3	233139
Bamongola	38281	35.6	3636	3.4	65662	61.0	107579
Habibpur	65199	38.7	7966	4.7	95232	56.6	168397
Old Malda	47866	32.8	4138	2.8	94016	64.4	146020
Barind	230059	35.1	22688	3.5	402388	61.4	655135
English Bazar	90100	28.2	5127	1.6	224411	70.2	319638
Manikchak	54947	30.9	5999	3.4	116626	65.7	177572
Kaliachak I	71291	29.2	17440	7.2	155056	63.6	243787
Kaliachak II	54543	33.3	6806	4.2	102522	62.6	163871
Kaliachak III	74299	34.6	6886	3.2	133536	62.2	214721
Diara	345180	30.8	42258	3.8	732151	65.4	1119589
Malda	834408	31.6	80419	3.0	1722205	65.3	2637032

Source: Government of India Census, 1991.

We find only one third of the population working. Table 3.39 shows the distribution in the blocks and regions. We find total main workers to be high in Barind (35.1 percent).

Table 3.40 shows the distribution of main workers in to different types at Block level. The pattern is distinctly different for Diara region, particularly for English Bazar. This is primarily because of large urban population in he block. Its seen that Harishchandrapur II has the maximum number of cultivators while Manikchak has the maximum number of agricultural labour.

Table 3.40: Distribution of Main Workers in Malda: Block Wise (1991)

	Cultivators		*Agricultural Labourers*		*Household Industry*		*Other Workers*	
	Popu-ation	*Perc-entage*	*Popu-ation*	*Perc-entage*	*Popu-ation*	*Perc-entage*	*Popu-ation*	*Perc-entage*
Harishchandrapur I	15766	38.0	19395	46.8	1031	2.5	5263	12.7
Harishchandrapur II	24011	50.5	17372	36.5	828	1.7	5371	11.3
Chanchal I	16956	39.2	16409	37.9	1155	2.7	8775	20.3
Chanchal II	20103	47.6	16736	39.6	655	1.6	4728	11.2
Ratua I	20957	43.4	18978	39.3	681	1.4	7699	15.9
Ratua II	13464	37.1	16528	45.5	426	1.2	5882	16.2
Tal	111257	42.9	105418	40.7	4776	1.8	37718	14.6
Gazole	38337	48.7	30475	38.7	1677	2.1	8224	10.4
Bamongola	17935	46.9	15012	39.2	691	1.8	4643	12.1
Habibpur	27674	42.4	24681	37.9	2109	3.2	10735	16.5
Old Malda	14314	29.9	13429	28.1	2292	4.8	17631	36.8
Barind	98260	42.7	83597	36.3	6769	2.9	41233	17.9
English Bazar	11055	12.3	19717	21.9	4246	4.7	54673	60.7
Manikchak	15788	28.7	26517	48.3	3426	6.2	9216	16.8
Kaliachak I	13015	18.3	20746	29.1	6194	8.7	31336	44.0
Kaliachak II	15330	28.1	18021	33.0	3074	5.6	18119	33.2
Kaliachak III	23809	32.0	14362	19.3	1136	1.5	34992	47.1
Diara	78997	22.9	99363	28.8	18076	5.2	148336	43.0
Malda	288514	34.6	288378	34.6	29621	3.5	227287	27.2

Source: Government of India Census, 1991.

While interacting with the farmers in the district we find the problem of labour supply, specially during the harvesting and sowing season. Table 3.41 shows the level of availability of labour in the region. It is seen that 39.5 percent of the respondents face the problem of labour supply severely. This is likely to impact the overall productivity adversely.

Table 3.41: Availability of Labour in Malda: Regionwise

	Very easy	*Easy*	*Medium*	*Difficult*	*Very Difficult*
Tal		24.4%	36.2%	39.4%	
Barind	3.7%	16.3%	57.8%	22.2%	
Diara		2.9%	34.3%	60.8%	2.0%
Malda	1.4%	15.4%	43.7%	39.0%	0.5%

Derived from Primary Survey result of 364 respondents.

This problem is faced as the farmers use hired labours in seasons when labour demand rises. Table 3.42 shows the composition of the type of labour. It is noticed that almost cent percent cultivators use hired labour and this practice is spread across regions. In Table 3.40 we had seen that of the total workforce 34.6 percent work as agricultural labour. During the lean season these labourers work in construction industry in the nearby towns.

Table 3.42: Type of Labour in Malda: Region Wise

	Hired	*Family*	*Child*	*Hired/Family*
Tal	40.5%	1.6%		57.9%
Barind	30.6%	0.8%	1.6%	66.9%
Diara	32.4%			67.6%
Malda	34.7%	0.9%	0.6%	63.9%

Derived from Primary Survey result of 352 respondents.

Another interesting feature of labour in the district is the mode of payment adopted to pay the agricultural labour. Table 3.42 shows the findings. 63.1 percent of the respondents are found to be paid/pay in cash while a major chunk of 33.3 percent are paid with cereals along-with cash.

Table 3.43: Mode of Payment of Labour in Malda: Region Wise

	Cash	*Cash/Cereals*	*Cash/Others*
Tal	74.80%	25.20%	0.00%
Barind	88.89%	11.11%	0.00%
Diara	13.86%	73.27%	12.87%
Malda	63.09%	33.33%	3.58%

Derived from Primary Survey result of 363 respondents.

d) Infrastructural Services: Infrastructural services viz. marketing facilities, transport and accessibilities, credit facilities etc. are essential for modern farm operations. These factors individually or collectively influence the agricultural patterns and productivity. Therefore, these factors are important to analyse, to understand the variability of agricultural productivity and to propose measures to increase productivity.

Marketing Facilities:

Market is a center of business activities, which direct the flow of goods from producer to consumer. An effective and efficient marketing system from the point of a view of farmer is one, which facilitates easy and smooth channeling of the farm produce at right price and at a time when the producer so desires.

Now, we discuss the present marketing pattern of the major crops in the district.

Paddy and Rice:

The progressive cultivators generally sell their paddy to the wholesale traders in the assembling markets and also to rice mill in the district. The small growers sell their paddy to village Mahajans or Farias who visit door to door in the village. The itinerant merchants very often process the paddy into rice in husking mills and sale the rice to the local traders, retailers and consumers. The small and marginal farmers sell their paddy in the nearest hat or to the Farias immediately after the harvest for urgent need of cash to repay the loan or advance.

Jute:

Farias, unemployed youths of cultivators' family and also some growers cum-Farias purchase jute at village level visiting door to door and sale the same to the big traders and their agents in the primary markets. They also sale to J.C.I. when the price offered by the J.C.I. is profitable as compared to that offered by the traders. The progressive farmers also bring their jute in the primary market for direct sale to traders and agent of jute mills. The traders send the jute, to jute mills at Calcutta after grading and bailing the same in bailing press installed at their premises. J.C.I., C.A.D.P. and co-operative are the active institutions in marketing of jute in the district.

Vegetables:

The small Farias usually bring the vegetable from farm to primary assembling markets where the stock are sold to wholesalers who in turn sale to retailers in the consumers markets in towns of the district. Vegetables are brought to the markets or hats from the farm in bullock carts and tanga. The Aratdars in the secondary market virtually control the price of vegetable in the local markets.

Oil Seeds:

Traders, their agents, village merchants and Farias procure oil seeds from village farms or primary markets. The stock thus procured is sold to wholesale traders and agents of oil mills in the secondary market in the district

Mango:

Mango is one of the most important commercial crops of the district. Mango orchards are sold even at the primary stage of fruiting. Plucking is done by contract labour and the fruits are graded (according to the size) and packed in buskets at garden point. The baskets are brought from garden to pukka road point in bullock carts and tangas to be loaded in trucks for sending to its destination in secondary and terminal markets at distant places/cities towns. There are also a number of itinerant merchants operating in mango marketing who make sizeable profit at the cost of producers. Advance trading as well as sell and resell of orchards at different stages of fruits is a unique feature of mango marketing in the district.

Wheat:

The progressive cultivators dispose of the stocks in secondary/primary market/hats while small and marginal cultivators dispose the produce at farm gate in the village. In primary market/hats the farias are very active. They even procure wheat roaming from village to village and sale in the secondary and big primary markets/hats.

The wholesalers again dispose of the stock into atta for sale in local markets/hats. A majority portion of the stock is converted into atta by the wholesalers for wholesale trade.

Understanding the importance of Marketing Facilities some important measures taken by the Government of West Bengal are i) Market Intelligence Scheme ii) Agricultural Regulated Market iii) National Grid of Rural Godown iv) Cold Storage facility.

Market Intelligence Scheme is one of the important activities for the Directorate of Agricultural Marketing in Malda district. It has an important role in determining the efficient system of marketing, which not only helps the farmers to get better price for their produce by dispensing their stock at the proper place and the right moment but also helps them to determine their cropping pattern. There are three market intelligence centers in three secondary markets of Malda district:. i) Englisbazar ii) Chanchal, and iii) Samsi. In each center there is one market level worker who observes the arrival and prices of agricultural commodities and reports the same to the Director of Agricultural Marketing, West-Bengal and Economic and Statistic Advisor to the Govt. of India. The main objective of this scheme is to introduce grading system in regulated market as well as rural areas. This helps the grower of Malda district to get remunerative price by grading their commodities.

But during rounds of field survey it was reported that hardly any farmer gets the benefits of this facility in the interior of the district. The response to the awareness about the scheme was satisfactory but they hardly get any information regarding the price from authorized services. The decision regarding the point of sale and the time of sale and the expected profit is guided by the farmers in network and compulsion of necessity.

Thus it is felt that to increase the effectiveness of Market Intelligence Scheme and bring about a shift in this service from a mere a data collection process to dissemination of information proper network needs to be established who regularly can interact with the farmers on the field.

Agricultural Regulated Market has been playing a major role for the smooth distribution of food crops, oil-seeds and cash crops to meet the supply and demand needs of the farmers, traders and consumers. At present, there are only two regulated market in the district, one in Englishbazar i.e. Diara region and another in Samsi of Tal region. The PS under the purview of English Bazar Regulated Market are English Bazar, Kaliachak, Gazole, Bamongola, Habibpur, Old Malda while Samsi regulated market supports Harishchandrapur, Chanchal, Ratua, Manikchak Police Stations. Thus it is found that the English bazar regulated market supports even the blocks of Barind region which do not have any regulated market of its own. The farmers of Barind region have to travel comparatively longer distance to access the facilities of English bazar regulated market. And to avoid this long distance and its cost implications the farmers of Barind region resort to sell their products to middle men. There is a necessity to develop a regulated market in the Barind region to support the requirements of this region.

National Grid of Rural Godown has been taken up by the Directorate of Marketing with an objective: construction of godown in the regulated market areas. In 2000, there were two godowns present in the regulated market area of i) Samsi Regulated Market for 1000 metric tones at principal market yard and ii) Chanchal sub-market yard under Samsi Regulated Market Committee of 500 metric tones. In this scheme both the Central and State Government is bearing 50 percent cost and the regulated market committee is bearing the rest 50 percent cost. These godowns were prepared with the intention that the farmers who come to sell their produce at regulated market can keep their unsold goods, and sell at a later date. Due to the absence of the rural godown scheme in Barind and Diara region farmers are unable to take the advantage of this scheme so either they have to carry their produce back and bring back on a later date which has a cost implication or else sell the produce at lower price. The middle-men take the benefit of this situation and try to exploit the farmers.

So there is an urgent necessity to assess the requirement storage facility in the district and especially in Barind and Diara region. While both the present godown are associated with Samsi Regulated Market, the non availability of godown facility in Englishbazar Regulated Market area is the sign of non-availability of primary infrastructural facility in the region. So it is suggested to develop godown facility in Englishbazar Regulated Market area at he earliest and gradually in Barind region. Table 3.44 shows the achievement of regulated market committee.

Table 3.44: Achievement of Regulated Marketed Committee in Malda District

	Samsi			English Bazar		
	Total Expenditure	*Total Income**	*Profit*	*Total Expenditure*	*Total Income**	*Profit*
1995-96	2,571,775	9,870,737	7,298,962	898,960	5,329,583	4,430,623
1996-97	4,138,118	12,230,673	8,092,555	4,574,568	7,412,027	2,837,459
1997-98	6,835,214	14,100,550	7,265,336	1,631,860	6,859,816	5,227,956

* Includes Market fee, License fee & other income.

From the above table it's seen that establishments of Regulated Market is a revenue-generating source. The initial capital investment require to built Regulated Market Committee is the major obstacle in proliferating the marketing facility across the district. But keeping in mind the importance of proper marketing facility in today's world setting up of such regulated market is felt to be of utmost necessity and a good business proposition in the long run.

Another important marketing facility is Cold Storage as this marketing infrastructure is necessary for carrying the agricultural produce from production season to consuming periods. Lack of inadequate scientific storage facilities is responsible for heavy losses to the farmers in terms of quality and quantity of crops. Seasonal fluctuation of prices is aggravated in the absence of these facilities. In 2000, Malda district had only one cold storage of 4000 metric tones capacity at Samsi (co-operative sector) in Tal region which is not sufficient for cultivators of the district. As we find in the recent past that there is a shift in cropping pattern throughout the district and it is more of cash crops, which can be supported by providing cold storage facility. More cold storage facilities are necessary in the district to serve the purpose of the cultivators.

Table 3.45: Market Density in Malda District (1998-99)

Blocks	*Geographical Area (ha)*	*No. of Market/ Hat*	*Average Area served by a market (ha)*
Harishchandrapur I	17,202	25	688
Harishchandrapur II	21,156	13	1627
Chanchal I	15,855	27	587
Chanchal II	20,550	14	1468
Ratua I	22,126	18	1229
Ratua II	17,210	8	2151
Tal	114,099	105	1087
Gazole	50,772	20	2539
Bamongola	20,380	21	970
Habibpur	39,234	19	2065
Old Malda	22,375	7	3196
Barind	132,761	67	1982
English Bazar	25,190	13	1938
Manikchak	31,654	17	1862
Kaliachak I	10,350	11	941
Kaliachak II	21,377	15	1425
Kaliachak III	23,617	12	1968
Diara	112,188	68	1650
Malda	359,048	240	1496

Source: Directorate of Agricultural Marketing, Malda.

After analyzing the availability of regulated markets we now take a look at the total market availability in the district. Table 3.45 shows the number of market for each block. But due to variability in the in the geographical area of the blocks these figures are not comparable. So we have calculated the geographical area that each markets/huts on an average serves. We find that there is a significant variation: 587 hectare for Chanchal-I while 3196 hectare for Old Malda. To analyse the market density we have considered the reciprocal of these value as if a market serves a lesser area it is considered vis-à-vis others. Considering the area that a market serves for the blocks. We calculated that average and the standard deviation and defind the upper limit and lower limit as mean +/- standard deviation. The blocks were then classified as high medium low based on their market density. It is noticed that majority of the majority of the blocks have medium market density Gazole and Old-Malda blocks of Barind region have low market density while Harishchandrapur I, Chanchal I, and Old-Malda Ihave high market density in Englishbazar block to be high in reality we find it has medium market density. The reason attributed for this is the concentration of market in Malda Town and lower number of huts in the block.

After analysing the market density in the district we now take a look at the point to whom the final product is sold by the primary cultivator. Table 3.46 shows the results and we find the farmers are unable to sell the products at points higher up in the chain. A major share (41.8 percent) is consumed by them, while 51.9 percent is sold in the local market. Middle man and Wholesaler play an important role in Diara region as 17.7 percent of the respondents sell their products to them.

Table 3.46: Market for Primary Cultivator in Malda: Region Wise

	Self consumption	*Local market*	*Middle man*	*Wholesaler*	*Others*
1. Tal	40.9%	56.7%	0.0%	0.0%	2.4%
2. Barind	48.9%	49.6%	0.7%	0.7%	0.0%
3. Diara	33.3%	49.0%	10.8%	6.9%	0.0%
Grand Total	41.8%	51.9%	3.3%	2.2%	0.8%

Derived from Primary Survey result of 367 respondents.

Therefore we find the marketing infrastructure which plays a vital role in providing of better prices of the produce to the farmers and also the good quality commodities to the consumer at reasonable prices is not developed in Malda district as a whole and Barind region in particular. So there is ample scope to develop these facilities and reap better harvests in the future.

Transport & accessibility:

Transport facility has a direct bearing on the cropping pattern and agricultural development of a region. Whatever a farmer produces at his farm he has to sell a certain portion of his produce in the market to obtain a good return, which needs an effective transport system so that goods may be speedily transported from producer to buyer. In those places where modern means of transportation is inadequate, there the surplus produce is often damaged either by adverse weather or by pests etc. With the help of the efficient transport system people can have access to the nodes or the market centers to avail all the necessary facilities for agriculture.

In Malda district most of the roads connecting the interior of villages with the main roads are kancha and narrow. Therefore to run the vehicle for transportation of farm produce is almost impossible. The condition of these roads during rainy season becomes poor. Bullock carts, rikshaw van and horse carts are only communicating system of rural people for transports of inputs.

After the evaluation of the importance of transport and accessibility in agricultural production it has been found that the district of Malda too, there is a variation in these parameters. The road density measured in terms of road length per thousand hectare has been used to measured the variability among different blocks and regions in Malda. While for the district as a whole it is found that the road density is 17.78 Km./th. Hect. The standard deviation in these road densities across the block/region is 8.28 Km./Th. Hect. As +- standard deviation encompasses majority of the blocks so using the cut off limits of mean +/- 1 standard deviation the blocks has been categorized as high/medium/low road densities. Gazole qualifies to have highest penetration of road as the N.H.34 happens to pass across the block. Manikchak, and Kaliachak III, which happens to be on the extremes of the district have low road density The variability of road density across regions in the district is found to be not pronounced so further analysis of that level is not made.

After analysing the market density in the previous sub section we now analyse the accessibility of the markets for purchase of inputs and selling of outputs. Table 3.47 shows the accessibility for the regions. In contrast to the market density we find market accessibility is difficult in Diara region. This is primarily due to the concentration of markets in Malda of Diara region. So farmers from far flung areas of Diara finds it difficult to access these markets.

Table 3.47: Access to Markets in Malda: Region Wise

	Easy	*Medium*	*Difficult*	*Very Difficult*
1. Tal	56.2%	19.2%	6.2%	18.5%
2. Barind	49.6%	23.7%	17.0%	9.6%
3. Diara	29.4%	3.9%	55.9%	10.8%
Grand Total	46.3%	16.6%	24.0%	13.1%

Derived from Primary Survey result of 367 respondents.

Credit facilities

In today's capital intensive agriculture, capital required to purchase machinery is high. To enable this institutional help and credit facility is a must. We now take stock of the availability of institutional help and credit facility in the district. Table 3.48 shows the availability of institutional help across the regions of the district.

Table 3.48: Availability of Institutional Help in Malda: Region Wise

	Easy	*Medium*	*Difficult*	*Very Difficult*
1. Tal	0.0%	0.0%	73.2%	26.8%
2. Barind	4.4%	2.2%	68.1%	25.2%
3. Diara	1.0%	9.8%	57.8%	31.4%
Grand Total	1.9%	3.6%	67.0%	27.5%

Derived from Primary Survey result of 364 respondents.

The table provides a clear indication that institutional help is unavailable in the district. 94.5 percent of the respondents are of the opinion that availability of institutional help is either difficult or very difficult. The situation is worse in the Tal region.

Other than institutional help the cultivators can avail the credit from various nationalised and co-operative banks. But on this parameter too the situation is no different. Table 3.49 illustrates the availability of credit facility in the district. It is found that 84.1 percent of the respondents find it difficult to avail credit from the institutions. The situation is worse in Tal region.

Table 3.49: Availability of Credit in Malda: Region wise

Difficult	*Very*	*Easy easy*	*Medium*	*Difficult*	*Very*
1. Tal	0.0%	5.5%	3.9%	25.2%	65.4%
2. Barind	3.7%	8.9%	3.0%	11.9%	72.6%
3. Diara	0.0%	17.6%	6.9%	11.8%	63.7%
Grand Total	1.4%	10.2%	4.4%	16.5%	67.6%

Derived from Primary Survey result of 364 respondents.

Thus we find that the credit availability and institutional help is virtually absent in the district. This acts as a great impediment to the overall increase of productivity in the district.

4

Perspective of Regional Agriculture

a) Land-use profile

Geographically land has been regarded as a specific area of the earth's surface. It is by far the most important asset of the nation and from the earliest times man has used it to satisfy his multiple needs. Land use is a primary indication of extent and degree to which man has modified the land resources. It is the application of human control in a systematic manner indicating an intimate relationship between prevailing ecological conditions and man. It is the result of a combination of both natural genesis and human influences which have been brought to bear on it, in the past and of those which are still active in the present (Vink, 1975).

Land use in an area is the cumulative out-come of historical events, the interaction of economic forces, with the natural environment, and the value of society. Land use is the surface utilization of all developed and vacant land on a specific point at a given time and space.

Land is the basic resource of human society. Land utilization is the use of land by man. The primary use of land is for crops, forest, pasture, etc. The term, land utilization, is also used for a varied utilization of land and soil. e.g. land under cultivation, pasture, barren land, orchards, fallow land, culturable waste, settlement, forest, water bodies, etc. According to Buck land utilization is the satisfaction which the farm population derives from the type of agricultural development, the provision for future production and the contribution to national needs.

Land-use shows the relationship between the society on the one hand and cultural advancement and resource planning on the other hand. The intensive use of lands depends upon population concentration, economic prosperity through better agricultural production, human establishment etc. On the other hand extensive use of land is related to sparse population, dispersed settlement, the absence of communication time and transportation. Only the systematic utilization of land can be able to promote economic and cultural advancement.

The most important objective of the development of agriculture in Malda district is to improve the living standard of the people in rural areas. On the other hand the economic development and the prosperity of the rural people in this district mainly depend upon agriculture. Adequate infrastructural facilities are required to accelerate the production and productivity of agriculture in this district. To understand the prevailing situation of agriculture in Malda district an inventory of land use is attempted here, because land use not only reflects the foundation of rural economy but also is the key to understand, the priorities and needs of the population. Agricultural production can be increased by increasing area under cultivation, double cropping and by reorganization of institutional factors. Yield of crops per hectare can be increased by accelerating more efficient use of factors of production, like environment labour, capital and application of new agricultural technology. In the following sections we examine existing agricultural land use in Malda district and the pattern of change over the years.

Classification of land

Land classification means dividing the land into different categories according to single factor or as a set of factors. Therefore land classification may be of many types depending upon the factors taken for classification. Any classification of land in any part of the world is guided primarily by the classification made by Stamp, who in his pioneer work, "The Land of Britain. Its use and Misuse" has classified land into six major categories.

In the international land use classification nine major land use classes are recognized. On the other hand in the United States of America the widely used schemes of land use classification are based on land capability classes. A. K. Philbrick has classified the land of China into seven categories. Generally the land utilization of Japan is classified into rice land, high land with dry agriculture, forested land and uncultivated land.

In India various schemes have been worked out to classify the land into different uses. The classification of land for the country as a whole is not applicable to the area under study.

The existing pattern of land-use in the Malda district are officially classified into following categories –

i) Geographical area

ii) Area under non agricultural use

iii) Forest

iv) Barren and uncultivable land

v) Permanent pastures

vi) Land under miscellaneous trees and groves.

vii) Cultivable waste land

viii) Land other than current follow

ix) Net area under cultivation

x) Current fallow

xi) Net sown area

xii) Gross cropped area

xiii) Area sown more than once

It would be suitable for a general understanding to comprise the above-mentioned categories into following categories. These are –

I) Waste land (including barren and uncultivated land and land for non agricultural use)

II) Cultivable or culturable waste land (including

culturable waste land), pastures and land under groves and trees)

III) Fallow land

IV) Net sown area

V) Total cropped area.

The Table 4.1 shows the proportion of each category of land to gross cultivated area in each of the 15 blocks in Malda district. Appendix 4.1 provides the details of the categories of land use.

Table 4.1 Land Use Pattern: Block wise (1998-99) (%)

	Geographical	*Waste*	*Cultiva-*	*Fallow*	*Net*
		Area	*Land*	*ble Waste*	*Land*
Sown		*in Hectare*		*Land*	
Area					
Harishchandrapur I	17,202	15.2	2.5	2.3	80.1
Harishchandrapur II	21,156	17.0	2.5	21.4	59.0
Chanchal I	15,855	14.9	2.1	0.6	82.3
Chanchal II	20,550	18.8	2.8	7.3	71.1
Ratua I	22,126	15.5	2.5	22.6	59.4
Ratua II	17,210	16.5	2.5	2.9	78.0
Gazole	50,772	14.8	2.7	3.0	79.5
Bamongola	20,380	15.1	2.6	5.0	77.3
Habibpur	39,234	10.4	2.5	7.7	79.4
Old Malda	22,375	18.1	2.5	6.8	72.6
English Bazar	25,190	22.2	2.5	4.0	71.3
Manikchak	31,654	16.6	2.5	3.2	77.8
Kaliachak I	10,350	32.6	3.0	0.5	63.9
Kaliachak II	21,377	55.0	2.7	1.2	41.1
Kaliachak III	23,617	28.1	2.2	1.1	68.6
Tal	114,099	16.4	2.5	10.5	70.6
Barind	132,761	14.1	2.6	5.3	78.0
Diara	112,188	28.1	2.5	2.3	67.1
Malda	359,048	19.1	2.5	6.1	72.3

Source: Malda District Annual Plan Report, 1998-99 (calculated).

It is seen from the Table 4.1, that the total area under wasteland is 19.1 percent of total area. Wasteland includes barren and uncultivated land and land for non-agricultural use. The barren and uncultivated land includes all such land which are practically useless or unproductive or unfit for cultivation. These lands are either rugged or sandy wastes or alkaline tracts which cannot be brought under cultivation except at a high cost. On the other hand land for non-agricultural use indicates those lands which cannot be brought under cultivation unless at a very high cost. The largest amount of area lying as a waste land is found in Kaliachak – II block, which occupies 55.0 percent land, because the soil of this block is medium to highly alkaline moreover presence of organic carbon is also medium low to medium. There are 10 blocks like Harishchandrapur – I, Harishchandrapur- II, Chanchal – I, Chanchal – II, Ratua – I , Ratua II, Gazole, Bamongola, Old- Malda and Manikchak the area of the waste land is recorded between 14 percent to 20 percent. There is a concentration of wasteland, above 20 percent found in English Bazar, Kaliachak – I and Kaliachak –III. Low amount of land is lying as a waste in Habibpur block (10.4 percent).

Cultivable or culturable wastelands are definitely cultivable but at present lying as waste on account of number of limitations. The total area of the culturable wasteland in the district is 2.5percent, which varies 2.1 percent in Chanchal I to 3.0 percent in Kaliachak – I block, i.e. the variation among blocks are low. In Malda district out of 15 blocks only eight blocks have a high proportion of culturable wasteland i.e. above 2.50 percent. Harishchandrapur-II, Chanchal – II, Ratua – II, Gazole, Bamongola, Old Malda, Kaliachak- I and Kaliachak- II blocks fall in this group. Other seven blocks provide a medium amount of culturable wasteland i.e. below 2.50 percent.

The term fallow land is applied to the lands not under cultivation at the time of reporting. The total area of fallow land in the district is about 6.1 percent. There are two blocks where more than 20 percent of land is kept fallow viz. Harishchandrapur II and Ratua I. Another four blocks have the share of fallow land between 4 percent and 8 percent viz. Chanchal II, Bamongola, Habibpur and Old Malda while nine blocks viz. Harishchandrapur I, Chanchal I, Ratua II, Gazole, English Bazar, Manikchak, Kaliachak I, Kaliachak II and Kaliachak III, have less than 4 percent of the area as fallow. Thus it is found that against the belief that in modern times with advanced techniques of agriculture, it is no longer necessary to keep agricultural land as fallow, in Malda district proportion of fallow land is significant in certain blocks. The main purpose to keep the land follow is to recoup the fertility lost by continuous cultivation. This objective can be fulfilled by growing crops in rotation with Legumes and by the use of fertilizers and organic manures. But in the district this practice is not prevalent using any scientific crop rotation technique.

Net sown area represents the extent of the cultivated area actually sown during an agricultural year. Net sown area comprises a total of 72.3 percent of the total area of the Malda district. A remarkable disparity is observed within the district, 'Net sown area' ranges from 41.1 percent in the block of Kaliachak –II to 81.3 percent in the Chanchal I block. In between these two extremes, there is a certain percentage in which a set of blocks can be accommodated. There are ten blocks which exceeds more than 70 percent of the Net sown area, viz. Harishchandrapur I, Chanchal I, Chanchal II, Ratua II, Gazole, Bamongola, Habibpur, Old- Malda, English bazar and Manikchak. Only two blocks Kaliachak I and Kaliachak III where net sown area varies from 60 percent to 70 percent while in Harishchandrapur II the percentage is less than 60 percent mark.

In the district mulberry cultivation in Kaliachak I and mango orchards in English Bazar, Old Malda and Ratua II are more economic which enables these blocks to sustain. But with proper implementation of crop rotation and scientific usage of land if the waste land (19.1 percent) culturable waste land (2.5 percent) and fallow land (6.1 percent) is put to plough the overall production and productivity levels can be increased to a considerable extent.

Land use: Intensity of Change

The land use categories provide an understanding of changing geographic character of the area. The pattern of land use is mainly conditioned by three sets of factors

i) Physical

ii) Economic framework

iii) Social, institutional and legal factors

The changing pattern of agricultural land use is largely concerned with the village population whose livelihood is dependent on agriculture. An increase in one type of land use must necessarily produce a decrease in another. In this aspect the study of changing spatial pattern of land use categories similarly reflects the changing socio-economic values of the region.

Table 4.2: Land use Dynamics: Malda District (%)

Sl. No.	*Type of Land Use*	*1980-81*	*1990-91*	*1998-99*	*Variation in '80s*	*Variation in '90 s*
1	Net Sown area	69.2	78.0	73.1	8.8	-4.9
2	Fallow land	5.0	0.1	5.3	-4.9	5.2
3	Uncultivated Land	6.1	2.3	2.1	-3.8	-0.3
4	Land not available for cultivation	19.1	19.1	19.1	0.0	0.0
5	Forest	0.4	0.4	0.3	0.0	-0.1
6	Pasture	0.3	0.1	0.1	-0.1	0.0
	Total area of the District (hectares)	3,59,048	3,59,048	3,59,048	3,59,048	3,59,048

Source: Malda District Annual Plan Report, 1980-81, 1990-91 & 1998-99 (calculated).

Table 4.2 shows the land use dynamics for the eighties and nineties in Malda District. The table describes land use under 6 broad categories. It has been noticed that in 1981 the net sown area was 69.2 percent of the district's total area and within 10 years this has increased to 78.0 percent. But in the next eight years it has decreased to 73.1 percent. This translates to an increase of 8.8 percent in eighties while a decline of 4.9 percent in nineties. The table also reveals the fact that in 1990-91 the proportion of fallow land had decreased to 0.1 percent and uncultivable land decreased to 2.3 percent, which accounted for the rise in the net sown area. In 1998-99 increase in fallow land to 5.3 percent is at the cost of net sown area. For the district the forest cover is minimum and it has declined in the 90's. Even the area under pasture has declined in the 80's. The constant figure of 19.1 percent for land not available for cultivation confounds the theoretical proposition that the cost of converting these tracts for cultivation is not economical. So to conclude we find that with the expansion of agriculture and modernization the share of uncultivated land is on the decline whereas it is the fluctuating share of fallow land that determines the net sown area.

b. Ground Water Potentials

The water provides essential basis and foundation for agriculture, particularly where rainfall is concentrated in a specific period and is erratic. With the advent of high yielding variety of seeds demanding costly inputs like fertilizers, agricultural implements etc. farmers are eager to ensure crop production and for this adequate and timely irrigation is important. Due to vagaries of monsoon and use of artificial supply of irrigation through DTW, STW, and canal irrigation substantial lowering of ground water table has happened.

The investigation on surface water by Sub-division IV-D Malda under the State Water Investigation Directorate, Calcutta, was conducted through an extensive survey for assessment of ground water resources at a number of places of different blocks of Malda District. The findings state that in this district ground water is used for both irrigation and drinking purposes. Malda district is confronted with the problem of low level of under ground water in the 'Barind' region on one hand, while on the other in 'Tal' and 'Diara' regions where good quality under ground water is available but some blocks face the problem of arsenic. In Barind where the water table is very low, the quality of water is poor for both irrigation and drinking purposes.

Table 4.3 shows the water level below the surface at a number of places in different blocks of Malda district, for the year of 1998 and 1999. It reveals that in general the water depth in Barind region is comparatively more than Tal and Diara. For the district the variation of water depth is significant as in the pre-monsoon period, the range is 2.01 metre (Harishchandrapur I, B.D.O., January-1999) to 21.73 (Habibpur, B.D.O., January –1998). In the post monsoon period the range is even stark and ranges between 1.78 metre (Pakua More G.P., November, 1998) to 25.83 metre (Habibpur-B.D.O., November, 1999). It is seen that the water depths of pre monsoon and post monsoon period do not vary much in Tal and Diara region while in Barind region significant variation is observed. This gives an indication that that in Barind region, to sustain agriculture in the winter months D.T.W. should be the main recourse for irrigation. The high water level of Tal and Diara needs to be judiciously exploited for enhancing the crop yield.

Table 4.3: Depth of Water Table At Selected Places in Malda (in metre)

	1998			*1999*		
	Pre-Monsoon		*Post-Monsoon*	*Pre-Monsoon*		*Post-Monsoon*
	Jan.	*April*	*Nov.*	*Jan.*	*April*	*Nov.*
TAL						
1) Harischandrapur – I						
B.D.O-	3.56	4.06	5.11	2.01	6.03	n.a
Kurshida A.P.O.-	n.a	n.a	1.9	3.71	3.92	n.a
2) Chanchal – I						
Block Seed Farm	4.16	4.56	1.67	4.32	9.01	n.a
Kharba Gram Panchayat	3.8	4.32	1.58	3.57	6.9	n.a
3) Chanchal – II						
Jalalpur Gram Panchayat	4.75	n.a	5.15	5	5.87	n.a
4) Ratua – I						
Block Seed Farm	4.64	5.04	n.a	n.a	5.21	n.a
Bhalooka Irri. Banglow	5.24	5.9	3.82	5.37	6.23	n.a
Gobarjana A. P. O.	5.06	5.56	5.55	5	6.05	n.a
Bhado A. P. O.	5.72	n.a	n.a	4.17	6.28	n.a
BARIND						

1) Old MALDA						
Malda P.W.D. Godown	6.7	8.22	2.95	2.85	8.57	n.a
Mandilpur Block - Seed Farm	7.56	9.5	3.92	7.31	10.24	n.a
Yatradanga Gram Panchayat	10.93	n.a	10.72	10.2	15.28	n.a
2) Gazole						
GazoleBlock Seed Farm	4.22	5.91	1.45	3.05	4.97	n.a
Balarampur A.K.K.	5.74	7.88	5.28	5.18	6.2	n.a
3) Bamongola						
Palkrishnapur B.S.F.	10.84	11.66	10.22	10.17	11.76	n.a
Pakuamore G.P.	3.29	3.79	1.78	3.43	6.8	n.a
4) Habibpur						
Habibpur B.D.O.	21.73	22.25	18.6	21.33	25.83	n.a
Habibpur B.S.F.	17.22	11.68	4.16	8.46	13.77	n.a
DIARA						
1) Englishbazar						
Englishbazar B.S.F.	n.a	6.55	3.82	3.72	7.33	n.a.
Milky Health Centre	5.26	5.56	3.36	6.1	5.71	n.a
Fulbari G. P.	5.93	n.a	5.38	5.18	5.39	n.a
2) Manikchak						
Nurpur health Centre	4.06	4.74	3.06	3.15	4.67	n.a
Kalindri H.C.	4.73	n.a	3.58	5.42	5.42	n.a
3) Kalichak – III						
Bainshnabngar H.C.	n.a	n.a	3.27	3.07	3.28	n.a
Birnagar H.C.	n.a	n.a	2.43	2.23	2.48	n.a

B.D.O. – Block Development Office, G.P. – Gram Panchayat, H.C. – Health Centre, B.S.F. – Block Seed Farm, A.P.O. – Anchal Pradhan Office

Source : Ground water sources of Malda, State Water Investigation Directorate (West - Bengal) 1998 – 1999.

Besides this general trend, there are pockets, where water table is either low or high determined by local slope, soil texture, soil structure and permeability factors. The water table reaches surface level during the monsoon and seepage is noticed particularly in saline-alkaline soils. Water logging is a common problem in Tal areas and in low-lying depressions. In such areas proper drainage is required for soil moisture regulation during rainy seasons.

After a through discussion with the officials 'Agri-Mechanical', 'Agri-Irrigation' department, and farmers it is suggested to adopt water shed approach which may serve as an alternative to fulfill irrigation need of agriculture.

c) Intensive Cultivation Programmes

Number of schemes and programmes to increase agricultural production as well as the productivity has been launched from time to time during the last two decades in different blocks of Malda district.

The areas under intensive agricultural approach follow the package concept. In this scheme programmes are selected on the basis of the careful study of their potentiality with favourable condition for agricultural production. These programmes are based on 'field approach' for which the village ten workers are asked to prepare appropriate farm plan for individual farmers with respect to crops which the farmers can grow. These programmes are as follows:

Integrated Cereal Development Programme (ICDP)

The ICDP was launched in 1994-95 in Malda district. This programme covered 9 blocks viz. Harishchandrapur I, Harishchandrapur II, Chanchal I, Chanchal II, Gazole, Old Malda, Habibpur, Bamongola, and Manikchak. The other 6 blocks are not included, because this programme is only applicable to the blocks where coverage of cereal is more than fifty percent. The basic objectives of the ICDP are:

i) To give demonstration to the farmers for a) proper seedbed treatment and b) integrated pest management.

ii) To educate farmers about sprinkler irrigation.

iii) To provide power tiller to the farmers at a subsidized rate of Rs. 30,000.

Special Jute Development Programme (SJDP)

SJDP is a Government of India scheme. This programme was also launched in 1994-95 in Malda district, covering eight blocks namely Harishchandrapur-I, Harishchandrapur-II, Old-Malda, Habibpur, Manikchak, Kaliachak-I, Kaliachak-II and Kaliachak-III. This programme was launched with the objective of improvement of the quantity and quality of jute. The main objectives of this programme are:

1) To give the demonstration to the farmer
2) To provide seeds at a subsidized rate.

Accelerated Maize Development Programme (AMDP)

This programme was launched in 1999 for entire Malda district to increase the production of maize. The main objectives of this scheme is to give demonstration, training and subsidized sale of agricultural implements to farmers. It is found that the farmers couldn't adopt this programme properly.

National Pulse Development Programme (NPDP)

This is a central government sponsored scheme. This programme was launched in 1994-95 in Malda district for all blocks to increase both quantity and quality of pulses. Under this scheme farmers are provided with agricultural implements at a subsidized rate.

Sugar Cane Development Scheme (SCDS)

It is a state government. sponsored scheme. This programme was initially launched in 80's and covered only six blocks, viz. Ratua I, Ratua II, Manikchak, Kaliachak I, Kaliachak II, and Kaliachak III. Under this scheme demonstration centres are created in each of the above-mentioned blocks which provide demonstration to farmers for inter cropping system. In intercropping system sugarcane are planted in autumn and spring seasons. '*Ratoon* management' is an important part of this scheme. In this management seeds are not used for further production, rather crops are used as seeds.

Seeds Multiplication Scheme (SMS)

It is a central government sponsored scheme. In this scheme, farmers are helped with agricultural implements at subsidized rate. State level training centres are created under the scheme, which provides demonstration to the farmers on seed multiplication to meet the existing shortage and for more economic development.

National Watershed Development Programme in Rain fed Areas (NWDPRA)

In the year of 1986, National watershed Development Programme was launched for rainfed areas in Malda District and covered eight blocks, viz. Habibpur, Bamongola, Old Malda, Gazole, Manikchak, Kaliachak I, Kaliachak II and Kaliachak III, where irrigation potential is less than 30percent. The main objective of this scheme is to increase the coverage with better technology.

Integrated Seed Development Scheme (ISDS)

This programme was launched in Malda district in the year of 1992 and covered Ratua I, Ratua II, Bamongola and Habibpur. Mainly it is a research-oriented scheme. This scheme is applicable to areas that are not easily accessible. Under this scheme the farmers of remote area are provided with seeds and mini kits of 2 kg. pack from the research centres for experimental cultivation.

5

Cropping Pattern, Crop Combination Region

It is well known that the growth of agricultural production depends on both area and productivity growth. The productivity growth can be further decomposed into yield growth and cropping pattern change. The former measures the impact of changes in output per unit of area while the later captures shift of acreage from one crop to another.

In this chapter we attempt to analyse the cropping pattern prevailing in the district, the changes happening, the growth trend of various crops, the crop combination and its changes. The chapter has been divided into 4 sections viz. a) cropping pattern, b) changing cropping pattern, c) growth trend analysis and d) crop combination analysis.

5.a Cropping pattern

The cropping pattern means both the time and space sequence of crops. The variety of cropping pattern is the result of physical economic and social factors. It is due to the variation in various components of physical environment- relief, climate, vegetation and soil. The economic factor affect cropping through a comparative return, which a farmer receives from a particular crop or a combination of crops. (Bishinoi, 1981)

Cropping pattern also depends on nature and availability of irrigation facilities. Where water is available, not only different crops can be grown but even a double or triple cropping will also be possible. When new irrigation facilities are provided thewhole method of production may also change. (Dayal, 1965)

Thus cropping pattern gives an indication of the relative importance a region gives to any particular crop. It is important to analyse cropping pattern as farmers in each agro-climatic region try to follow the cropping pattern to match geographical condition and also invite new technology to introduce a new pattern, to maximize farm income.

For the purpose of this section we have analysed the area under cultivation for each of the 13 crops individually at the block level for the period 1993-94 to 2000-01. Individual years show variation in area under cultivation for each crop. This is mainly because of cyclical pattern of crop cultivation adopted by the farmers, natural calamities etc. To make a comment in the cropping pattern of the districts and its blocks we have avoided the cyclic nature and considered the average area under cultivation for each crop at block level for the period 1993-94 to 2000-01.

We then calculated the share of each crop to the gross cropped area. We found for any block the top six-crop command at least three quarter of the gross cropped area. So for the purpose of analysis we have clubbed the remaining crops. The Map No-5.1 provides an illustration of the cropping pattern, at the block level.

Analysing the cropping pattern, block wise we find in Harishchandrapur-I, aman (34.6 percent), boro (17.6 percent), wheat (13.9 percent) and jute (13.4 percent) are the major crops. [The figures in the parenthesis denote the area of individual crop as percentage of gross cropped area]. The major crops stated here are purely based on the cut off limit of 10 percent, i.e. if the area cropped is greater than 10 percent then we consider the said crop as the major crop.

The major crops for the other blocks are provided below:

Harischandrapur II: aman (36.2 percent), boro (22.3 percent) and wheat (12.0 percent. The other crops are having a share less than 10 percent individually.

Map No: 5.1

CROP DISTRIBUTION IN MALDA: BLOCK WISE (93-94 to 00-01)

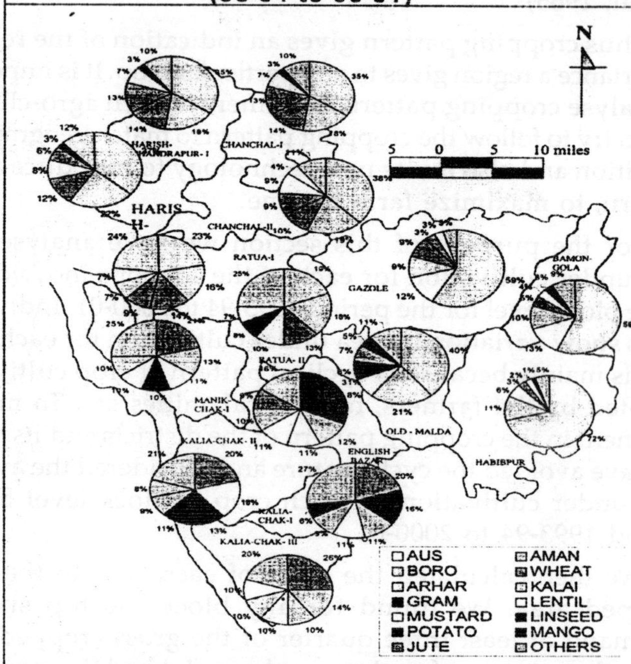

Chanchal I: aman (33.6 percent), boro (16.9 percent), wheat (12.6 percent), Jute (10.5 percent and mustard (10.3 percent).

Chanchal II: aman (37.2 percent), boro (19.3 percent) and wheat (10.0 percent).

Ratua I: aman (22.4 percent), boro (16.3 percent) and wheat (13.9 percent).

Ratua II: boro (19.2percent), aman (18.4 percent), wheat (12.5percent) and mustard (10.2 percent).

Gazole: aman (58.7 percent) and mustard (12.0 percent).

Bamongola: aman (56.2 percent), mustard (13.0 percent) and boro (10.1 percent).

Habibpur: aman (70.7 percent), and boro (11.1percent).

Old Malda: aman (39.3 percent), and boro (21.1percent).

English Bazar: mango (31.3 percent), boro (11.9 percent), mustard (11.2 percent), aus (11.0 percent) and aman (10.0 percent).

Manikchak: wheat (21.0 percent) kalai(13.4percent), aus (10.6 percent) and mango (10.2 percent)

Kaliachak I: wheat (20.2 percent), mango (15.6 percent), boro (11.0 percent) and mustard (10.8 percent)

Kaliachak II: wheat (20.8 percent), aus (18.2 percent), mango (12.8 percent) and gram (10.5 percent)

Kaliachak III: wheat (25.1 percent), aman (14.4 percent), kalai (10.3 percent), mustard (10.2 percent) and boro (10.1 percent)

We have also analyzed the cropping pattern at region level shown in the Map No-5.2. This illustrates that while aman (30.5 percent), boro (18.6percent) and wheat (12.5 percent) are the major crops in Tal region. Aman (57.5 percent), boro (12.0 percent) and mustard (10.0) percent are for Barind region. Diara has a different crop combination with wheat (19.0 percent), mango (13.5 percent), aus (11.0 percent) and boro (10.3 percent) are the major crops.

For Malda district as a whole the cropping pattern as

Map No 5.2
CROP DISTRIBUTION IN MALDA: REGION WISE
(93-94 to 00-01)

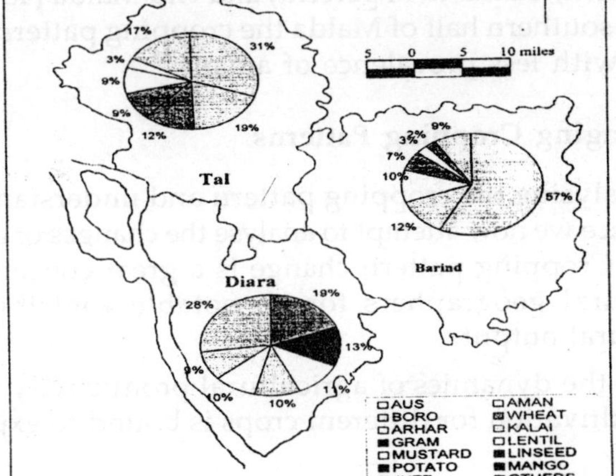

Map No: 5.3

CROP DISTRIBUTION IN MALDA: MAJOR CROPS (93-94 to 00-01)

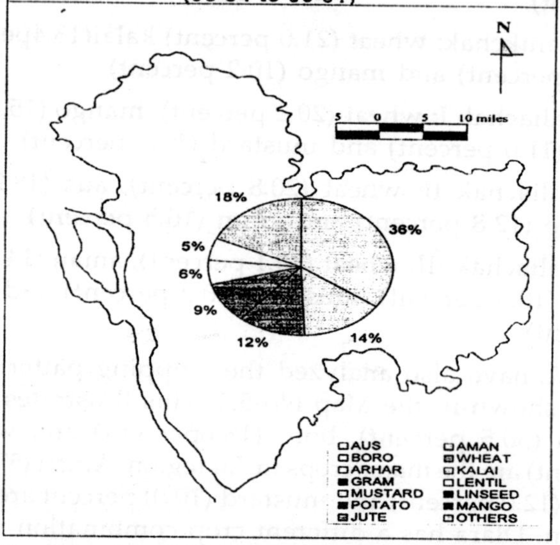

shown in the Map No-5.3 It is interesting to note that aman commands around 37 percent of gross cropped area for the four blocks viz. Harishchandrapur-I, Harishchandrapur-II, Chanchal-I and Chanchal-II in the northern part of the district. Aman also commands the majority shares in the three eastern blocks of Gazole, Bamongola and Habibpur. Aman is found to have a varied share in the central part of Malda i.e. Ratua-I (23 percent), Ratua-II(18 percent) and Old Malda (40 percent) while in southern half of Malda the cropping pattern is more diverse with less prevalence of aman.

5.b Changing Cropping Patterns

After analysing the cropping pattern and understanding its importance we now attempt to analyse the changes of cropping pattern. Cropping pattern change is a great concern to the agricultural geographers for its notable contribution to agricultural output.

With the dynamics of agricultural productivity the area under cultivation for different crops is bound to experience

Map No: 5.4

CHANGING CROPPING PATTERN IN MALDA (93-94 to 96-97 vs 97-98 to 00-01)

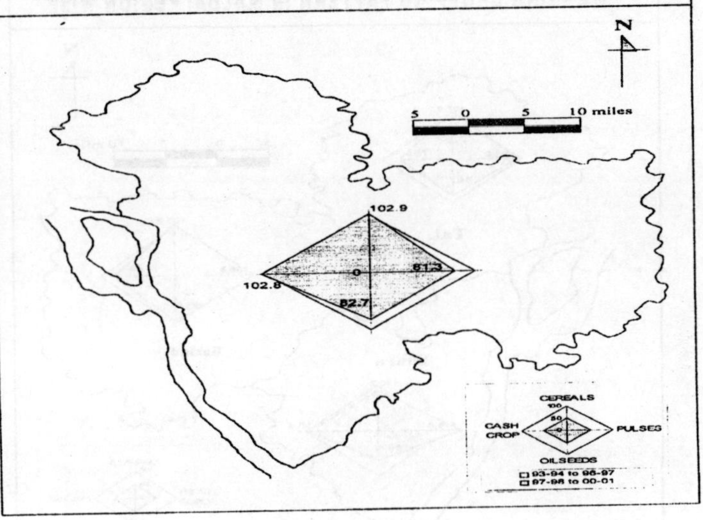

Map No: 5.5

CHANGING CROPPING PATTERN IN MALDA: BLOCK WISE

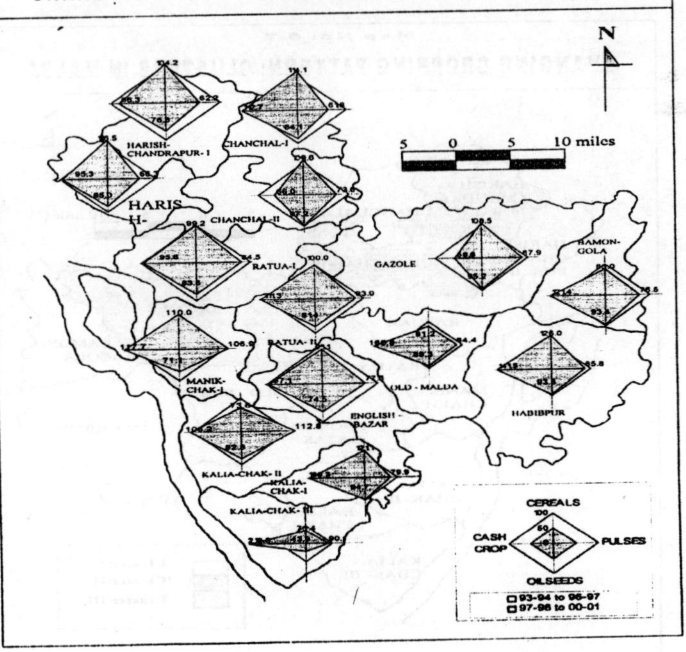

Map No: 5.6

CHANGING CROPPING PATTERN IN MALDA: REGION WISE

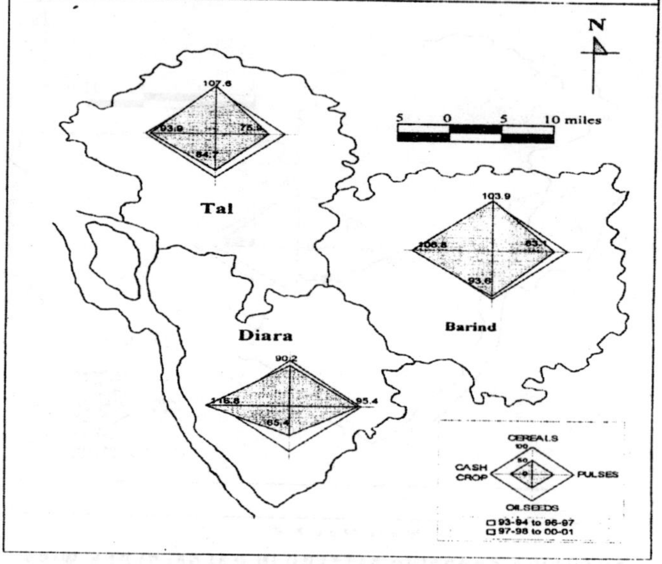

Map No: 5.7

CHANGING CROPPING PATTERN: CLUSTERS IN MALDA

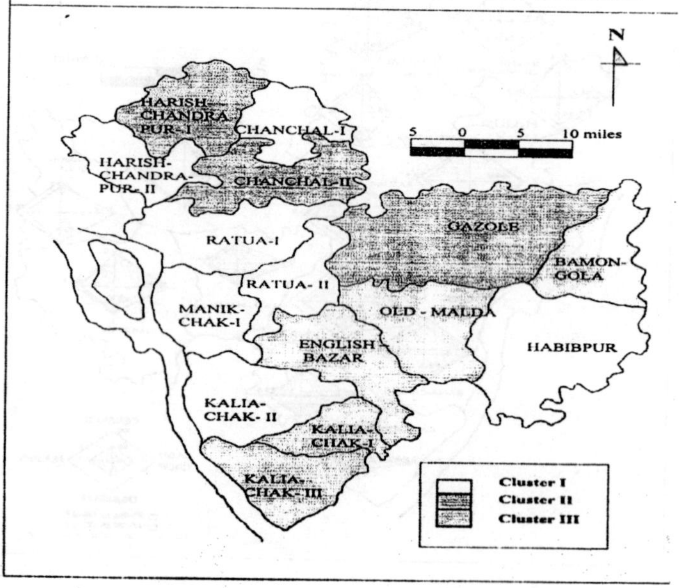

a shift. The causes for this shift can be

1) Increase in returns of any particular crop
2) Technological feasibility
3) Change of preference
4) Non-availability of resources.

In this section we attempt to analyse the changing cropping pattern of crop cultivation in the district. The objective of this section is to identify the cropping pattern in each region and analyse the changing nature of it.

Methodology:

To estimate the pattern of the shift at the block level we have considered the area under cultivation for individual crops. This analysis makes a comparative study between Period I (1993-94 to 1996-97) and Period II (1997-98 to 2000-01). The analysis is made at the crop group level viz. Cereals (Aus, Aman, Boro and Wheat), Pulses (Arhar, Gram, Kalai and Lentil), Oil-seeds (Mustard and Linseed) and Cash crop (Potato, Mango and Jute) as breaking these crop groups to individual crops makes the analysis complex and inappropriate to draw conclusions. Using the average area for Period I as base (=100) the average area for Period II is calculated.

Results:

For all crop groups as the index for Period I is equated to 100, so the index value for Period II gives an indication whether the average area in absolute terms have increased or decreased at the block level.

Map no. 5.4 show the changing cropping pattern using radar diagram for the Malda district as a whole, wherein the North, East, South and West axes of the radar diagram represent Cereals, Pulses, Oil-seeds and Cash crops respectively. The 'yellow' shade represents the base period while the 'green' shade indicates the index for Period II.

For the district as a whole it is observed that area under cereals have increased in Period-II (102.9 percent of Period-I). Similar increase, of 2.8 percent is noticed, for cash crops too. For pulses and oilseeds the area under cultivation in Period-II, have decreased to 81.3 percent and 82.7 percent of Period-I respectively.

We now analyse the changing cropping pattern at the block level. Map 5.5 provides the nature of change in the cropping pattern at the block level.

From the map we find that in Harishchandrapur I while the area under cultivation for cereals have increased to 104.2 percent of Period I in Period II, for pulses, oilseeds and cash-crops it has declined to 62.2 percent, 76.3 percent and 86.3 percent respectively. Thus we find that the area under pulses has been significantly hit.

In Harischandrapur-II, area under cereals have increased in Period-II, by 16.5 percent of Period-I. In period-II decline of pulses, oilseeds and cash crops to 63.7 percent, 85.0 percent and 95.3 percent respectively depicts the shift to cereals in the block. The causes of increase for cereals can be explained by multiple cropping of paddy.

In Chanchal-I the area under cereals and cash crops have both increased to 114.1 percent and 112.7 of Period-I respectively. This increase is at the cost of decline in pulses and oilseeds to 59.0 percent and 84.1 percent respectively.

For Chanchal-II we find a drop in pulses, oilseeds and cash crops to 71.7 percent, 97.2 percent and 66.0 percent respectively. Only cereals have increased to 109.6 percent over the period.

A peculiar pattern is noticed for Ratua-I, wherein for all crop groups viz. cereals, pulses, oilseeds and cash crops there is a decline of 99.2 percent, 82.8 percent, 83.6 percent and 95.6 percent respectively.

In Ratua-II where cereals maintained same area under cultivation and area under cash crops increased by 11.3 percent, there is a decline for pulses and oilseeds to 82.0 and 81.4 respectively.

In Gazole a severe drop in area under cash crop is noticed. This drop is primarily because of decline in jute cultivation. There is a decline in pulses and oilseeds to 79.7 percent and

95.2 percent respectively. In Period-II only cereals cultivation in the block increased to 108.5 percent of Period-I.

In Bamongola a different pattern of crop changed is noticed. Here, area under cereals pulses, oilseeds have declined to 85.0 percent, 74.3 percent and 93.4 percent respectively, while area under cash crop has increased to 121.4 percent.

For Habibpur, cereals and cash crops are the two major crop groups where in the area under cultivation have increased to 126 percent and 141.5 percent. This major increase in cash crops is not to be considered very seriously as it is basically the impact of low base for cash crops. For pulses and oil seed the area has declined to 76.8 percent and 93.3 percent respectively.

In Old Malda while there is a drop in area under cereals, pulses and oilseed to 81.2 percent, 76.6 percent and 89.3 percent respectively, a sharp rise to 166.8 percent is noticed for cash crop. This sharp rise is causes by the rise in the mango and jute cultivation.

A peculiar trend is noticed in English Bazar as the area under cultivation for all major crop groups have declined. The figures of Period-II for cereals, pulses, oilseed, and cash crop are 91.1 percent, 73.4 percent, 74.5 percent and 97.1 of Period-I, respectively. The cause for this decline can be attributed to the urbanization of the block.

Manikchak, portrays a different pattern of change, as in this blocks the area under cultivation have increased for cereals, pulses and cash crops to 110.0 percent, 103.5 percent and 117.7 percent respectively. This increase for three major crop groups have been achieved at the cost of oil seeds, which has declined to 71.1. This rise is mainly due to effective use of multiple cropping.

In Kaliachak-I a phenomenal increase of cash crop is noticed. It has increased to 168.3 percent mainly due to more area coming under mango orchards. Area under cereal cultivation has also increased by 21.1 percent while, area under pulses and oilseed cultivation have declined to 71.8 percent and 91.7 percent respectively.

In Kaliachak-II the change in the pattern is of an increase of pulses and cash crop (109.6 percent and 106.2 percent) and that of a decline for cereals and oilseeds to 73.6 and 82.8 percent.

Finally, Kaliachak-III shows a pattern, which is marked by staggering growth to 218.8 percent in area under cash crop. This impressive growth has been achieved by more area coming under jute cultivation. For cereals and pulses the decline to 75.4 and 79.4 percent is noticed. A prominent feature for this block is a severe drop in area under oilseed to 43.8 percent. This drop is primarily because of the drop in area under mustard cultivation.

When we consider the change comparatively in larger domain i.e. region, (Map 5.6 depicts the change of area under cultivation in a comparative form at the region level) we find that cereals have gained in Tal and Barind region as in Period-II 107.6 percent and 103.9 percent of Period-I area is under cereals cultivation for the two blocks. It has decreased for Diara region to 90.2 percent. Thus a marginal increased is noticed for area under cereal cultivation for the district as a whole (102.9 percent of Period-I).

The area under pulses cultivation has declined across regions. The decline is severe in Tal (74.1 percent of Period-I), Barind (76.6 percent of Period-I) and moderate for Diara (89.4 percent of Period-I). Thus total area under cultivation for the district has declined by 19.7 percent.

For oilseed cultivation too we observe a declining trend in the area under cultivation. But the rate of decline varies between blocks; while the decline of 34.6 is severe in Diara it is moderate in Tal (15.3 percent) and Barind (6.4 percent).

For cash crop cultivation there is a marginal increased of 2.8 percent noticed for the district. The region wise break-up is as follows: Tal- decline of 6.1 percent, Barind- growth of 6.8 percent and Diara- growth of 16.8 percent.

Thus we find that there is a change in the cropping pattern in the district with marginal rise for the area under cereals and cash crops and a drop in pulses and oilseeds. When we compare the total area under cultivation for all these crop groups combined we find a marginal drop of 1.9 percent. This is mainly due to drop in area under cultivation for 1998-1999 due to flood.

This analysis at region level do not help in analyzing the factors that have driven this change as we make a simplistic assumption that the pattern of change within a region is similar across the blocks. To overcome this, the approach adopted is of clustering the blocks based on the composition of change in cropping pattern. In this direction we have analyzed the indices for Period II and tried to group them based on the commonality of change. For this cluster analysis has been applied and the acceptable number of cluster has been defined as three. For the purpose of cluster analysis the indices for each block vs crop is categorized in a scale of 1 to 5 as shown in the Table 5.2. The scale has been assigned as in Table 5.1.

Table 5.1 Scale used for Index Range: Cluster Analysis

Index Range	*Scale*
< 85	1
85-95	2
95-105	3
105-115	4
>115	5

Table 5.2 Block wise Index of Area under Crop Groups for 1997-98 to 2000-01

(Base 1993-94 to 1996-97)

	CEREALS		*PULSES*		*OILSEEDS*		*CASHCROP*	
	Index	*Scale*	*Index*	*Scale*	*Index*	*Scale*	*Index*	*Scale*
Harishchandrapur I	104.2	3	60.4	1	76.8	1	86.3	2
Harishchandrapur II	116.5	5	63.7	1	85.0	1	95.3	3
Chanchal I	114.1	4	59.0	1	84.1	1	112.7	4
Chanchal II	109.6	4	71.7	1	97.2	3	66.0	1
Ratua I	99.2	3	82.8	1	83.6	1	95.6	3
Ratua II	100.0	3	82.0	1	81.4	1	111.3	4

Gazole	108.5	4	79.7	1	95.2	3	58.6	1
Bamongola	85.04	2	74.3	1	93.4	2	121.4	5
Habibpur	126.0	5	76.8	1	93.3	2	141.5	5
Old Malda	81.2	1	76.6	1	89.3	2	166.8	5
English Bazar	91.1	2	73.4	1	74.5	1	97.1	3
Manikchak	110.0	4	103.5	3	71.1	1	117.7	5
Kaliachak I	121.1	5	71.8	1	94.7	2	168.3	5
Kaliachak II	73.6	1	109.6	4	82.8	1	106.2	4
Kaliachak III	75.4	1	79.4	1	43.8	1	218.8	5

We then attempted to group blocks based on the pattern of shift. The initial cluster centers for the blocks and the final centers is shown below in Table 5.3 and Table 5.4 respectively.

Table 5.3: Initial Cluster Centers

	Cluster		
	I	*II*	*III*
CEREALS	5.00	4.00	1.00
PULSES	1.00	1.00	1.00
OIL	2.00	3.00	1.00
CASH	5.00	1.00	4.00

Table 5.4: Final Cluster Centers

	Cluster		
	I	*II*	*III*
CEREALS	4.14	3.67	1.40
PULSES	1.29	1.00	1.60
OIL	1.29	2.33	1.40
CASH	4.14	1.33	4.40

The cluster-wise number of blocks are Cluster I: 7, Cluster II: 3 and Cluster III: 5.

Map 5.7 shows the different blocks that form these clusters. By the pattern of change in the cropping pattern we find that Cluster I comprising of Harishchandrapur II, Chanchal I, Ratua I, Ratua II, Habibpur, Manikchak, Kaliachak I shows spectacular growth in area under cereals and cash crops cultivation while a severe decline in pulses and oil seeds cultivation. The inference that can be drawn from this shift is that in these blocks there is a reallocation of cultivable area happening.

For cluster II the blocks Harischandrapur-I, Chanchal-II and Gazole shows a similar pattern of change. Herein the area under cultivation for pulses and cash crops have declined severely while for oilseeds there is a marginal decline. Area under cereal cultivation has moderately increased in these blocks.

Cluster-III comprising of Bamongola, Old-Malda, English Bazar, Kaliachak-II and Kaliachak-III shows a different pattern of change from the previous clusters in terms of change in area under cereal cultivation. Herein there is a decline for area under cereal cultivation. For oilseeds and pulses too there is a decline noticed in this cluster. It is the cash crop which has significant increased its area in this cluster.

5.c Growth Trend Analysis

This section attempts to illustrate the trend of area under each crop over the period. The following figures show the area under each crop group for the individual blocks (Fig 5.1 for cereals, Fig 5.2 for pulses, Fig 5.3 for oil-seeds and Fig 5.4 for cash crops). Fig 5.5 shows the trend for each region viz. Tal, Barind and Diara. The trend for each cluster formed in the previous section is shown in Fig 5.6. We then show the trend of the crop groups in Malda district as a whole in Fig 5.7.

To facilitate comparison across blocks and then across regions we have considered the area under each crop group as a percentage of total geographical area of the particular block or region. Please note that the percentage for certain crop groups in the figures are greater than hundred percent in certain years. This happens as the analysis is done on crop group basis and not at individual crop level i.e. multiple cropping is possible.

After analyzing the spatial pattern of various crop groups and illustrating the trend of area under cultivation for each crop groups we have found that cash crops have gained area under cultivation during the period. But the analysis was unable to estimate whether the rise or decline is statistically significant. Moreover, it failed to identify the crop in particular which has affected the shift. To overcome this and to identify the dragging and lagging crops at the region level we analyzed the growth trends. This section analyses the trends in growth rates over the period 1993-94 to 2000-01 for the major crops of Malda District

Methodology:

Time series data for 8 years (1993-94 to 2000-01) of major crops of Malda viz. aus, aman, boro, wheat, arhar, kalai. gram, lentil, mustard, linseed, potato, mango, jute are used in this analysis.

The exponential function $Y=AB^t$ was fitted to the data to compute the compound growth rates. Compound growth rate (r) =(Antilog b) 1* 100. The compound growth rates were tested for their significance by the students 't' test.

Similar studies for the calculation of growth trend use indexing of the actual area. In our case this is not required as the problem arising due to use different unit of measurement is not applicable here.

The co-efficient (e.g. 0.056) given in the tables to explain trend growth can be interpreted as 5.6 compounded annual growth.

Result discussion:

In the following paragraphs we discuss the trend of area under cultivation for four crop groups. The analysis for Malda and its three regions reveals some interesting trends.

Cereal: There is no significant fixed pattern emerging for area under cultivation of cereals in Malda (Table 5.5). But the decline of 13.7 percent is significant for aus. For boro a significant growth of 5.5 percent is observed over the same period. For aman, which happens to command, maximum area under cultivation in the district though shows a slight increase in the area under cultivation but the growth rate is not significant. In contrast wheat's minor decline is also not significant over the period.

When these growth rates are analyzed across region we find the decline of aus to be most prominent in Diara and Barind region, and comparatively low in Tal. For aman the general trend is of growth but the growth of 1.8 percent in Tal is significant. For boro the growth rates of 6.3 and 9.3 percent for Tal and Diara respectively are significant.

Table 5.5: Growth trend of cereals in Malda: Region wise (1993-94 to 2000-01)

		Tal	Barind	Diara	Malda
AUS	co-eff	-0.099	*-0.122*	*-0.177*	*-0.137*
	t-stat	-1.6	-2.5	-4.6	-4.4
Aman	co-eff	*0.018*	0.018	-0.049	0.017
	t-stat	2.2	0.7	-0.3	0.9
Boro	co-eff	*0.063*	0.011	*0.093*	*0.055*
	t-stat	3.6	0.7	4.2	8.5
Wheat	co-eff	-0.028	0.046	-0.019	-0.010
	t-stat	-1.4	1.8	-0.8	-0.6

PS: italicised co-efficients are significant at 5% level of confidence.

The growth rates for wheat over the period across region are found to be insignificant.

Pulses: The growth rates for area under cultivation for pulses are found to be insignificant for Malda as a district (Table 5.6). For individual crops viz. arhar, kalai, gram and lentil the growth rates are insignificant either. Though insignificant but there is an overall general decline of pulses cultivation in Malda district. Region wise analysis shows significant decline of only arhar in Diara region (26.0 percent) and kalai in Barind region (8.7 percent). A decline is noticed for individual crops across region but none of the decline rates are significant.

Table 5.6: Growth trend of pulses in Malda: Region wise (1993-94 to 2000-01)

		Tal	Barind	Diara	Malda
Arhar	co-eff	-0.200	-0.260	*-0.260*	-0.219
	t-stat	-0.8	-1.1	-3.3	-1.9
Kalai	co-eff	-0.028	*-0.087*	-0.030	-0.033
	t-stat	-0.5	-3.1	-0.3	-0.7
Gram	co-eff	-0.133	-0.134	-0.062	-0.088
	t-stat	-1.1	-0.6	-0.8	-0.9
Lentil	co-eff	-0.046	0.014	-0.012	-0.014
	t-stat	-0.4	0.1	-0.5	-0.2

PS: italicised co-efficients are significant at 5% level of confidence.

Oilseeds: The general trend for the area under cultivation for oilseeds is of decline in the district in the given period (Table 5.7). This trend is seen across the regions. But the decline is not significant at individual region level. When we individually consider the two crops viz. 'Mustard' and 'Linseed' we notice a similar declining trend. Again the drop is not significant for the individual regions for Mustard. The analysis does not improve for the Linseed at region level.

Table 5.7: Growth trend of oilseed in Malda: Region wise (1993-94 to 2000-01)

		Tal	Barind	Diara	Malda
Mustard	co-efficient	-0.015	0.004	-0.074	-0.021
	t-stat	-0.3	0.1	-1.4	-0.5
Linseed	co-efficient	-0.110	-0.147	-0.285	-0.146
	t-stat	-0.7	-0.8	-1.5	-0.9

PS: shaded co-efficients are significant at 5% level of confidence.

Cash crops: For the district as a whole no definite trend emerges for the cash crop during the 1993-94 to 2000-01 (Table 5.8). When we consider the crops individually for the district as a whole, the analysis throws significant growth (1.7 percent) for Mango. The change over the period is insignificant and negligible for Jute and Potato. But considering the crops individually for the region throws some interesting facts. For Jute the growth trend is opposite for Tal and Diara region. For Tal the decline (2.8 percent) is significant; but for Diara the scenario is just opposite with a significant growth (14.3 percent). Though we get significant growth for Mango at the district level but the growth rates at region level is not significant.

Table 5.8: Growth trend of Cash Crop in Malda: Region wise (1993-94 to 2000-01)

		Tal	Barind	Diara	Malda
Potato	co-efficient	-0.016	0.019	-0.044	0.000
	t-stat	-0.1	0.8	-0.7	0.0
Mango	co-efficient	0.003	0.052	0.014	*0.017*
	t-stat	1.1	1.0	1.3	4.5
Jute	co-efficient	*-0.028*	-0.093	*0.143*	-0.015
	t-stat	-2.4	-0.5	3.3	-0.5

PS: italicised co-efficients are significant at 5% level of confidence

The above analysis is based on the regions defined by the physiographic divisions but as in this chapter we have developed clusters based on the changing pattern of area under different crop groups we now analyse the significance of such change in these clusters. The methodology applied is similar to the growth trend analysis for the regions, which we have just discussed.

The following tables (Table 5.9 to Table 5.12) show the growth trend for area under individual crops for the individual clusters.

Fig 5.1 Trend of Area Under Cereal Cultivation: Block Wise (1993-94 to 2000-01)

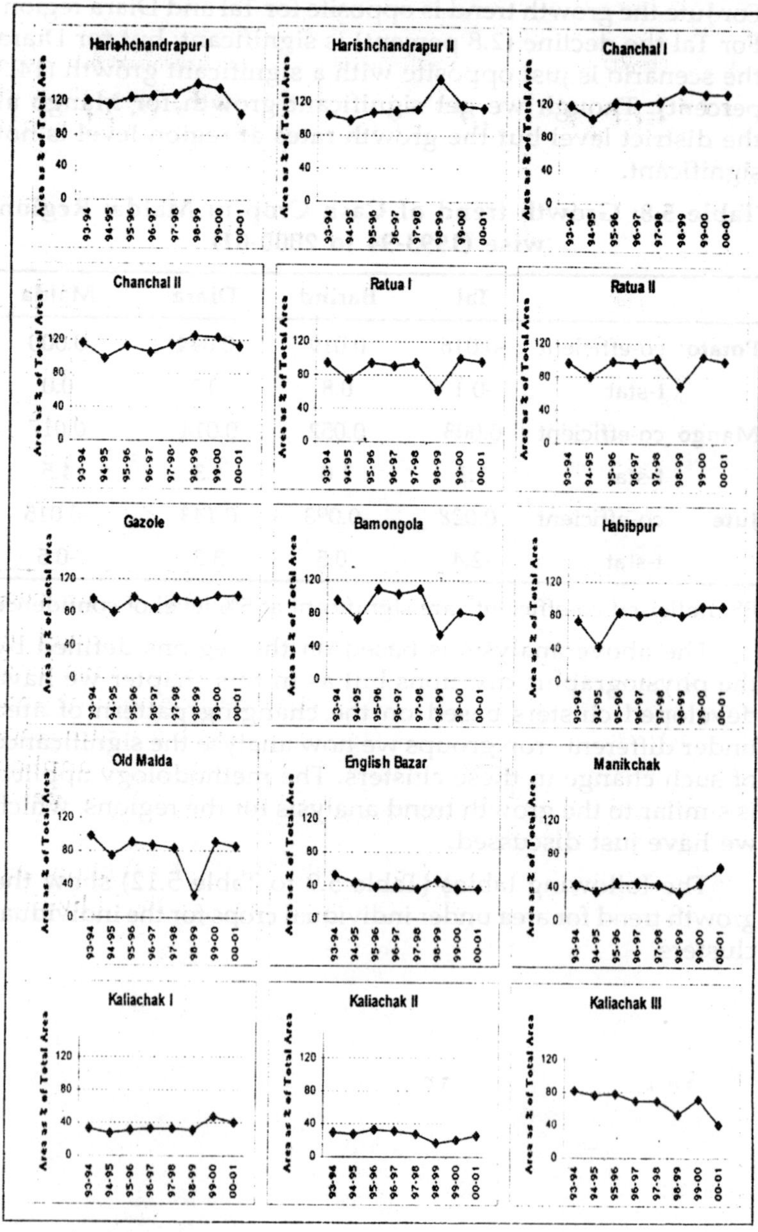

Fig 5.2 Trend of Area Under Pulses Cultivation: Block Wise (1993-94 to 2000-01)

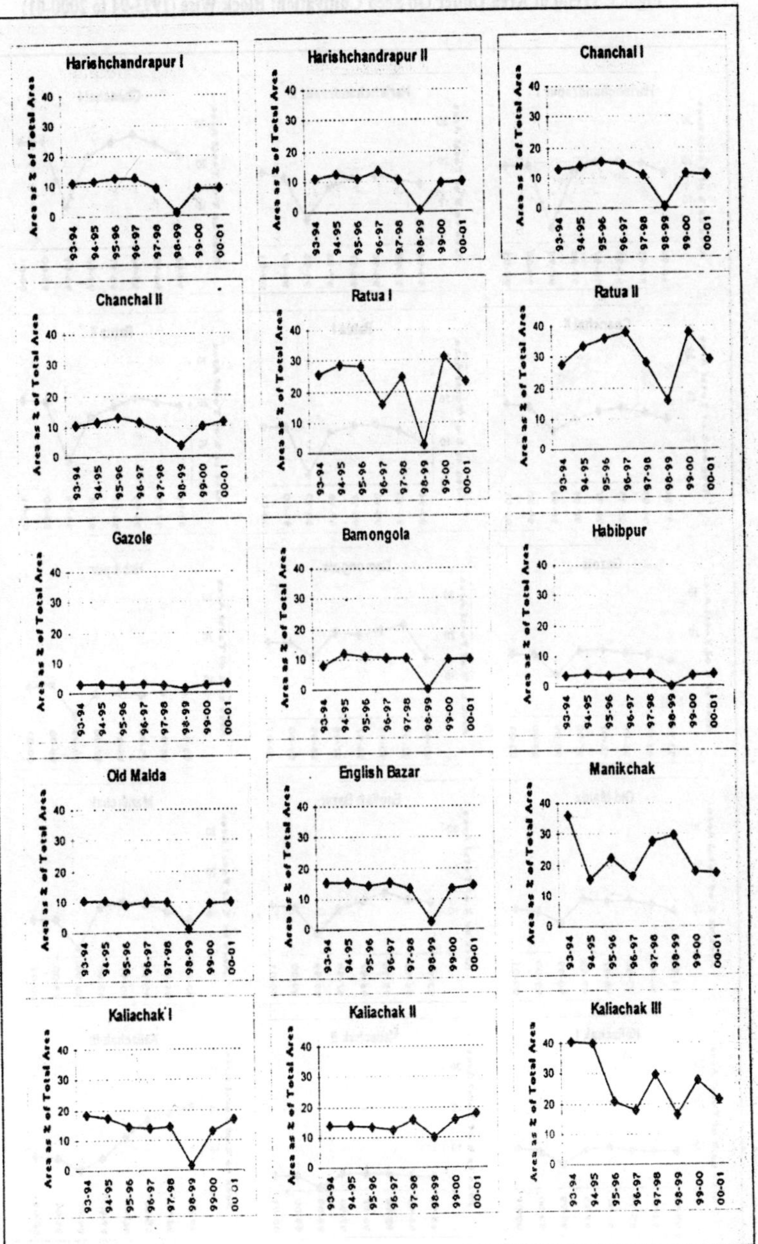

Fig 5.3 Trend of Area Under Oil Seed Cultivation: Block Wise (1993-94 to 2000-01)

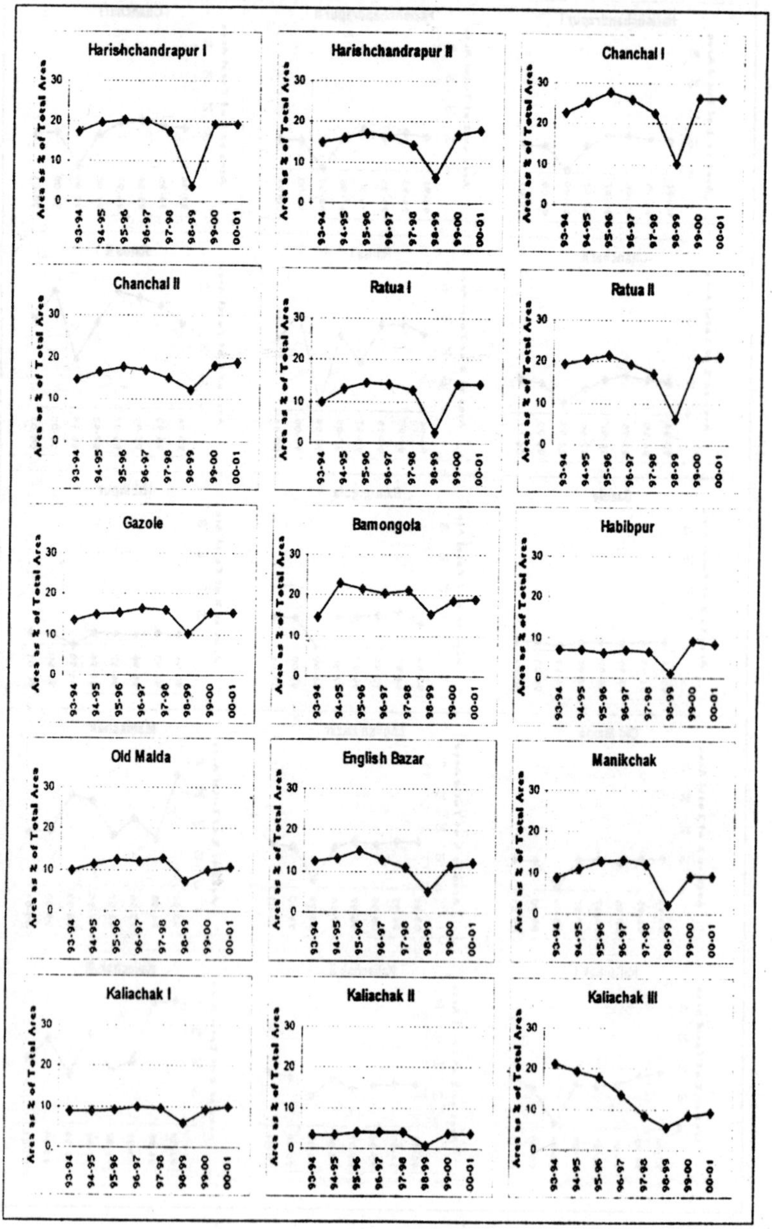

Fig 5.4 Trend of Area Under Cash Crop Cultivation: Block Wise (1993-94 to 2000-01)

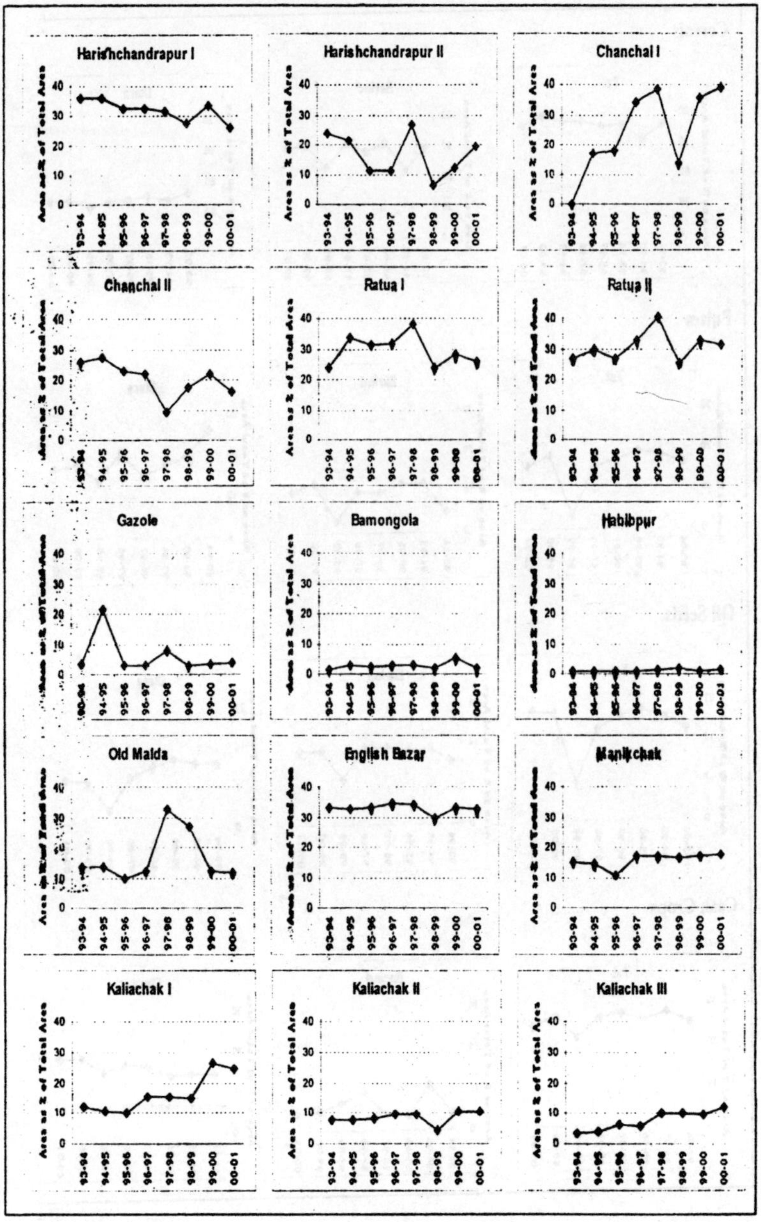

Fig 5.5 Trend of Area Under Cultivation: Region Wise (1993-94 to 2000-01)

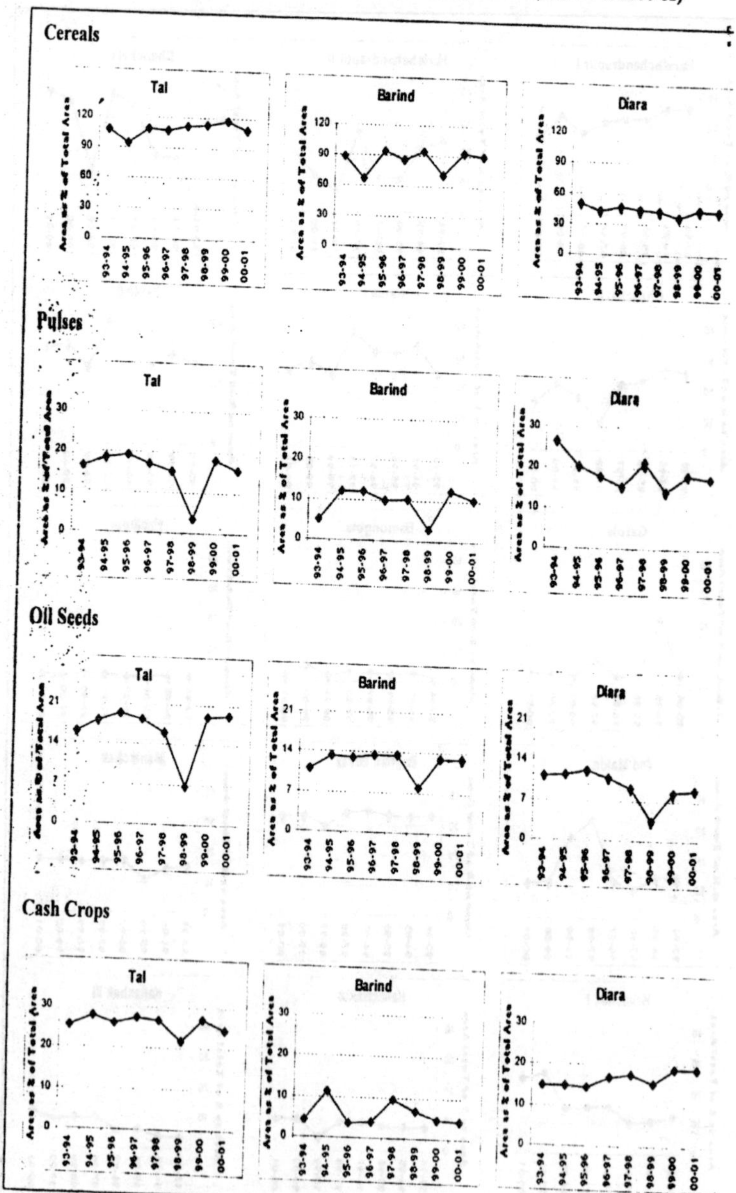

Fig. 5.6: Trend of Area Under Cultivation: Malda (1993-94 to 2000-01)

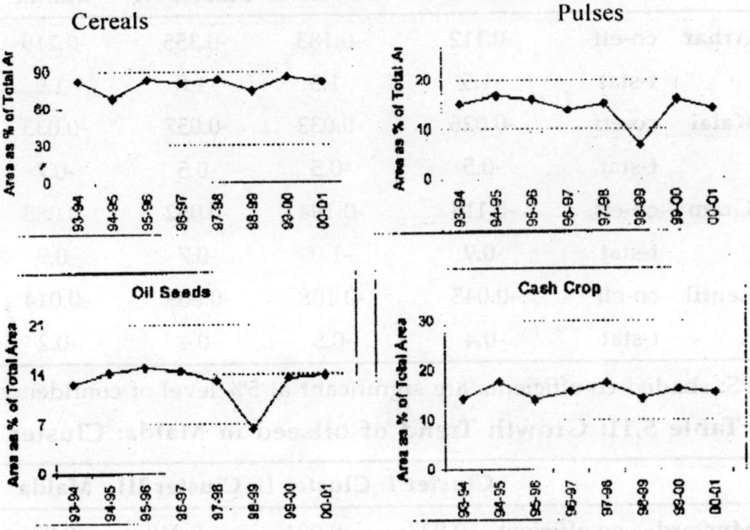

Table 5.9: Growth Trend of Cereals in Malda: Cluster wise (1993-94 to 2000-01)

		Cluster I	Cluster II	Cluster III	Malda
AUS	co-eff	*-0.093*	*-0.145*	*-0.182*	*-0.137*
	t-stat	-1.9	-2.2	-4.8	-4.4
Aman	co-eff	*0.041*	0.019	-0.050	0.017
	t-stat	1.9	1.4	-0.7	0.9
Boro	co-eff	*0.073*	*0.057*	0.015	*0.055*
	t-stat	8.0	3.7	0.9	8.5
Wheat	co-eff	0.014	-0.024	-0.043	-0.010
	t-stat	0.9	-0.8	-1.8	-0.6

PS: italicised co-efficients are significant at 5% level of confidence

Table 5.10: Growth Trend of Pulses in Malda: Cluster wise (1993-94 to 2000-01)

		Cluster I	Cluster II	Cluster III	Malda
Arhar	co-eff	-0.112	-0.183	-0.355	-0.219
	t-stat	-1.5	-1.3	-1.8	-1.9
Kalai	co-eff	-0.026	-0.033	-0.057	-0.033
	t-stat	-0.5	-0.5	-0.5	-0.7
Gram	co-eff	-0.118	-0.194	-0.052	-0.088
	t-stat	-0.9	-1.0	-0.7	-0.9
Lentil	co-eff	-0.043	-0.108	-0.009	-0.014
	t-stat	-0.4	-0.5	-0.4	-0.2

PS: shaded co-efficients are significant at 5% level of confidence

Table 5.11: Growth Trend of oilseed in Malda: Cluster

		Cluster I	Cluster II	Cluster III	Malda
Mustard	co-efficient	-0.023	0.001	-0.048	-0.021
	t-stat	-0.4	0.0	-1.8	-0.5
Linseed	co-efficient	-0.121	-0.138	-0.195	-0.146
	t-stat	-0.8	-0.8	-1.1	-0.9

PS: shaded co-efficients are significant at 5% level of confidence

Table 5.12: Growth Trend of Cash Crop in Malda: Cluster wise (1993-94 to 2000-01)

		Cluster I	Cluster II	Cluster III	Malda
Potato	co-efficient	-0.007	-0.011	0.006	0.000
	t-stat	-0.1	-0.2	0.2	0.0
Mango	co-efficient	*0.020*	*0.009*	*0.014*	*0.017*
	t-stat	4.6	2.2	3.5	4.5
Jute	co-efficient	0.023	*-0.100*	0.106	-0.015
	t-stat	1.1	-2.4	1.5	-0.5

PS: italicised co-efficients are significant at 5% level of confidence

From the above tables we find that the growth trends do not turn significant for individual crops even when we do the analysis at cluster level. This is because the clusters have been formed using crop group data and not individual crops. We now attempt to analyze the growth trend for the clusters using crop group data. Table 5.13 shows the growth trend and the significance level of each crop group for the clusters.

In the Table 5.13 too we do not find significant growth trend of the crop groups for the clusters. We had expected that the growth trend will be more significant when we use the crop group level data for the clusters but our hypothesis that 'the trend of area under different crop cultivation is similar to the pattern of change among these blocks' is negated as the clusters are formed with blocks which shows similar pattern of change over two periods Period I (1993-94 to 1996-97) and Period II (1997-98 to 2000-01) for all crop groups taken together and not on individual crop groups.

Table 5.13: Growth trend of crop groups in Malda: Cluster wise (1993-94 to 2000-01)

		Cluster I	Cluster II	Cluster III	Malda
Cereals	co-eff	*0.032*	0.012	-0.045	0.008
	t-stat	2.2	1.2	-1.8	0.6
Pulse	co-eff	-0.045	-0.066	-0.055	-0.038
	t-stat	-1.2	-0.9	-1.0	-0.8
Oil Seed	co-efficient	-0.023	0.001	-0.048	-0.029
	t-stat	-0.4	0.0	-1.8	-0.6
Cash crop	co-efficient	0.023	*-0.071*	0.031	0.002
	t-stat	1.7	-2.1	1.8	0.2

PS: italicised co-efficients are significant at 5% level of confidence

Thus to conclude this section we find that there is general tendency of decline in area under various crops. It is aman, boro and mango whose area under cultivation is on the rise. The drop in area of pulses and oil seeds needs to be considered by the policy makers seriously as this goes against the theory that with modernization in agriculture, multiple cropping is more prevalent resulting in general rise of net area cropped and farmers tend to reduce area under cereals to produce more of varied crops. One can raise the point that with progress in agriculture the productivity increases so in the district with lower area under various crops the production is not affected and moreover with urbanisation and land being used for other purposes the area under cultivation for various crops are on the fall. We are not in a position to defend this or refute this idea now. For this we will analyze the growth trend of yield and production in following chapters.

5.d. Crop Combination Region

Crop combination analysis is defined as the geographical investigation of agriculture, which purports to select various crops to be studied collectively in an area. It is a method of analysis, first developed by J.C. Weaver, for delimiting agricultural regions on the basis of multi crop pattern.

There are mainly two techniques with which we can establish crop combination, viz. semi-statistical and statistical. The former is subjective as the patterns of crop combination are established arbitrarily, whereas the later is objective where the patterns of crop combination is established by reckoning the least deviation of the actual crop percentages from the theoretical distribution.

The semi-statistical technique is very simple and does not require any complicated calculations. Being an arbitrary choice technique there is every chance of repetition in presentation and interpretation of crop combination.

The statistical technique is more accurate, scientific and popular than the semi-statistical one for establishing crop combinations. Moreover this approach has wider applicability and has the capacity to handle the strongly developed cropping diversity or even agricultural rediversification in an area.

Weaver's method consist of comparing the actual percentages of the cropped area occupied by the different field crops with theoretical distributions in which the cropped area is equally divided among the component crops in an enumeration unit. The purpose of the procedure is to establish and designate crop combinations which are established by the most closed resemblance in the actual crop percentages and the theoretical distributions. The ideal theoretical distributions are explicitly out lined in Table No. 5.14 as a basis to determine the identity and number of crops involved in the basic crop combination in the sub-clusters.

Now the problem is to accurately compare the actual percentages with in the individual regional units with the theoretical distribution as given in Table No. 5.14. The variance and standard deviation formulae were selected for this purpose and these may be stated as follows:

1. Variance = $\frac{\sum d^2}{n}$

2. Standard Deviation= $\sqrt{\frac{\sum d^2}{n}}$

Where d is the difference between the actual crop percentages in a given regional unit and the percentages in the theoretical distributions and n is the number of crops in a given combination.

Table 5.14: Theoretical distribution of cropped area

Monoculture = 1 crop accounts for 100.0% of total cropped area
2 crop combination = each crop 50.0%
3 crop combination = each crop 33.3%
4 crop combination = each crop 25.0%
5 crop combination = each crop 20.0%
6 crop combination = each crop 16.7%
7 crop combination = each crop 14.3%
8 crop combination = each crop 12.5%
9 crop combination = each crop 11.1%

The least sum of squared deviations and variance and lowest standard deviation and co-efficient of variation analysis for cropping in the Malda district for the year 1993-94 to 2000-01 is indicative of the magnitude of deviation of the actual percentage from the theoretical distributions (Table-5.15). The sum of the squared deviation is the lowest for 5 crop combination, the coefficient of variation is least for 4 crop combination, and the variance and the standard deviation do not reported the lowest even upto a 9 crop combination which includes even minor crops like lentil sharing only 3.5 percent of the total cropped area. The share of the 10th ranking crop when placed against the 1st ranking crop that is aman is considerably small. Therefore it suggested that either the sum of the squared deviations or coefficient of variation analysis should be used for the identification of the desired combination. The computation established both the identity and the number of crops in the ranked combination for the district as aman, boro, wheat, mustard and jute i.e. 5 crops: Am, B, W, Mu & J and 4 crops: Am, B, W & Mu. Doi (1959), Thomas (1963), Coppock (1964), Jasbir Singh (1974) and many others have modified this technique involving the examination the examination of cropland occupancy by various crops with the help of standard statistical algorithm, namely the least squares. It has been observed that the technique of least deviation of actual percentages from the standard theoretical combination values is of little help for the identification of crop combination in the enumeration units where the regional share of several crops is quite close to one another; the least squares technique may be adopted as a substitute to overcome this difficulty. Besides, the actual percentages of crops at first or second rank may be much higher than the crops at the lower ranks in the computed crop combination; such variation with a significant magnitude in actual percentages is shown in the combination only in a ranked format without giving any weight to the percentage strength of each crop or without any regard as to ratio between crops in crop combination. Though the Weaver's technique is mathematically sound, it requires much calculation work. Furthermore Weaver (1954) himself admits that this technique occasionally trend to show the lowest deviation for a crop combination which includes even a crop occupying as much as one percent at the total harvested cropland. A modified form of Weaver's technique has been put forward by Doi (1959).

Table 5.15 Analysis of Crop Combination for Malda district, (1993-94 to 2000-01)

Crop combination	Mono Culture	2 Crops		3 Crops			4 Crops				5 crops				
Crop Ranking	1	1	2	1	2	3	1	2	3	4	1	2	3	4	5
Crops	Aman	Aman	Boro	Aman	Boro	Wheat	Aman	Boro	Wheat	Mustard	Aman	Boro	Wheat	Mustard	Jute
Actual % of total Cropped Area	33.9	33.9	14.4	33.9	14.4	11.9	33.9	14.4	11.9	9.5	33.9	14.4	11.9	9.5	5.8
Theoretical Distribution of Crops in %	100.0	50.0	50.0	33.3	33.3	33.3	25.0	25.0	25.0	25.0	20.0	20.0	20.0	20.0	20.0
Deviation of Actual % from theoretical distributions (d)	66.1	16.1	35.6	0.5	18.9	21.4	8.9	10.6	13.1	15.5	13.9	5.6	8.1	10.5	14.2
(d^2)	4373.4	260.2	1268.1	0.3	358.9	458.6	78.6	112.6	171.1	241.0	192.3	31.5	65.3	110.8	202.8
$(\sum d^2)$	4373.4	1528.3		817.8			603.4				**602.7**				
Variance = $\frac{\sum d^2}{n}$	4373.4	764.17		272.6			150.85				120.55				
SD (σ) = $\sqrt{\frac{\sum d^2}{n}}$	66.132	27.644		16.511			12.282				10.979				
Co-efficient of Variation	66.132	55.287		49.532			**49.128**				54.897				

contd.

Table 5.15 contd.

Crop combination	6 crops						7 Crops						
Crop Ranking	1	2	3	4	5	6	1	2	3	4	5	6	7
Crops	Aman	Boro	Wheat	Mustard	Jute	Mango	Aman	Boro	Wheat	Mustard	Jute	Mango	Aus
Actual % of total Cropped Area	33.9	14.4	11.9	9.5	5.8	5.2	33.9	14.4	11.9	9.5	5.8	5.2	4.9
Theoretical Distribution of Crops in %	16.7	16.7	16.7	16.7	16.7	16.7	14.3	14.3	14.3	14.3	14.3	14.3	14.3
Deviation of Actual % from theoretical distributions (d)	17.2	2.3	4.7	7.2	10.9	11.5	19.6	0.1	2.4	4.8	8.5	9.1	9.4
(d^2)	295.9	5.2	22.6	51.7	119.0	131.4	383.5	0.0	5.6	23.1	72.7	82.5	87.9
$(\sum d^2)$	625.7						655.3						
Variance = $\frac{\sum d^2}{n}$	104.29						93.621						
SD (σ) = $\sqrt{\frac{\sum d^2}{n}}$	10.212						9.6758						
Co-efficient of Variation	61.272						67.73						

contd.

Table 5.15 contd.

Crop combination	8 Crops								9 Crops								
Crop Ranking	1	2	3	4	5	6	7	8	1	2	3	4	5	6	7	8	9
Crops	Aman	Boro	Wheat	Mustard	Jute	Mango	Aus	Gram	Aman	Boro	Wheat	Mustard	Jute	Mango	Aus	gram	lentil
Actual % of total Cropped Area	33.9	14.4	11.9	9.5	5.8	5.2	4.9	3.6	33.9	14.4	11.9	9.5	5.8	5.2	4.9	3.6	3.5
Theoretical Distribution of Crops in %	12.5	12.5	12.5	12.5	12.5	12.5	12.5	12.5	11.1	11.1	11.1	11.1	11.1	11.1	11.1	11.1	11.1
Deviation of Actual % from theoretical distributions (d)	21.4	1.9	0.6	3.0	6.7	7.3	7.6	8.9	22.8	3.3	0.8	1.6	5.4	5.9	6.2	7.5	7.6
(d^2)	456.6	3.6	0.3	9.1	45.5	53.2	57.6	79.7	517.9	10.7	0.7	2.7	28.7	34.9	38.5	56.8	58.1
$(\sum d^2)$	705.7								748.9								
Variance = $\frac{\sum d^2}{n}$	88.209								83.207								
SD (σ) = $\sqrt{\frac{\sum d^2}{n}}$	9.392								9.1218								
Co-efficient of Variation	75.136								82.096								

The modified format of Doi's technique solves the problem of Weavers technique simultaneously substituting the variance ($\frac{\sum d^2}{n}$) or least standard deviation ($\sqrt{\frac{\sum d^2}{n}}$) of Weaver with the sum of square deviations ($\sum d^2$).

The combination having the lowest $\sum d^2$ will be the crop combination.

In Doi's technique it is not required to calculate $\sum d^2$ for each combination but the crop combination is actually established by consulting one sheet table which presents critical values for various elements at different rank against cumulative percentage of elements at higher ranks; for an agricultural geographer elements here mean crops. The use of one sheet table requires only the summing up of actual percentages under different crops instead of findings the differences between actual percentages and theoretical distributions.

All those crops are included in the combination whose cumulative percentage is less than 50; or the critical value for all the elements at different ranks against 50 is zero. Therefore, the cumulative percentage starts from above 50 percent, which is contributed by the higher ranks, may be first one, two, or three crops or so on. In Malda the first crop, aman occupies 33.87 percent. The next crop, boro, is included in the crop combination which makes the sum of the first two crops 48.26 percent (Table 5.16).

Table 5.16 Crop wise % area & cumulative % cropped area for Malda. (1993-94 to 2000-01)

Crop	*% Cropped Area*	*Cumulative % cropped area*
Aman	33.87	33.87
Boro	14.39	48.26
Wheat	11.92	60.18
Mustard	9.48	69.65
Jute	5.76	75.41
Mango	5.21	80.61

Aus	4.91	85.52
Gram	3.57	89.09
Lentil	3.49	92.59
Kalai	2.91	95.50
Potato	1.79	97.29
Linseed	1.10	98.39
Arhar	0.00	98.39

Thus it is found that the district is 5-crop combination region for the period 1993-94 to 2000-01 using Doi's sum of least square method.

Table 5.16 shows the significance crops as shaded along with their percentage cropped area. It is found that 75.4 percent of the area is covered by these 5 crops. Jute with only 5.76 percent area of total cropped area gives an indication that the remaining crops are not that significant. For the period 1993-94 to 2000-2001, Map No 5.8 illustrates the crop combination for the blocks and Map No 5.9 for the regions. Map No-5.8 shows Habibpur to be a mono cropped region. Gazole and Bamongola as 2 crop region, Harishchandrapur-II and Old Maḷda as 3 crop region, Harishchandrapur-I as 4 crop Chanchal-I and Chanchal-II as 5 crop region, English Bazar as 6 crop region, Ratua-I, Ratua-II, Kaliachak-II and Kaliachak-III as 7 crop region while Manikchak and Kaliachak-I as 8 crop region.

Map No. 5.9, which analyses the cropping, pattern, for the regions, shows Tal as 5 Crop Region, Barind 3 crop region and Diara 8 crop region.

Thus we find that it is the less develop Barind region with poor irrigation facilities cannot adopt multiple cropping. In contrast Tal region has balanced between the *Kharif* and *Rabi* crops and are cultivating aman, jute in the summer months while boro, wheat, mustard in the winter months. Diara region has diversified further to have mango, gram and kalai along with wheat, aus, boro, mustard and aman as the major crops. This analysis shows that with proper irrigation facilities and a mix of food crop and cash crop, the crop combination can be made effective. This is likely to provide stability to the agricultural scenario of the district.

This analysis provides important information about the combination pattern in the district during the 90s but is unable to gauge the nature of change happening in the district. To gauge the change we divide the period 1993-94 to 2000-2001 into two sub periods: Period-I: 1993-94 to 1996-97 and Period-II: 1997-98 to 2000-2001. Similar crop combination analysis is then repeated for the two periods. The result of this analysis at block level is shown in Map-5.10 for Period-I and Map-5.11 for Period-II and at region level in Map 5.12 and Map-5.13 for the Period-I and Period- II respectively.

Thus Map-5.10 shows that during 1993-94 to 1996-97 while Habibpur was a mono crop region; Gazole and Bamongola are 2 crop region, Harishchandrapur-II and Old Malda have 3 crops; Harishchandrapur-I is the only 4-crop block, Chanchal-I and Chanchal-II are the 5-crop blocks; Ratua-II, English Bazar, Kaliachak-II and Kaliachak-III are 6 crops regions, Manikchak 7 crop region and Kaliachak-I as 8 crop region.

During Period I, we find Manikchak and Kaliachak-II are the only two blocks of Malda where aman do not feature as the significant crop. Otherwise all other blocks have aman as one of the principal crop though the relative position of aman in the hierarchy varies from block to block. It is in English Bazar, Kaliachak_I and Kaliachak-III that aman is not the most significant crop, otherwise in all other blocks it was top on the hierarchy.

Map 5.10 also shows the various significant crops in each block during the period 1993-94 to 1996-97. Though no fixed pattern is emerging but taking a closer look we find the blocks in the northern low land basically cultivated aman, boro, jute wheat and mustard as shown in the Map-5.12 explaining the crop combination pattern region wise for Period-I. In the western highland of Barind plagued with irrigation problem aman and mustard were the major crops, while in the southern part i.e. Diara, cultivation had really diversified with wheat, aus, mango, mustard, aman, boro, gram and kalai as the significant crops.

When we compare the above findings with the crop combination pattern for Period-II, (1997-98 to 2000-01), shown in Map 5.11, we hardly find any major change happening.

Map No: 5.8

PATTERN OF CROP COMBINATION IN MALDA: BLOCK WISE (93-94 to 00-01)

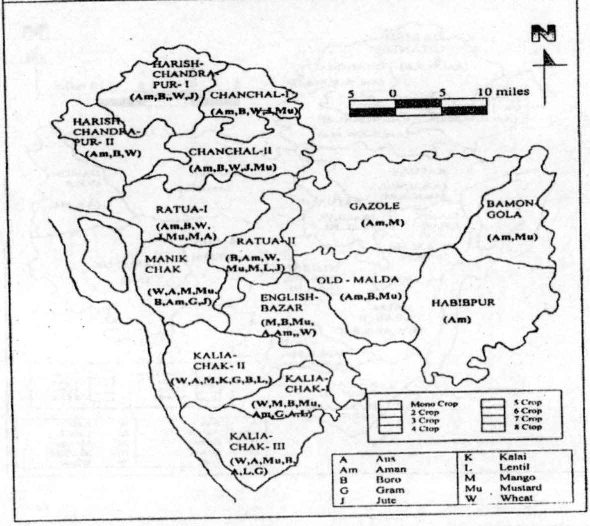

146

Map No: 5.9

PATTERN OF CROP COMBINATION IN MALDA: REGION WISE (93-94 to 00-01)

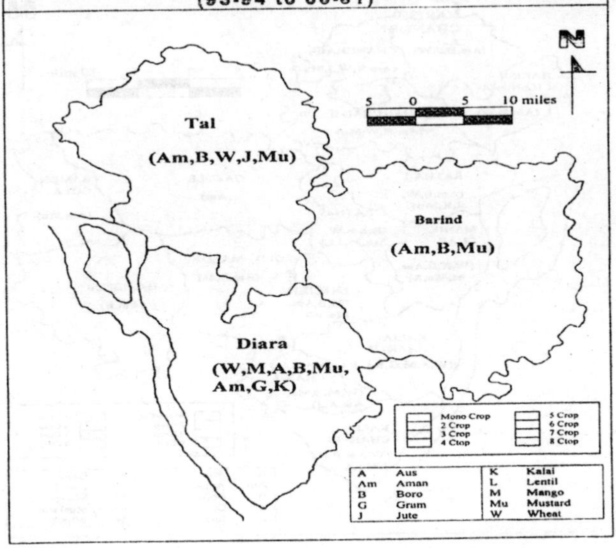

Map No: 5.10

PATTERN OF CROP COMBINATION IN MALDA: BLOCK WISE (93-94 to 96-97)

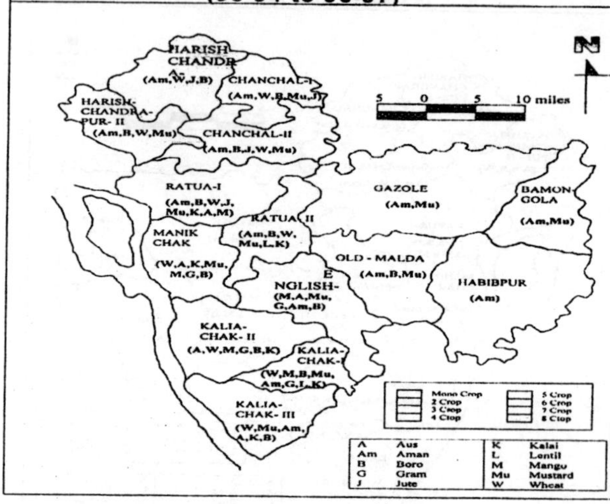

149

Map No: 5.11

PATTERN OF CROP COMBINATION IN MALDA: BLOCK WISE (97-98 to 00-01)

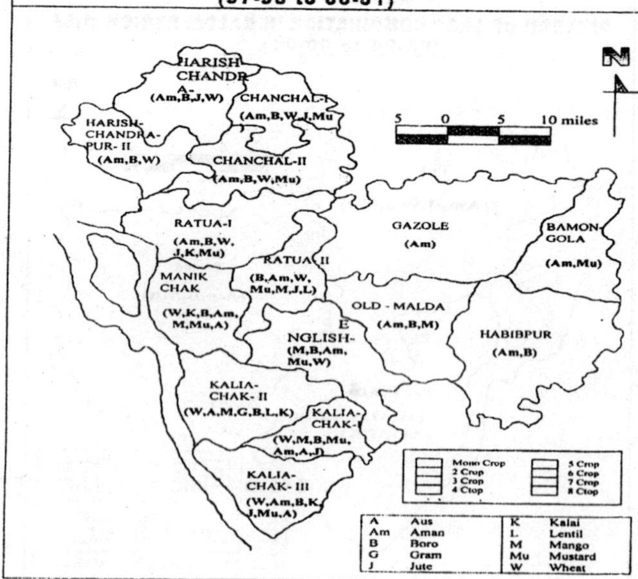

Table 5.17 shows the change in crop combination pattern in terms of significant crops cultivated.

Table 5.17: Number of Significant crops: Block wise

	Number of significant crops	
	Period I	*Period II*
Harishchandrapur I	4	4
Harishchandrapur II	3	3
Chanchal I	5	5
Chanchal II	5	4
Ratua I	8	7
Ratua II	6	7
Gazole	2	1
Bamongola	2	2
Habibpur	1	2
Old Malda	3	3
English Bazar	6	5
Manikchak	7	7
Kaliachak I	8	7
Kaliachak II	6	7
Kaliachak III	6	7
Tal	5	6
Barind	3	2
Diara	8	8
Malda	5	4

It is found that though the number of significant crops has not changed dramatically but the relative importance of individual crops have changed over the years. Thus we find over the decade of 90's there is no major change in the crop combination pattern in the blocks of Malda. In fact in some of blocks viz. Chanchal-II, Ratua-I, Gajole, English Bazar and Kaliachak I the number of significant crops have decreased. One may propose that 1998-99 being the flood year affect the number of crops in Period II; but one need to note that in this crop combination analysis number of significant crops is determined based on percentage of gross cropped area and not geographical area. Thus the crop combination of the district is skewed in favour of Diara region and heavily against

Map No: 5.12

PATTERN OF CROP COMBINATION IN MALDA: REGION WISE (93-94 to 96-97)

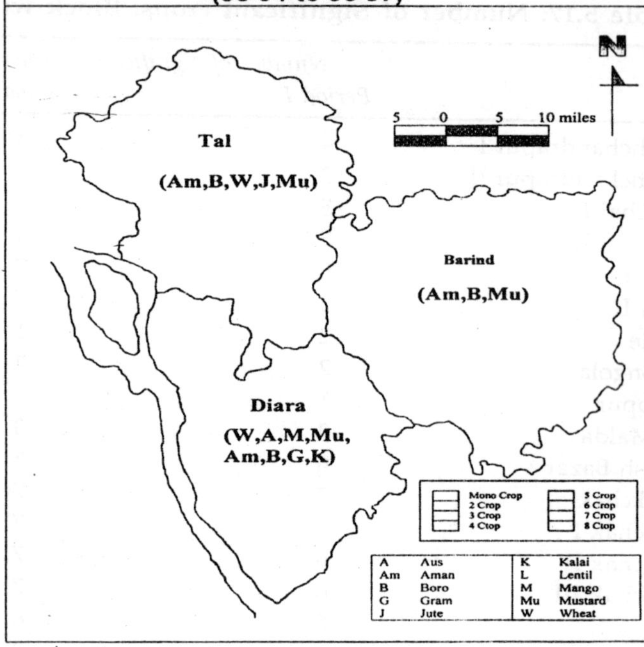

151

Barind region. This is primarily due to low irrigation facility of Barind.

To sum up the chapter, we find that

- The district is primarily a cereal producing area with aman and boro as the primary crops for all the blocks of Tal and Barind region. In Diara region wheat and mango assume greater importance.
- There is a definite pattern of the cropping pattern change in the district as it is found pulses and oilseeds are loosing the steam while cereals and cash crop are marginally growing.
- There is difference for sure in the change of cropping pattern between the regions, as it is found that the cereal cultivation is on the growth path in Tal and

Map No: 5.13

PATTERN OF CROP COMBINATION IN MALDA: REGION WISE (97-98 to 00-01)

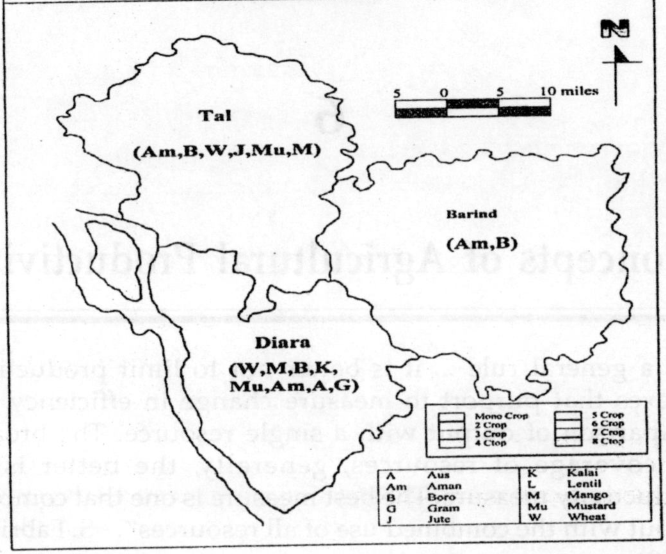

152

Barind, while it is not so for Diara; Diara shows a definite preference towards cash crops.

- There is no significant growth pattern observed for Malda district as a whole for the crops individually other than boro and mango increasing while aus declining.
- Further, Malda is found to be primarily a five-crop region, though there is wide regional variation as Diara is a eight cropped region against Barind a three cropped region and Tal a six cropped region.

These differences itself highlight the regional variation in the cropping pattern, pattern of change and crop combination for the district.

6

Concepts of Agricultural Productivity

"As a general rule ... it is better not to limit productivity indexes that purport to measure change in efficiency to a comparison of output with a single resource. The broader the coverage of resources, generally, the better is the productivity measure. The best measure is one that compares output with the combined use of all resources". - S. Fabricant (1959)

Productivity consciousness has acquired worldwide momentum. Higher productivity is necessary for the survival of any nation. It stands for proper utilisation of available resources to achieve the best result with minimum cost. Improvement in productivity is the only answer to the problems in the agricultural sphere and it is the only path to prosperity. In Malda it assumes special significance owing to the resource gap. In order to overcome the hurdle of shortfall in resources, stepping up of productivity is a must.

Frederick W. Taylor in his "Task Study" said, "Human work can be made infinitely more productive not by 'working harder' but by "working smarter'.

Productivity means the economic yield from each factor of production (land, labour, capital and organisation) and each input (raw materials, fuels, time and knowledge) or an overall yield of the joint factors and resources enumerated above in combination.

Productivity denotes the efficiency with which the various

inputs are converted into goods and services. However, it is a multi-faceted concept; no single definition can fully describe it. Technically, it signifies the ratio between the output and input. Productivity is said to be high when more output is derived from the same input, or the same output is obtained from a less input. It is well understood as the ratio of output to input with respect to given resources. When more is produced with the same expenditure of resources it may be termed as effectiveness; when the same amount is produced at less cost it may be termed as efficiency. The word productivity is broad enough to cover both.

In agricultural parlour productivity is not a synonym of fertility. Generally it is used to express the power of agriculture of a particular region to produce crops. In recent years many attempts have been made to define the meaning of agricultural productivity and a considerable amount of literature exist on this subject.

Agricultural productivity refers to the ratio between the output and input. The improvement of agricultural productivity generally implies more efficient use of factors of production like labour, land capital etc. It is also important to remember that productivity is a physical rather than a value concept, which describes the relationship between input and output. According to Dewett, productivity expresses the varying relationship between agricultural output and one of major capital and other complimentary factors remaining the same.

Many economists give their view about agricultural productivity. Some of them suggested, yield per acre should be considered to indicate agricultural productivity. A number of others criticized this concept because it considered only one factor i.e. land which is not the only factor of production. There are many other factors present or it can be said that productivity could also be measured in terms of per unit of labour and capital.

There are several concepts of productivity. Four of them are of relevance here, land productivity, labour productivity, capital productivity and total factor productivity.

a) Productivity of land

Among the four inputs of production, viz. land, labour capital and organisation, land is most permanent and fixed input. So attention may especially be focussed on the productivity of land. In a developing country productivity of land has a greater importance because the land secure the employment of a large number of population. In places where land resources are limited, the way out for raising the crop production is to keep pace with the growth of population and the demand for improved diets is by raising yields per hectare.

But raising productivity of land, doesn't necessarily mean only raising the yields of individual crops. The productivity of land may be increased by using the same land in different way. To increase the land productivity intensive cultivation system, multiple cropping systems can to be applied. Land productivity may increase also by progressively changing land from low value to high value crops. Japan, China, Taiwan are applying these processes.

There is a distinction present between the concepts of measurement of agricultural output in terms of calories and in terms of money values (M. Shafi) for example if in a certain region land is shifted from cereal to potatoes the output per hectare in terms of calories of human food is likely to increase, but its productivity in terms of money value may change up or down according to the relative prices of cereals and cash crop.

Again shifting of land from main crop potato to luxury vegetables may well increase it's productivity in terms of money, but will almost certainly reduce it in terms of calories (M. Shafi.)

In developing countries with rapid growth of population and with shortage of food supply, the first need may be to maximize the volume of total out-put in terms of calories.

When we consider land, then NSA and GCA area come into consideration, So

$$\text{Land Productivity} = \frac{\text{Total agricultural product of a year}}{\text{Net Sown area of the same year}}$$

Also, Land Productivity =

$$\frac{\text{Total agricultural product of a year}}{\text{Gross cropped area of the year}}$$

Here Net Sown area is better than Gross cropped area when we are bothered about partial productivity of Land because NSA capture both yield effect as well as cropping intensity effect while GCA captures only yield effect.

b) Productivity of Labour

If the productivity of land is of primary importance as a determinant of the total level of product, then agricultural production of labour is primary determinant of income of the population engaged in agriculture. Labour productivity is one of the ways to assess agricultural productivity. It can be arrived at by computing the money returned per agricultural worker. Labour productivity indicates the standard of living of the farming population in a certain region. The concept of labour productivity is somewhat more complex than land productivity. It is actually the labour productivity which should help in studying real gains achieved in agriculture in country like India where population pressure is tremendous.

Labour input considers the total number in the labour force. In order to take into account the intensity of labour, the number of man-hours worked in agriculture can also be considered. Similarly the total agricultural output may be taken as the gross farm output, or it may be taken as the value added by labour and other factors in agriculture i.e. the value of fertilizers, pesticides fuel and other inputs from out side the agricultural sector subtracted from the value of the output in order to determine the net contribution of agricultural sector (M. Shafi).

In agriculture, labour productivity has two important aspects. First it mainly affects the national prosperity that means the national income secondly, it naturally determines the standard of living of the agricultural population. In economic perspective national income will be increased if labour get a high wage per hour. Therefore, if a country wants to increase its prosperity it is required: a) to encourage technical assistance and improvement to the labour population, which helps to increase the agricultural productivity in an economy and, b) to stimulate a continual transfer of labour from low productivity to high productivity region. However there are two ways for raising the farmers standard of living; either, he may be paid more than the prevailing regional or world prices for a given amount of work, or the steps can be encountered to raise his out put. Output per man can be improved also by two ways: a) by giving each farm worker more land and livestock to look after and b) by making each unit and livestock capable of yielding a bigger output.

$$\text{Labour Productivity} = \frac{\text{Total agricultural product of a year}}{\text{Total number of labour force in that year}}$$

Here either number of male labour should be converted into equivalent number of female labour or vice-versa.

c) Productivity of Capital

Capital the other major factor of production plays an important role in determining the overall productivity. Capital productivity is a partial concept wherein the change in output is measured due to the impact of capital.

To find out partial productivity of capital we have

$$\text{Capital Productivity} = \frac{\text{Total agricultural product of a year}}{\text{Total gross fixed capital in agriculture that year}}$$

But, capital productivity is complicated to compute and difficult to interpret. This is mainly because of both diversity of farms and the purpose for which capital may be utilized in agricultural production process. Capital is generally utilized for the purchase of land, land reclamation for land improvement, irrigation process, livestock purchase, feeds, seeds fertilizers, agricultural implements and machinery etc.

d) Total factor productivity

Productivity measures are subdivided into partial or total measures. As discussed partial measures are the amount of output per unit of a particular input. But, partial measures of productivity can be misleading, as there is no clear indicator of why they change. For example, land and labour productivity may rise due to increased use of tractors, fertilizer or output mix (move to high value crops). To account for at least some of those problems a total measure of productivity, the Total Factor Productivity (TFP) was devised. TFP is the ratio of an index of agricultural output to an index of agricultural inputs. The index of agricultural output is a value-weighted sum of all agricultural production components. The index of agricultural inputs is the value-weighted sum of conventional agricultural inputs. These generally include land, labour, physical capital, livestock and chemical fertilizers and pesticides. Growth in TFP is referred to as the Solow residual. It is generally considered a measure of technological progress that can be attributed to changes in agricultural research and development (R&D), extension services, human capital development such as education and physical, commercial infrastructure, as well as government policies and environmental degradation (Ahearn., 1998). Change in TFP can also be due to unmeasured inputs or imperfectly measured inputs.

This is the ratio of the output to the total input needed for its production, including not only work hours and capital, but also any other input that might be involved. This might be the investment made in human beings to raise the quality of labour or that made to improve productive knowledge through research and development, or by the introduction of organisational, managerial and social innovations.

Total factor productivity is clearly a more accurate indicator of the economic efficiency than land or labour or capital productivity. However, mainly because of the difficulties involved in quantifying various intangible inputs to total factor productivity, land and labour productivity is far more widely used. It is important to bear in mind that land and labour productivity, is affected not only by capital input, but also by other factors, which affect the efficient use of both capital and hours of work. These other factors consist not only of investment for education, training, research and development, but also of non quantifiable factors such as the relationship, climate and worker and management attitudes towards productive efficiency and competitiveness.

So to calculate Total factor Productivity (TFP) the following relationship can be used.

$$\text{TFP} = \frac{\text{Total production of a year}}{\text{Total of the weighted Input Indices}}$$

To calculate the weighted input indices generally Land, Labour and Capital are given 0.50, 0.26 and 0.24 weight respectively; but this is not a fixed one, it can change with situations. The other method to calculate TFP is to use total differential equation of the various inputs used.

e) Factors Influencing Growth in Agriculture

Researchers originally limited themselves to examining the roles of labour and physical capital in economic growth. The failure to adequately explain growth led them to examine the roles of other factors and to develop endogenous growth theory. Investment in infrastructure has been cited as an important source of growth in agriculture (Jayne *et al.*, 1994). However, Ferreira and Khatami (1996) claim that economic literature has not reached a consensus on the direction of causality between infrastructure and development. Nor can investment be viewed in isolation of policy reform which has been shown to be a vital stimulus of production (Auraujo Bonjean, Chambas and Foirry, 1997; Lachaal, 1994; Lin, 1992; McMillan, Whalley and Zhu, 1989; Wiens, 1983); as have institutions (North, 1994). Public investment in forms of human capital: education, extension, training and technology research have also been shown to increase productivity (Antholt, 1994; Beal, 1978; Evenson and McKinsey, 1991; Pray and Evenson, 1991; Pardey, Roseboom and Craig, 1992; Rosegrant and Evenson, 1992).

Nelson (1964 and 1981) recognized that there are important interactions between capital formation, labour allocation, technical progress and productivity. This calls into question whether the growth due to physical capital can be separated from growth attributed to other inputs. Unless a production technology is a fixed Leontief process, there is always some degree of substitutability among categories of inputs. However, since inputs are not perfect substitutes, the lack of adequate investment can slow down production growth. Estimates of the elasticity of substitution in agriculture between hired labour and capital equipment vary from 0.32 in the short run (Brown and Christensen, 1981) to 1.78 percent (Lopez, 1980) in the long run.

Most measures of TFP incorporate inputs and physical capital, leaving human and social capital, technology, institutions, infrastructure and policy to "explain" growth in TFP. Social and human capital are the on-farm human elements that mediate how policy, technology, institutions and infrastructure affect input and physical capital use. Human capital directly affects whether and how technology will be adopted. Technology choice in turn, affects the inputs and physical capital used. That is, technology is embodied in the types of inputs and how they are used. Social capital affects access to physical capital (e.g. land directly or through land titling and loans) and variable inputs (e.g. through credit or cooperatives).

In general, researchers have estimated TFP and then focused on how one or several of these factors might be driving its growth (Antle, 1983; Nehru and Dhareshwar, 1994; Evenson and McKinsey, 1991; Rosegrant and Evenson, 1992). Usually, they have done so using the change in TFP as a dependent variable in a regression with explanatory variables that represent measures of technology, human capital and policy (which are not easily quantifiable or assignable in constructing the production indices). In the following sections, policy is divided between budgetary policies that affect investment in R&D and infrastructure, political and economic policies and political stability.

Human Capital

Human capital directly influences agricultural productivity by affecting the way in which inputs are used and combined by farmers. Improvements in human capital affect acquisition, assimilation and implementation of information and technology. Human capital also affects one's ability to adapt technology to a particular situation or to changing needs.

Schultz's (1963) classic work attributed between 21 to 23 percent of the growth in U.S. income, between 1929 and 1957, to education of the labour force. Contemporaneously, Griliches (1963) focused on minimizing the unexplained portion of growth in U.S. agriculture by adjusting labour for quality, using education. When he included research and extension expenditure as an input to production, he found that virtually all the "unexplained" growth could be explained by economies of scale, R&D and labour quality changes. Romer (1986) and Lucas (1988) provide theoretical grounds for human capital being the driving force behind economic growth.

Jamison and Lau (1982) explored the role of farmer education and extension on farm efficiency. They found that farmer education and extension were not only important to enhancing production on Thai, Korean and Malaysian farms, but that there was an interaction effect between education and extension. In contrast, they found physical capital had an insignificant impact on production and profits. On the other hand, some researchers are finding evidence that returns to education are low, especially for those who stay in agriculture. In their summary of the findings on the determinants of rural poverty for six country studies based on econometrically estimated income equations, Lopez and Valdes (2000) conclude that the return to education in farming is surprisingly small in most cases. An increase in one year in the average level of schooling raises per capita annual income of the family by less than US$ 20 per person in most cases. The main contribution of education in rural areas appears to be to prepare young people to emigrate to urban areas and towns.

Using an econometric approach, Nehru and Dhareshwar (1994) examined sources of TFP growth in 83 industrial and developing countries for the period 1960-1990. They found that human capital formation was three to four times more important than raw labour in explaining output growth. Using human capital as a separate variable, they found that the countries with the fastest growing economies have based their growth on factor accumulation (human capital, labour and physical capital), not growth in efficiency or technology.

Research and Technology Transfer

Research increases the set of available technologies, hence agricultural R&D expenditures are used as a proxy for agricultural technological change. However, the development of technology does not always result in its adoption. In some cases this may be because the technology being developed is not appropriate, that is, it does not meet the needs of agricultural producers. Hence, researchers focus on public expenditure as an explanatory variable in TFP growth. Additionally public research has been shown to lead private research (Chavas and Cox, 1992).

Several caveats arise in focusing on public R&D to explain growth in agricultural TFP. Public R&D expenditures are used as proxy for R&D results, yet there is not an exact correspondence between expenditures and technology. Even when technology is produced, researchers may have different goals than farmers, e.g. yield maximization rather than profit maximization or risk minimization or improvement in commercial crops rather than staple crops. Additionally, when an appropriate technology does result, the process of technology adoption in agriculture is widely recognized as one that occurs over many years in which some adopt quickly and others wait for extension or the results of their neighbours to convince them to adopt.

Bearing this in mind, researchers have found that public investment in developing and extending agricultural technology is justified by the high rates of return to such investment. In a survey of studies on Asia, Pray and Evenson (1991) found rates of return to national research investment from 19 to 218 percent, returns to national extension investment from 15 to 215 percent and returns to international research investment of 68 to 108 percent. A report of the Taskforce on

Research Innovations for Productivity and Sustainability indicated that the returns to research, though variable, were always high, from 22 to 191 percent. Using an index number approach to calculate TFP for several crops in India, Rosegrant and Evenson (1992) and Evenson and McKinsey (1991) used econometric analysis to identify sources of growth in TFP. Rosegrant and Evenson (1992) found that public research accounted for 30 percent of growth and extension for about 25 percent, with rates of return for each respectively of 63 percent and 52 percent. Evenson and McKinsey (1991) found that public investment in India in research accounts for over half of growth, while extension contributes about one-third and infrastructure accounted for very little growth. They calculated internal rates of return of 218 percent for public research, 177 percent for public extension and 95 percent for private research expenditures in India.

Block (1994) compares econometric estimates of TFP for Sub-Saharan Africa between 1963 and 1988. He uses three different methods of aggregating agricultural output: official exchange rates, purchasing power parity and wheat units. He finds that one-third of the growth in agricultural TFP in Sub-Saharan Africa is due to research expenditures. In India, Rao and Hanumantha (1994) attribute continued growth in agriculture, despite a sharp decline in physical capital formation, to better utilization of existing infrastructure, fertilizer and high yielding varieties.

While the returns to research are high, the technology is not always adopted. For example, high yield varieties (HYV) of wheat and rice have been introduced on less than one-third of the 423 million hectares planted to cereal grains in the Third World. Specifically, in Asia and the Middle East 36 percent of the grain area was HYV, 22 percent in Latin America and one percent in Africa (Wolf, 1987). This implies there is much potential for increasing agricultural productivity using existing technology. However, the use of HYV requires increased use of fertilizer, but external debt in Latin America and poverty and inadequate water supply in Africa have made fertilizer use and hence HYV unprofitable. Jahnke, Kirschke and Lagemann (n.d.) also attributed low adoption of HYV in Africa to lack of appropriate technology development and few extension services directed to women. Additionally, nontraditional crops have rarely been the focus of improved varieties or technology and potential exists to develop them to increase agricultural production.

Public Investment and Policy

Public policy and budgetary decisions regarding infrastructure also have a profound effect on agricultural production. The financing aspects of public R&D and human capital development were discussed above, but both physical and institutional infrastructure affect the development and transfer of technology. For example, irrigation systems and roads may be required to make a technology profitable to implement. Reforms in pricing policy or the marketing system may be needed to provide incentives.

A serious conflict arises with structural adjustment reforms. Budget cuts in public services often accompany market reforms. While fiscal restraint may be required to stabilize the economy in the short run, cuts in human capital development, public R&D, and infrastructure have a detrimental long-term effect on productivity growth. Policy makers need to choose carefully to mitigate the deleterious impacts of budget cuts on future growth.

Using an econometric approach, Jayne *et al.* (1994) demonstrated the complementarity of public policies and public investments in facilitating the use of new technology. They point to the sharp decline in public investments and growth in Zimbabwe during the 1980s. Pal (1985) underscores the complementarity of public policy towards investment in irrigation technology and private variable input use.

The importance of policy reform is increasingly viewed as fundamental for agricultural productivity gains. Liberalizing markets so prices can send proper signals to producers is the fundamental objective of structural adjustment programs in developing countries and policy reform in economies in transition. Assigning property rights is viewed as a means of promoting development through the efficient and responsible use of resources (North, 1994) and therefore underlies the distribution of capital in economies in transition, land reform and most land policy. Block (1994) discusses the complementarity of economic reform and technical change, but cautions that policy reform offers a one-time effect.

An example of the relation between policy reform and productivity is the implementation of China's "responsibility system" (RS) in 1980-81, which linked productivity to material reward, resulted in increased crop yields "for every major crop" (Wiens, 1983). McMillan, Whalley and Zhu (1989) calculated that in response to the RS and price reforms, output in the Chinese agricultural sector increased by over 61 percent between 1978 and 1984. They attribute 78 percent of the increase to the RS and 22 percent to higher prices for crops. They calculate the RS increased productivity in agriculture by 32 percent. Lin (1992) calculated that 42 to 47 percent of the growth in agricultural output was attributable to the RS during the same period.

In another example, price reforms in Egypt implemented in 1986 resulted in increased wheat and maize yields from 1987 to 1993. Rice production increased by 62 percent, while yields increased by 42 percent (Khedr, Ehrich and Fletcher, 1996). Bevan, Collier and Gunning (1993) contrast the performance of agriculture in Kenya and Tanzania. In Kenya where there was little intervention production of food and cash crops increased by 4.6 and 5.5 percent per annum, respectively. In Tanzania, where policies controlled prices and taxed export crops, agricultural production stagnated until policy reforms were instituted in 1984.

Using an econometric approach to estimate TFP for the United States dairy industry 1972-1992, Lachaal (1994) examined how protectionist policies in the form of direct subsidies to agriculture reduced productivity growth in the United States dairy industry. Lachaal showed that government subsidies encouraged using materials at the expense of feed and raised the cost of production by 1.8 percent for each 10 percent increase in subsidy. The subsidy policy was the source of technical inefficiency, creating biases that distorted factor usage.

Political Stability and Conflict

Another aspect of policy that can influence or hinder agricultural production is the political situation. In a study of the productivity growth of 83 industrial and developing countries between 1960 and 1990, Nehru and Dhareshwar (1994) found that the economies that perform the worst are those involved in wars (particularly civil wars) and those that have the most price distorting policies. They explore a variety of policy variables and find that apart from political stability and the initial endowments of a county, virtually no other policy variable is associated with growth.

The World Food Summit Plan of Action items 2 and 3 (1996b) recognize the role of government in providing an environment conducive to investment, through guarantee of rights and law as well as policies encouraging investment. Corruption is the extreme case where law enforcement breaks down and incentives are lacking. While long-standing institutionalized bribery can be seen as simply an added cost of doing business, pervasive corruption and violence increase risk and result in capital flight, disinvestment and jeopardize assistance.

7

Measurement of Agricultural Productivity

Productivity as defined in agricultural geography means output per unit of input or per unit of area respectively, and the improvement in agricultural productivity is generally the result of a more efficient use of the factors of production, viz. environment, arable land, labour, capital and the like. Productivity, is a difficult theme, both in concept and in terms of measurement of its level. Therefore, any definition that is adopted is bound to suffer from certain weaknesses. It is important to remember, however, that productivity is a physical rather than a value concept, which describes the relationship between the output and the major inputs like land, labour and capital. The regional differences in agricultural productivity are the result partly of natural advantages of abiotic environment (soils and climate) and partly of farming efficiency as controlled by cultural ecology. Farming efficiency refers to the properties and qualities of various inputs and the manner in which they are combined and put to use for production. Increases in agricultural productivity is largely related to the choice of inputs, and their relative quantities, and the techniques and the skill with which they are used in the production processes.

The level of agricultural productivity or performance, as a concept, means the degree to which the economic, cultural, technical and organizational variables (i.e. the man-made frame) are able to exploit the abiotic resources of the area for agricultural production (Jasbir Singh, 1979). The regional variations in physical output from the soils are the result partly of natural circumstances and partly of human manipulations of the land resources. The regional differences in yields per unit area indicate the magnitude and the direction of the inter-play of a multitude of factors. Furthermore, the level of agricultural productivity or performance is a dynamic concept, as any modification in physical factors and improvement in non-physical bases of farming effect *agriculturaproductkunde* per hectare.

The method of mapping of spatio-temporal characteristics of the level of agricultural productivity provides a rational base for future orientation in agricultural planning. The pattern of change in level of agricultural productivity in relative terms is a reliable index of the agricultural development in the past. Besides, it can be used as an effective measure for delimiting the areas where even agrarian development could not bring about significant changes and modifications in the crop structure and agricultural production, and which may thereby be termed as *weaker areas* or *area of poverty*.

Measuring the independent control of land, labour and capital on agricultural productivity is extremely difficult because they are complementary rather than isolated aspects. Thus a measure of land productivity, for example, output per hectare would not necessarily be an indicator of land potential, but rather a measure of collective utilization of land, labour and capital. In the same way, labour productivity, for example, output per adult-male unit farm work force or man-days is also a reflection of innate land potentiality and the degree of capital investment. Capital productivity means output per unit of input in monetary values but land and labour efficiency ultimately needs methods which can assess the output and input ratio, and the input should include land, labour and capital.

a) Approaches of the Study

Several techniques adopted for computing efficiency in level of agricultural productivity per unit area per unit of time, or per unit of farm work force, etc. are detailed below:

1. Assessing the value of agricultural production per unit area
2. Measuring production per unit of farm labour or man-hour
3. Determining output in relation to input, or output-input ratio and profitability of farming measured in terms of the return for the sum total of human efforts or paid-out-cost in relation to the output (Khusro, 1964)
4. Expressing production of agriculture in terms of grain equivalents per head of population (Buck, 1967; E. de Vries, 1967; Clark and Haswell, 1967)
5. Considering output per unit area or yields per hectare after grading them in ranking order, thereby deriving the ranking coefficient (Kendall, 1939; Stamp, 1960; Shafi, 1960)
6. Giving weightage to the ranking order of the output per unit area with the percentage share under each crop (Sapre and Deshpande, 1964; Bhatia, 1967)
7. Using the carrying capacity of land in terms of population (Stamp, 1958, 1967)
8. Determining an index of productivity (Enyedi, 1964; Shafi, 1972, 1974)
9. Calculating the index number of agricultural efficiency by expressing the per unit area carrying capacity (in terms of population) of the component enumeration unit as a percentage of the per unit area carrying capacity for the entire region (Jasbir Singh, 1972, 1974)
10. Computing the crop yield and concentration indices ranking coefficient (Jasbir Singh, 1976)
11. Involving the area, production and price of each cultivated crop in each of the constituent areal unit of the region, and then relating the out-turn in terms of money of the unit to the corresponding productivity of the region (Hussian, 1976)

12. Delimiting agricultural productivity by computing the intensity and spread indices of three variables, i.e. (i) yield, (ii) grain equivalents, and (iii) cropping system (Singh, V. R., 1979)

Of these, the first three techniques seem to require such statistics as are not readily available and even easily accessible in most of the underdeveloped and developing countries of the world. Technique (3), however, has little validity in a subsistence farm economy where (i) foodgrains dominate and constitute 75 to 85 per cent of all agricultural production, (ii) the major output is retained for domestic consumption, and (iii) most of the inputs are provided by the farmer.

Technique (4) which advocates measuring agricultural progress in terms of grain equivalent per head of population was used for the first time by Buck in 1967. He realized that in a subsistence agricultural economy as in China, productivity expressed in terms of monetary value has no meaning because the crops may be grown for local domestic consumption, and only a small portion of it may be sold for cash. To him, therefore, the natural unit for measuring the level of agricultural productivity in such a community appeared to be the conversion of kilograms of agricultural products into grain equivalents. He considered all grains to be equal in food value. He converted agricultural products other than food grains into grain equivalents according to the local market price at which they are exchanged against food grains which are grown predominantly in a locality.

Technique (5), which works on the basis of hectare-yield statistics of crops, indicates the efficiency of agriculture more adequately. The spatial variation in physical output from land is the result of combinations of natural environment and human activities. Kendall (1939) developed method of determining agricultural efficiency based on output per unit area and devised a system of ranking coefficient.

Sapre and Deshpande (1964) introduced technique (6). They have, in fact, modified the ranking coefficient approach by giving weightage to the area under different crops. They have used the weighted average of ranks instead of the simple average of ranks. The weighted ranks of various crops are proportionate to the percentage of cropland under each crop. The weighted average of ranks seems to have an inherent weakness which arises from not taking into account the harvested regional strength of crops.

The technique (7) of carrying capacity of land (in terms of population) was suggested by Stamp (1958) in his Presidential Address to the International Geographical Congress at Rio de Janerio in 1956. Stamp (1960) has opined, making some allowances for quality, that higher the output per unit area, greater is the efficiency of the farmer. He had taken into account, first, a standard nutrition unit, this is, to what extent food and land are required to support one average human being and to produce that much amount of food respectively; second, the caloric value of some leading food crops since 90 percent of the world population depends upon food grains. In this approach the production of crops is converted into calories, which then can be used to measure the optimum carrying capacity of land in terms of population. In a sense the carrying capacity is a measure of farming efficiency.

While discussing geographical types of agriculture, Enyedi (1964) devised technique (8) for determining an index of productivity coefficient. Enyedi's formula of productivity index is:

$$\text{Productivity Index} = \frac{Y}{Y_n} \div \frac{T}{T_n}$$

Where Y is the total production of the selected crop in unit area,

Y_n is the total production of the same crop on national scale,

T is the total cropped area of the unit area, and

T_n is the total cropped area at national scale.

Enyedi's technique is appreciable in the sense that it determines the productivity index of an area with reference to national level. However, the technique does not consider that in certain cases the productivity index is influenced by the magnitude of the area under a particular individual crop.

Besides, when the district yield is less than the national yield, its productivity index is higher than the national level.

Technique (9) is a modified form of technique (7) and is considered most useful for measuring agricultural efficiency. In those parts of the world which suffer from food shortage, what matters most in many countries is the actual amount of food produced. After making some allowances for the quality of production (i.e. to change the crop production into caloric values) and the usages and the wastages in the form of seed, cattle feed, storage losses, etc. it can be inferred that higher the caloric output per unit area greater is the carrying capacity of land in terms of population and hence the efficiency of farming. The carrying capacity of agricultural areas, i.e. their maximum caloric return from the soils can be considered as their index of efficiency. The variations in caloric productivity per unit area are the result of differential interaction between the combination of environmental conditions and the combination of human activities.

Technique (10) introduced by Jasbir Singh, (1976) in order to assess the regional differences in the levels of food production and to delimit the weaker areas from the point of view of agricultural production is enough to focus attention only on the important food crops of a region or a country lying in the Oriental World since they are the dominant, primary and secondary crops in terms of agricultural land occupancy. The average food crop yields and proportions of these crops in the total harvested area have been used as twin-elements for measuring the index of the level of food production. For an objective measurement of the level of agricultural productivity, the relative crop yield and concentration indices arranged in ranking order and computed into average ranking coefficients, would give a measure which one may call the crop yield and concentration indices ranking coefficient. The procedure may be explained as follows:

$$Y_i = \frac{Y_{ae}}{Y_{ar}} \times 100$$

Where Y_i is the crop yield index,

Y_{ae} is the average yield per hectare of crop 'a' in the component enumeration unit,

Y_{ar} is the average yield of the crop 'a' in the entire region or country

$$C_i = \frac{P_{ae}}{P_{ar}} \times 100$$

Where C_i is the crop concentration index,

P_{ae} is the percentage strength of crop 'a' in the total harvested are in the component enumeration unit, and

P_{ar} is the percentage strength of crop 'a' in the total harvested area in the entire region or country

The crop yield and concentration indices thus derived for all the regional units and the crops are ranked separately. Yield and concentration ranks for individual crops are added and thereafter divided by 2, thus giving the crop yield and concentration indices ranking coefficient. The equation is :

$$\text{Crop yield and concentration indices Ranking coefficient for crop 'a'} = \frac{\text{Crop yield index ranking of crop 'a'} + \text{Crop concentration index ranking of crop 'a'}}{2}$$

The result thus derived will give us an idea of the level of agricultural productivity: the lower the ranking co-efficient, the higher the level of agricultural productivity and vice versa.

Technique (11), put forth by Hussain (1976) for establishing agricultural productivity of the Sutlej-Ganga plains of India, converted the agricultural production into money value of a regional unit in proportion to the whole region. This approach revealed that other things remaining the same, higher the return in terms of value in money, greater is the productivity of land. However, because of variations in crop, combinations and crop prices, this approach suffered in its application in the global perspective.

Singh V. R. (1979), too, advocated approach (12) with which he tried to present a two-dimensional picture of agricultural productivity consisting of intensity and spread. Intensity and spread of three variables, namely, (i) yield, (ii) grain equivalents, and (iii) cropping systems have been taken into consideration to formulate agricultural productivity regions. Logically, this approach seems equally reliable and dependable, but a long chain of formulae makes the procedure excruciatingly lengthy involving enormous and cumbersome calculations. Moreover, this technique does not mirror the agricultural productivity of an area. Rather, two separate maps for intensity and spread have to be drawn, and thereafter they have to be superimposed for identifying the categories, so subjectivity and personal bias may inadvertently enter into one's inferences at this stage.

To conclude, the techniques for measuring agricultural productivity, efficiency or performance levels should present useful tools for generalizing the overall performance of an area at a given point of time and may possibly be between two points of time to find out dynamic trends in it. Such techniques should have wide applicability so as to comprehend the level of agricultural development. Regional imbalances in farm production obviously call for an intensive effort on the farm so that per unit area yield disparities might be narrowed down.

An analysis of spatial patterns of levels of agricultural productivity is significant for several reasons, the major ones of which may be identified as follows:

1. The overall picture does not, however, give the exact idea of the regional differences in the agricultural production and, that for proper understanding of the situation regional studies are indispensable; and here the regional imbalances in the levels of agricultural productivity have to be recognized.
2. In the age of specialization there is an urgent need to synthesize the two subjects of geography and agriculture for well guided and sound agricultural planning and implementation of package programmes

in a country where farming is the mainstay of a large proportion of population and food shortage clouds are always hovering.

3. It may have to be recognized that the impact of the new strategy varies from one regional unit to another, depending on the variable combinations of physical environs and socio-economic, cultural and human circumstances.
4. A survey of spatial differences in the levels of agricultural productivity or efficiency may be useful for differentiating areas whose performances are poor in comparison with other, in spite of the new agricultural strategy.
5. It may help in the delimitation of agricultural production typologies, or areas of prosperity, parity and poverty.

Finally, the geography of agricultural productivity may attempt, first, to map, describe, and interpret the regional imbalances in levels of productivity; second, to demarcate areas with relatively poor performances, and third, since any agricultural revolution rests on capricious nature, it must be reduced either by following irrigation agriculture or dry farming technology. Such attempts will suggest for the acceleration of farm production future agricultural programmes will have to be made flexible and re-examined, re-adjusted and re-cast from time to time in the light of past experiences and accomplishments in the field of agricultural productivity.

b) Measurement of Agricultural Productivity

Our basic idea in this section is to find the regional disparity in productivity amongst the blocks and regions for individual crop. So through this analysis we intend to identify the regions whose yield for individual crops are high. In the previous section we have seen the latest techniques of measuring agricultural productivity wherein population is used as a parameter; but with the objective of identifying regional variation in productivity, inclusion of population as a parameter is felt unwarranted.

We have seen that Enyedi's method attempt to find productivity index using the relation

$$\text{Productivity Index} = \frac{Y}{Y_n} \div \frac{T}{T_n}$$

Where: Y is the total production of the selected crop in unit area,

Y_n is the total production of the same crop on national scale

T is the total cropped area of the unit area, and

T_n is the total cropped area at national scale.

But it is felt that considering the total area of each crop for the block and district is misguiding. We should rather use the relevant area for each crop at the block and region level; so, in our analysis we have modified Enyedi's technique for determining an index of productivity co-efficient, which is discussed below.

Methodology

Productivity index has been calculated using the relation

$$\text{Productivity Index} = \frac{Y}{Y_n} \div \frac{A}{A_n}$$

Where Y, is the total production of the selected crop in the block/region.

Y_n is the total production of the same crop at district level.

A is the total cropped area of the particular crop in the block/region.

A_n total crop area for the same crop at district level

For the purpose of ignoring the fluctuation of the individual years for productivity of individual blocks we have considered the average area and average production in our analysis (Appendix-VII.i to VII.xiii). To gauge the change in productivity over the period we have divided the entire period 1993-1994 to 2000-01 into Period I (1993-94) and Period II (2000-01). We then calculated the productivity index for individual crop for both the periods (Appendix-VII.xiv & VII.xv). We have found that the productivity index varies between 0.12 (Jute- Kaliachak in Period-II) and 6.43 (Jute-Bamongola in Period-II). To enable comparative analysis across blocks it was felt to classify the productivity indices into 5 classes, viz. Very Low (V.L.), Low (L), 'Medium' (M), High (H), and 'Very High' (V.H.).

Table 7.1 shows the ranges in which these productivity indices have been classified

Table 7.1: Categorization of Productivity Indices

Category	*Value*
Very Low	Less than 0.9
Low	0.9-1
Medium	1-1.1
High	1.1-1.2
Very High	Grater than 1.2

Thus we are able to identify the level of productivity index for individual crops at block/region level for Period-I and Period-II as discussed above and classify into 5 classes and have plotted Map 7.1 to 7.13. These maps provides the snapshots of the variation in the productivity at the block / region level and also the pattern of change in the productivity.

Cercals: Map 7.1 to 7.4 which analyses the productivity for aus, aman, boro and wheat respectiely shows some interesting pattern.

Aus: It is found that in general the productivity of aus in the blocks of Diara region are comparatively higher than other blocks. Moreover the productivity in Harishchandrapur-I, English-Bazar, Manikchak and Kaliachak-I have increased over the years to 'Very High' level. It is interesting to note that the productivity for Harishchandrap ır-II, Chanchal-I,

Chanchal-II, Ratua-II, Bamongola and Habibpur have fallen. This change at the block level has resulted in a decline in the productivity for 'Tal' in Period-II over Period-I and increase from 'Low' to 'High' in Diara region over the same period.

Aman: The peculiarity of productivity level of aman in the district and block level is that while in Period-I the level of productivity was 'Low' for all blocks except Ratua-I, Gazole Manikchak with 'Medium' productivity, in Period II there is a wide variation in the productivity levels as Kaliachak-I has become a 'Very High' productive block with Gazole and Habibpur showing 'high' productivity. The productivity of the English Bazar blocks of the district in Period-II has sharply fallen. Aman which happens to be the prime crop of the district requires more attention and thereby increased productivity is expected. The appalling situation of the district is explained by decreasing productivity of aman in many blocks. At region level the direction of productivity change is found to be different, while for 'Tal' the productivity declined from 'Low' to 'Very Low'. Barind maintained its productivity level while Diara's productivity increased from 'Low' to 'High'. This single crop is able to explain that Diara region is improving with higher productivity.

Boro: The other major crop of the district has shown varied productivity levels in Period-II while 'Medium' productivity level in Period-I with an exception in Manikchak ('Low') and Habibpur ('Very Low'). In Period-II Harishchandrapur-II and English Bazar have increased their productivity to 'Very High' level while Gazole has improved its productivity to 'Medium'. But, it is alarming to find the productivity of Ratua-I, Old-Malda, Bamongola, Manikchak, Kaliachak-I, Kaliachak-II and Kaliachak-III to be declining.

At region level Tal and Barind maintained their 'Medium' and 'Low' productivity level respectively over the years whereas Diara's productivity have declined from 'Medium' to 'Very Low' level.

Wheat: Like other cereals wheat also shows the similar pattern of uniform 'Medium' Productivity level in Period-I while varied productivity level in Period-II. Harishchandrapur,

English Bazar and Kaliachak-III are the blocks where the productivity increased sharply while for the blocks of Barind region wheat productivity is on the decline. Wheat, a winter crop which requires irrigation facility, is not supported in the Barind region as the region's irrigation facility is not adequate. At region level even Tal shows a decline in productivity.

Pulses: Map 7.5 to 7.8 analyses the productivity for arhar, kalai, gram and lentil individually. The findings are discussed here.

Arhar: For arhar the general level of agricultural productivity during Period-I is 'Low' while in Period-II is 'Very Low'. The block standing out during the two Periods are: Period-I: Harishchandrapur-II, 'Very High'; Old-Malda, 'Medium'; Period-II Gazole and Kaliachak-III, 'Very High'. Thus barring these two blocks the general trend gives an indication that there is a change in agricultural productivity of arhar is distinct. This productivity fall happens along with a decline in area under cultivation of arhar, as discussed in Chapter 5.

Kalai: The level of crop productivity for kalai matches the regional demarcation as in Period-II, Tal region is found to have 'Very Low' productivity, Barind 'Very High' productivity while Diara 'High' productivity. This regional variation was not at all evident in Period-I where all the blocks, except Harishchandrapur-I, were having 'Medium' productivity. This productivity pattern provides an indication of potential of kalai cultivation in Barind region. But this potential needs to be studied along with area under cultivation as kalai is not found as a significant crop in the Barind region (Findings of Chapter 5)/

Gram: In case of gram the productivity and its pattern are similar to that of cereals. In Period-I the blocks are having 'Low' productivity level. Against this in Period-II the blocks show varied productivity levels. Harishchandrapur-I, Habibpur and Kaliachak-III are the blocks wherein productivity has increased significantly. But the rise of productivity in Habibpur is unable to resist the decline in productivity of Barind region as a whole as other there blocks

Map No: 7.1

CROP PRODUCTIVITY INDEX: AUS

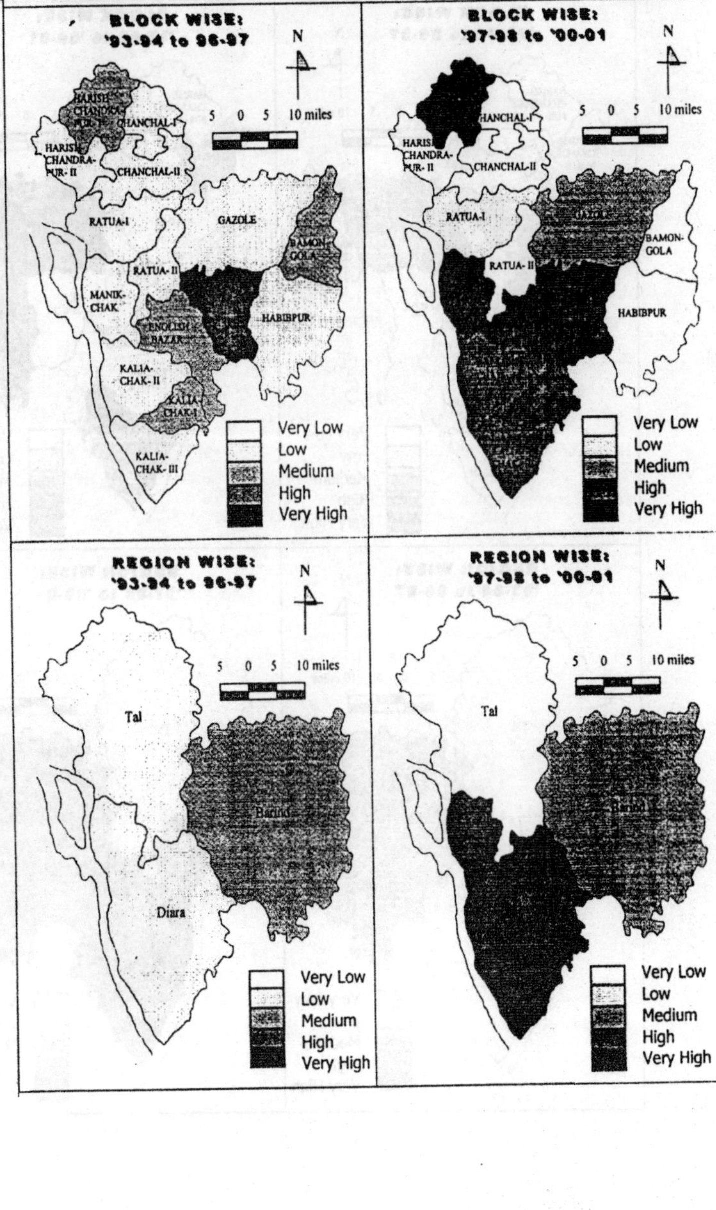

Map No: 7.2

CROP PRODUCTIVITY INDEX: AMAN

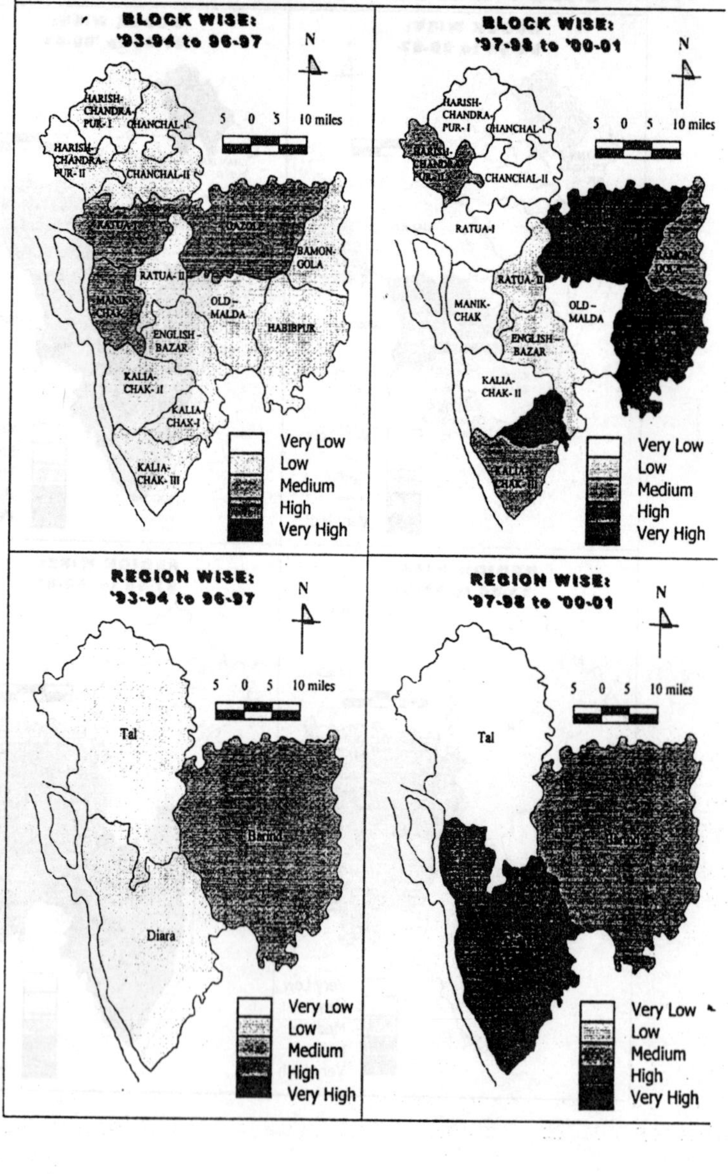

Map No: 7.3

CROP PRODUCTIVITY INDEX: BORO

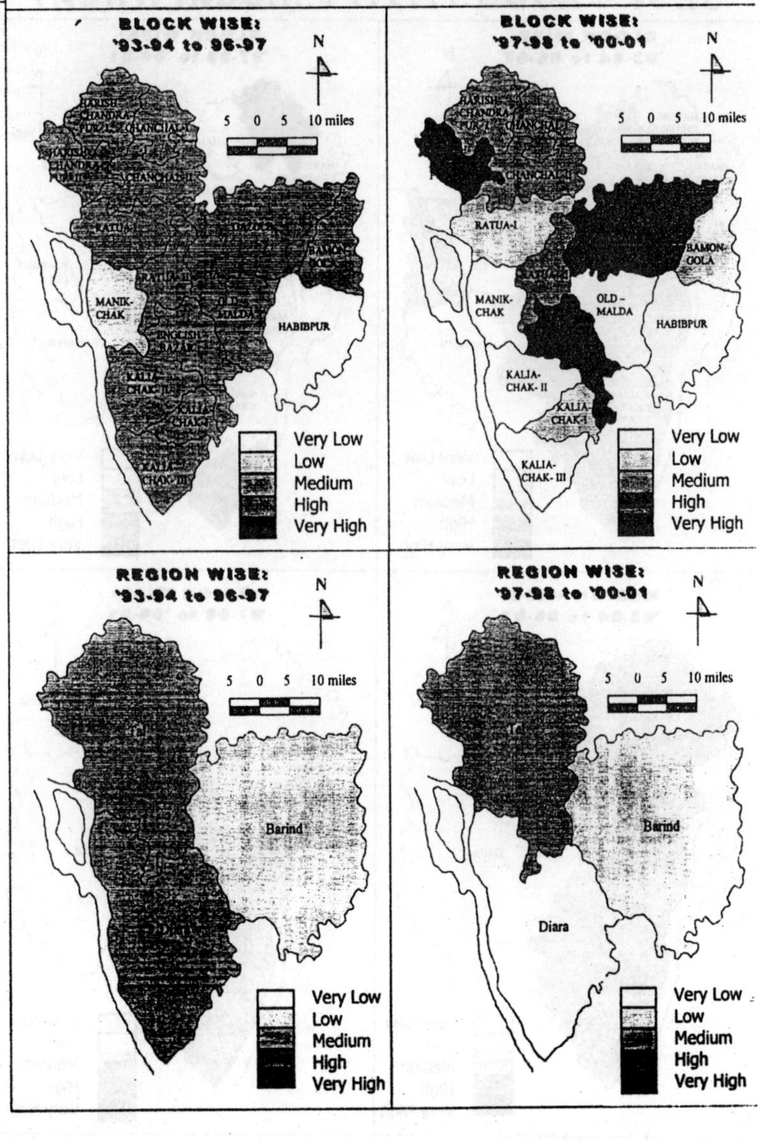

Map No: 7.4

CROP PRODUCTIVITY INDEX: WHEAT

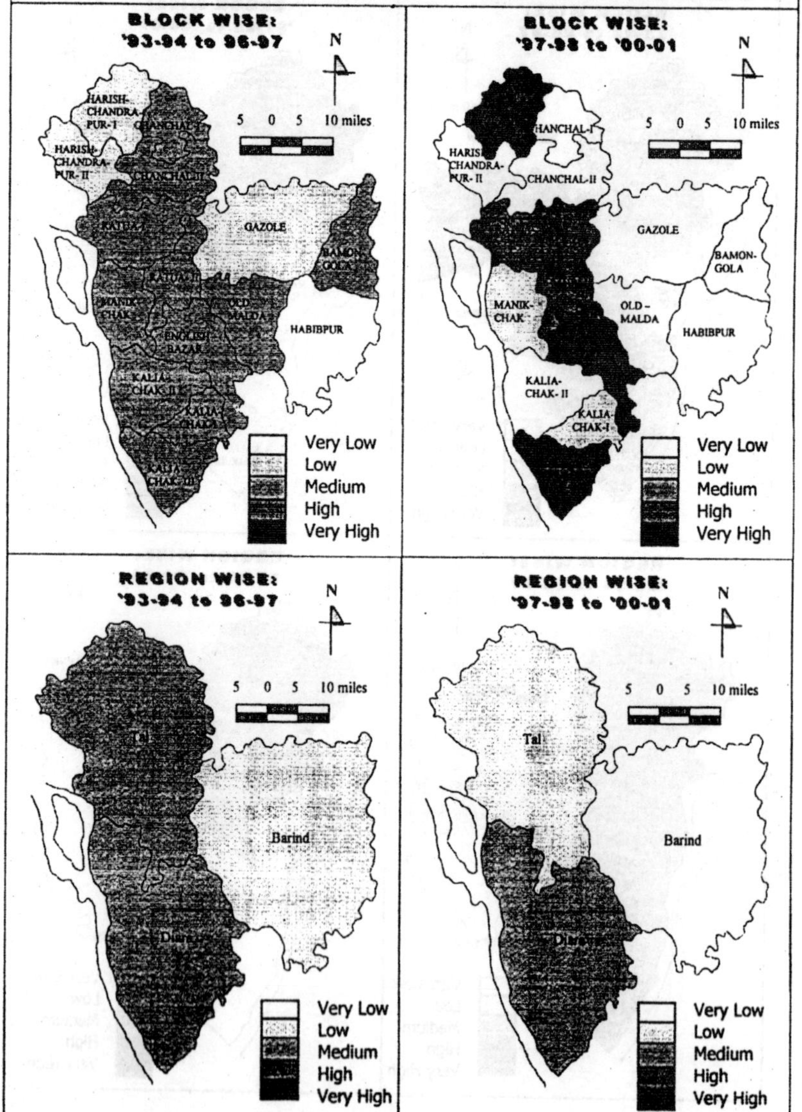

viz. Gazole, Bamongola and Old-Malda slide to 'Very Low' level.

Lentil: the productivity of Lentil across blocks in Period I is comparatively more uniform than Period II. In Period I while Old Malda is having 'Very High' productivity, Ratua I, Bamongola, Kaliachak II show 'Low' productivity and English Bazar and Kaliachak I have 'Very Low' productivity. Others have 'Medium' productivity. In Period II, Ratua II and Kaliachak II have graduated to have 'Very High' productivity. The productivity of Old Malda has sharply dropped to 'Very Low' level. At regional level Tal shows a moderate increase in productivity over the years, while Barind's productivity has fallen.

Oil seeds: Map 7.9 and 7.10 show the variation of the productivity level of mustard and linseed, respectively at block and region level.

Mustard: Mustard shows a definite regional pattern of Productivity level in Period II. Eastern blocks of Gazole, Bamongola and Old Malda have increased their productivity index to 'Very High' level while in western blocks viz. Ratua I, Manikchak and Kaliachak II, the productivity has fallen to 'Very Low' level. This shift has caused Barind's productivity to increase to 'High' level while Diara's productivity has fallen to 'Very Low' level.

Linseed: Linseed productivity is found to be low in maximum number of blocks in Period-I with exception of Chanchal-II "Very High"; Kaliachak-II 'Very Low' So the disparity was not so pronounced in Period-I. In period-II the blocks of Diara region and Old-Malda have progress substantially to 'Very High' productivity level. This is in contrast to the fall in productivity of the central belt consisting of Ratua-I, Ratua-II, Gazole, Bamongola and Manikchak.

Cash Crop: Map 7.11 to 7.13 provides an illustration of the productivity level of potato, mango and jute for the period 1993-94 to 1996-97 and 1997-98 to 2000-01 at the block and region level.

Potato: In Potato too the pattern of diversity is similar to that of the other crops as in the Period-I the blocks were

Map No: 7.5

CROP PRODUCTIVITY INDEX: ARHAR

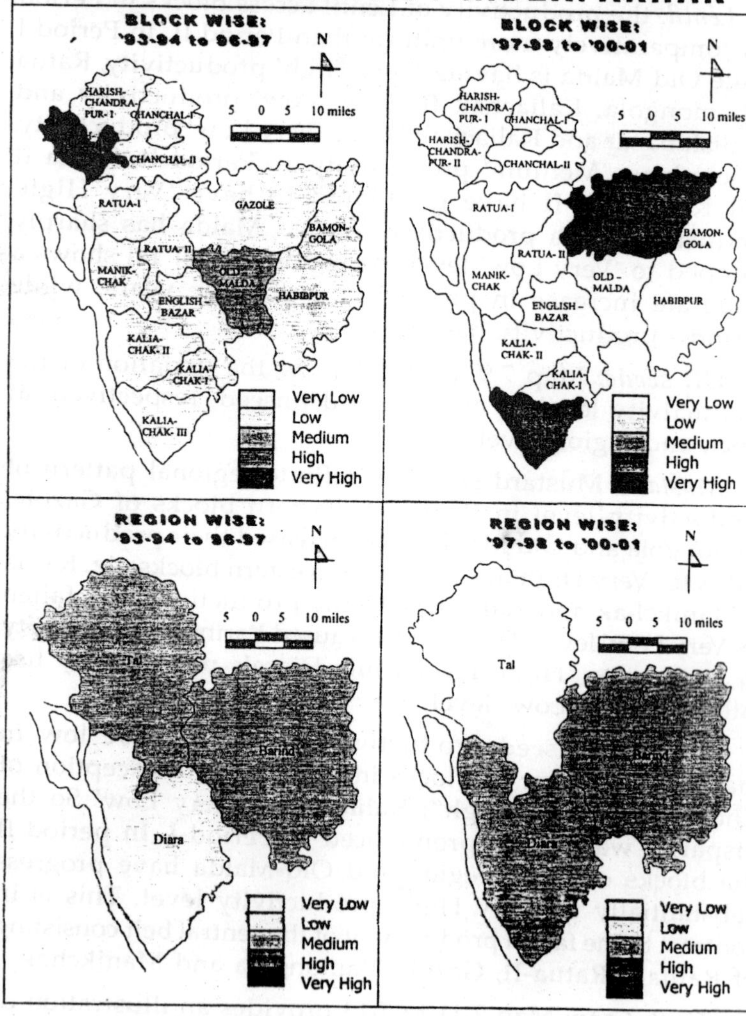

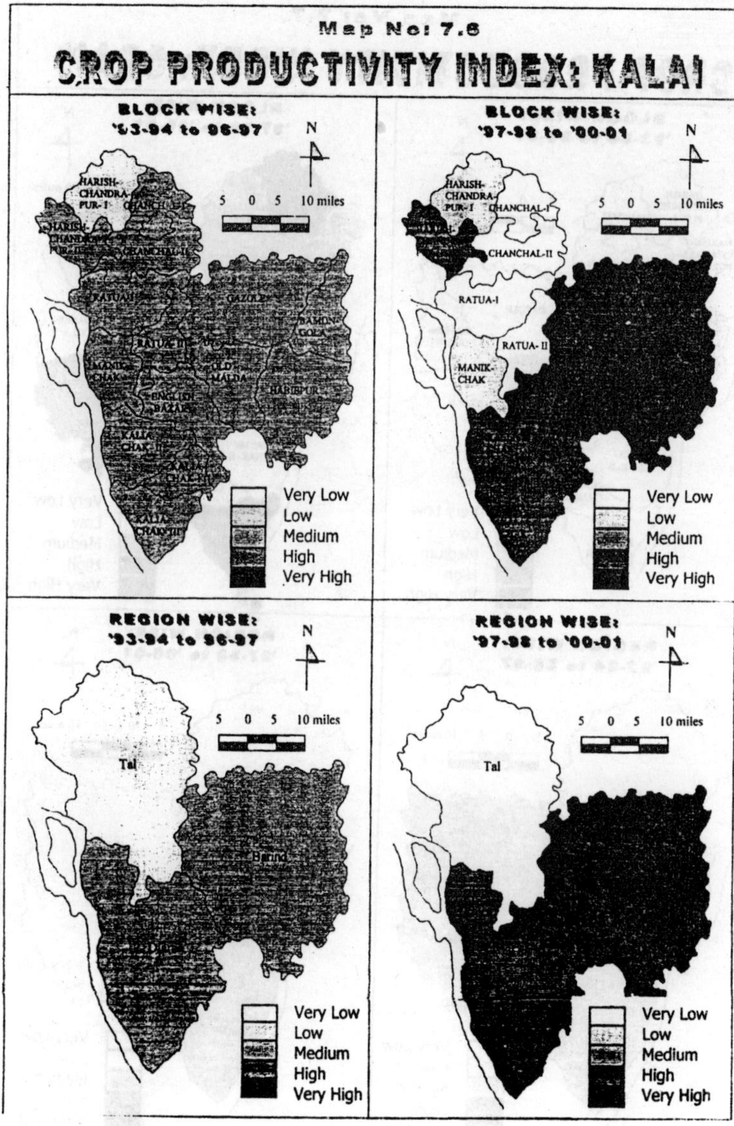
Map No: 7.8
CROP PRODUCTIVITY INDEX: KALAI
BLOCK WISE:
'93-94 to 96-97
BLOCK WISE:
'97-98 to '00-01
REGION WISE:
'93-94 to 96-97
REGION WISE:
'97-98 to '00-01
HARISH-CHANDRA-PUR-I
CHANCHAL-I
CHANCHAL-II
RATUA-I
RATUA-II
MANIK-CHAK
GAZOLE
BAMON-GOLA
OLD MALDA
ENGLISH BAZAR
HABIBPUR
KALIA-CHAK
Tal
Barind
5 0 5 10 miles
N
Very Low
Low
Medium
High
Very High

Map No: 7.7

CROP PRODUCTIVITY INDEX: GRAM

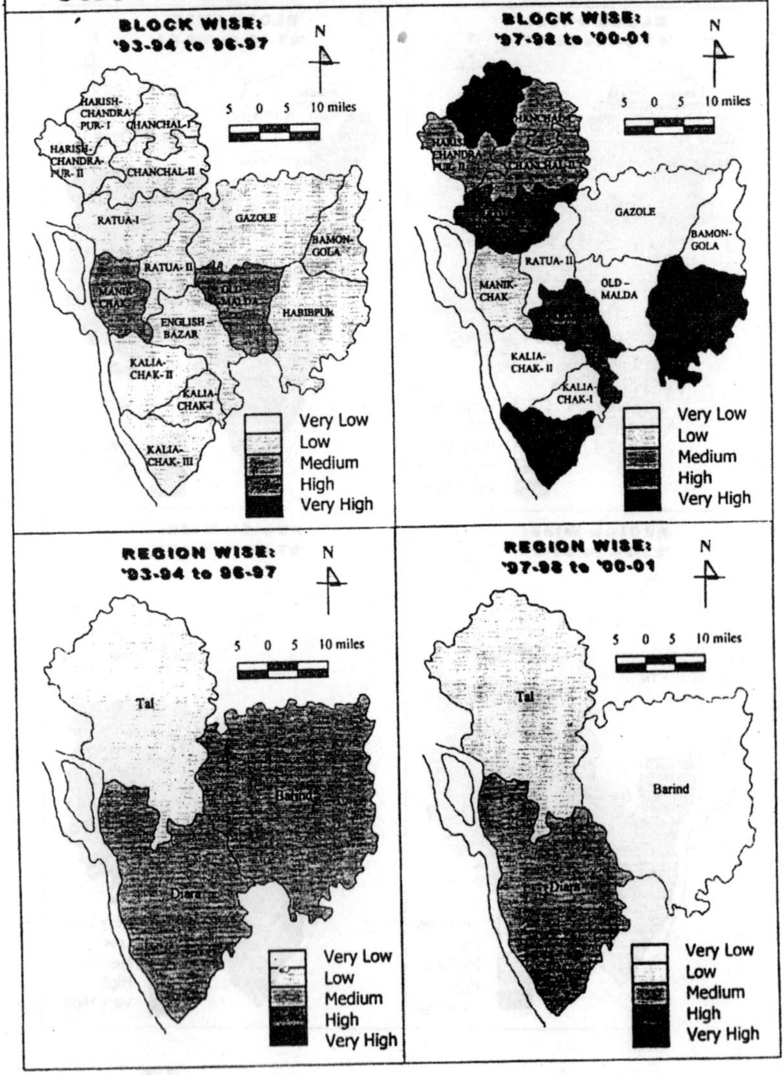

Map No: 7.8

CROP PRODUCTIVITY INDEX: LENTIL

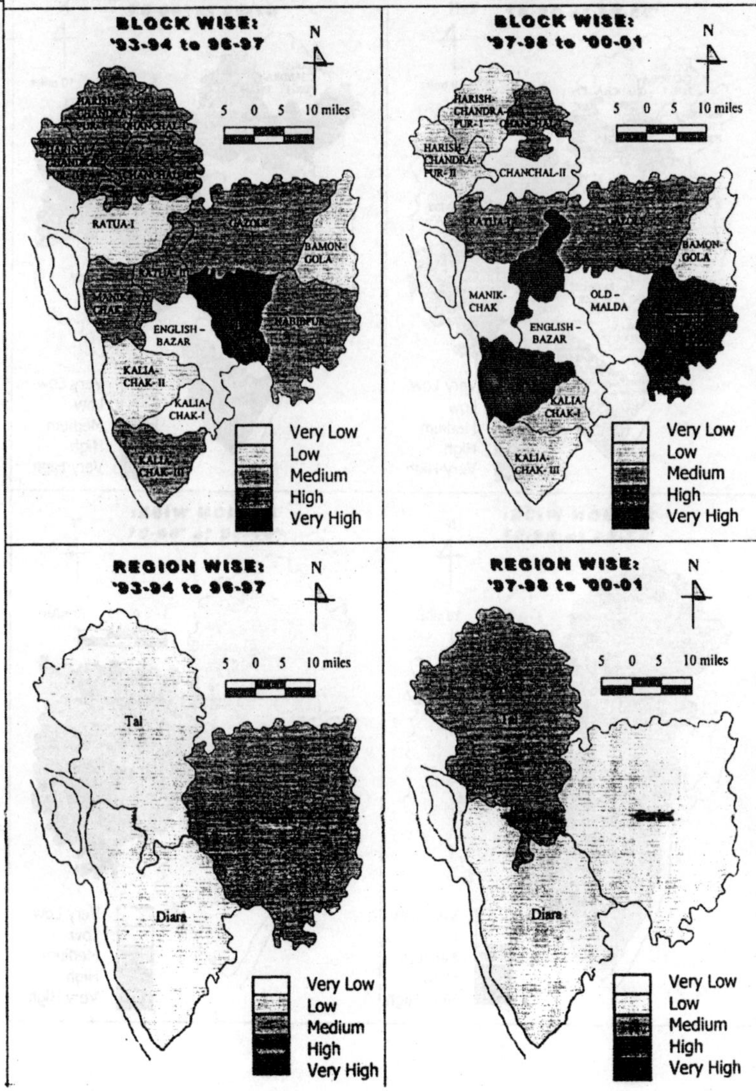

Map No: 7.9

CROP PRODUCTIVITY INDEX: MUSTARD

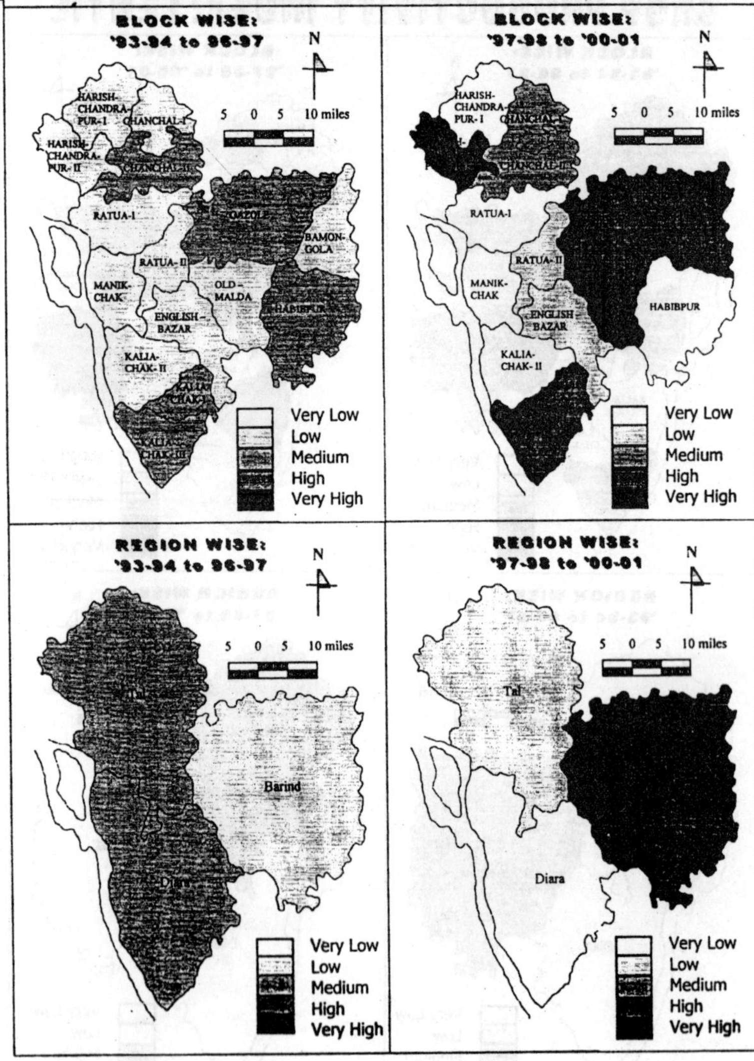

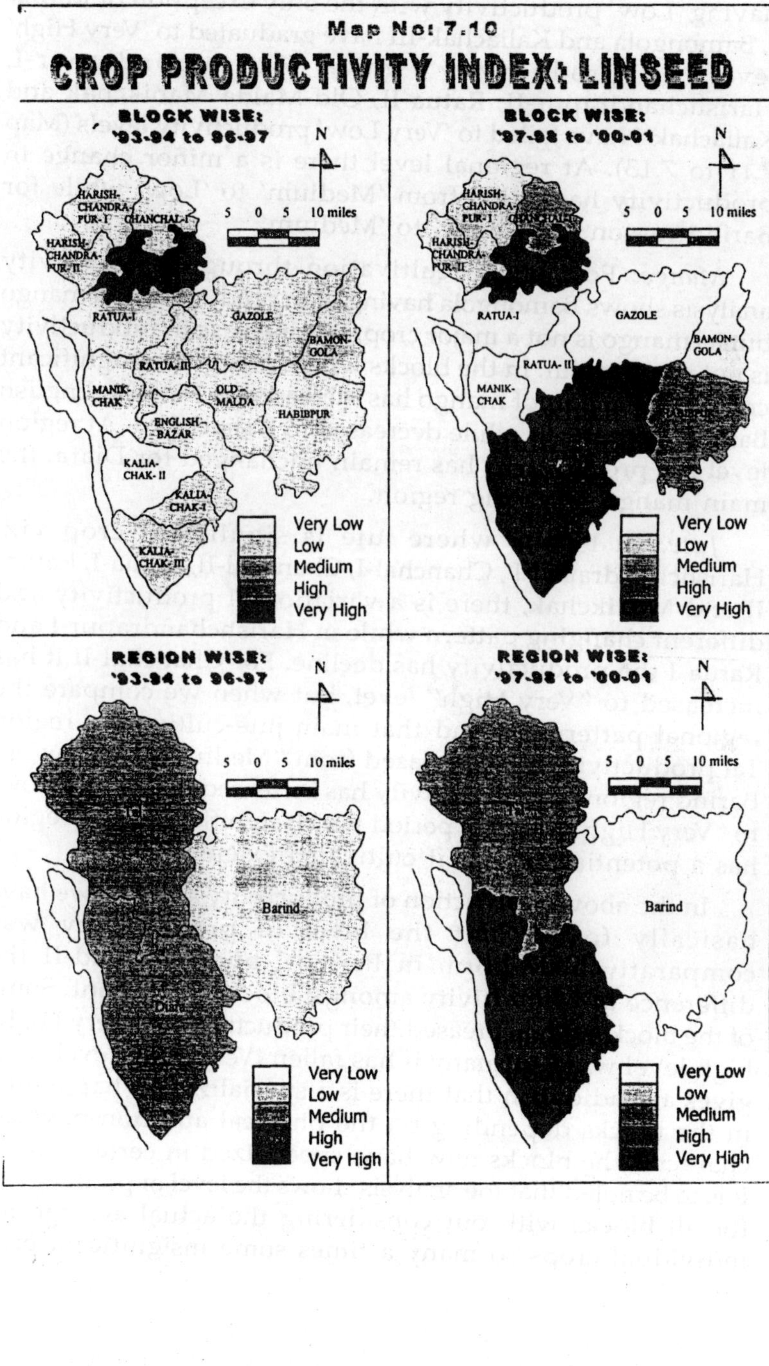
Map No: 7.10
CROP PRODUCTIVITY INDEX: LINSEED
BLOCK WISE:
'93-94 to 96-97
N
5 0 5 10 miles
HARISH-CHANDRA-PUR-I
CHANCHAL-I
HARISH-CHANDRA-PUR-II
RATUA-I
GAZOLE
BAMON-GOLA
RATUA-II
MANIK-CHAK
OLD-MALDA
HABIBPUR
ENGLISH-BAZAR
KALIA-CHAK-II
KALIA-CHAK-I
KALIA-CHAK-III
Very Low
Low
Medium
High
Very High
BLOCK WISE:
'97-98 to '00-01
N
5 0 5 10 miles
HARISH-CHANDRA-PUR-I
HARISH-CHANDRA-PUR-II
RATUA-I
GAZOLE
BAMON-GOLA
RATUA-II
MANIK-CHAK
Very Low
Low
Medium
High
Very High
REGION WISE:
'93-94 to 96-97
N
5 0 5 10 miles
Barind
Very Low
Low
Medium
High
Very High
REGION WISE:
'97-98 to '00-01
N
5 0 5 10 miles
Barind
Very Low
Low
Medium
High
Very High

having 'Low' productivity with the only exception of Ratua-I, Bamongola and Kaliachak-III have graduated to 'Very High' level of productivity while Harishchandrapur-I, Harishchandrapur-II, Ratua-II, Old-Malda Manikchak and Kaliachak-I have failed to 'Very Low' productivity levels (Map 7.11 to 7.13). At regional level there is a minor change in productivity has fallen from 'Medium' to 'Low' while for Barind reason from 'Low' to 'Medium'.

Mango: For mango cultivation through productivity analysis shows Bamongola having high productivity in mango but as mango is not a major crop, this increase in productivity is not meaningful. In the blocks where mango is a significant crop productivity of mango has increased in Ratua-I, English Bazar, Kaliachak-II while decreased in Kaliachak-I. At region level the productivity has remain unchanged for Diara, the main mango culvating region.

Jute: In blocks where jute is significant crop viz. Harishchandrapur-I , Chanchal-I, Chanchal-II, Ratua-I, Ratua-II and Manikchak, there is a variation of productivity and different changing pattern while in Harishchandrapur-I and Ratua-I the productivity has decline. For Chanchal-II it has increased to "Very High" level, but when we compare the regional pattern we find that main jute-cultivating region Tal productivity has decreased from "Medium" to 'Low'. In Barind region the productivity has increased from 'Very Low' to "Very High" over the period which signifies that the region has a potential for jute if cultivated extensively.

In the above sub-section of productivity analysis we have basically found that the level of productivity was comparatively uniform in Period-I but in Period-II the difference in productivity amongst blocks significant. Some of the blocks have increased their productivity to "Very High" high level while in many it has fallen 'Very Low' level. This gives an indication that there is a specialization happening in the blocks depending on the physical and non-physical character the blocks now have specialized in certain crops. It is to be noted that the analysis shows the level of productivity for all blocks with out considering the actual acreage for individual crops so many a times some insignificant crop

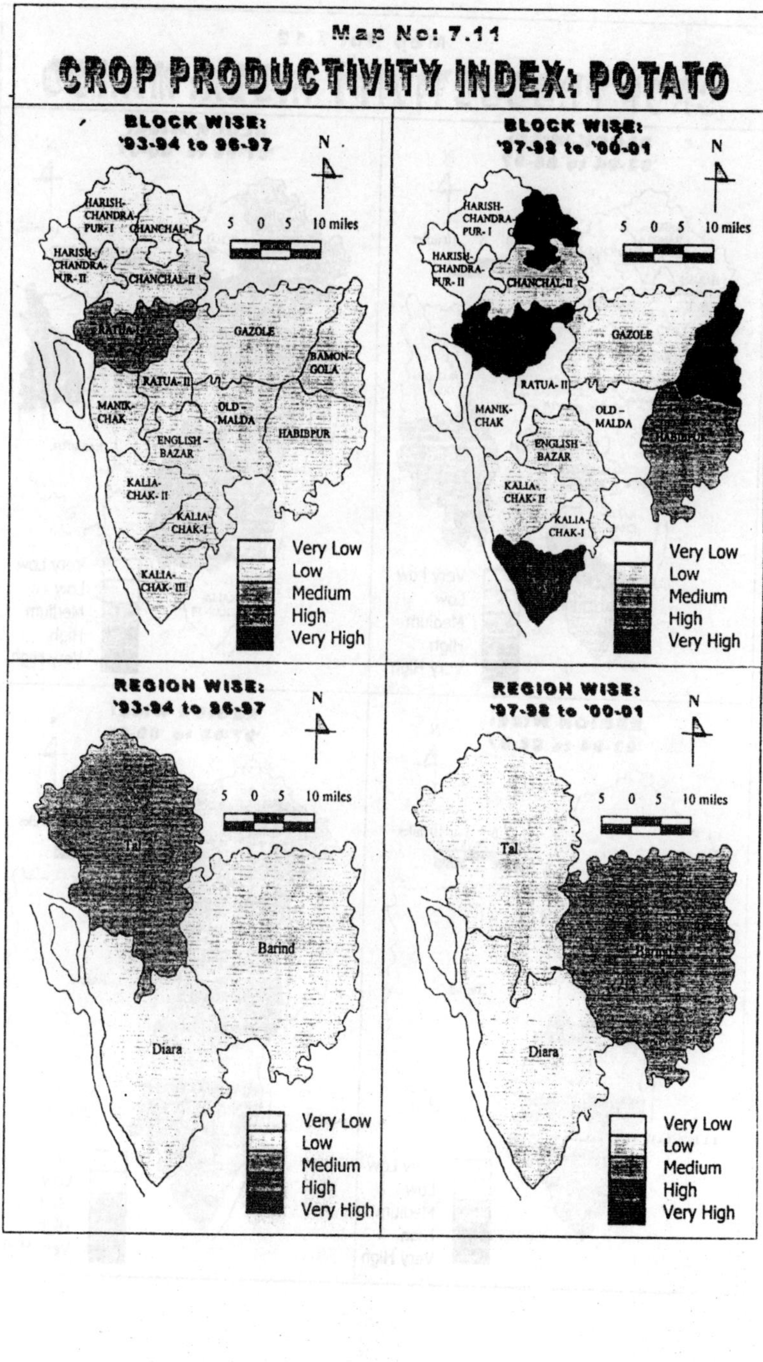
Map No: 7.11
CROP PRODUCTIVITY INDEX: POTATO
BLOCK WISE:
'93-94 to 96-97
N
5 0 5 10 miles
HARISH-CHANDRA-PUR-I
CHANCHAL-I
HARISH-CHANDRA-PUR-II
CHANCHAL-II
RATUA-I
GAZOLE
BAMON-GOLA
RATUA-II
MANIK-CHAK
OLD-MALDA
HABIBPUR
ENGLISH-BAZAR
KALIA-CHAK-II
KALIA-CHAK-I
KALIA-CHAK-III
Very Low
Low
Medium
High
Very High
BLOCK WISE:
'97-98 to '00-01
N
5 0 5 10 miles
HARISH-CHANDRA-PUR-I
HARISH-CHANDRA-PUR-II
CHANCHAL-II
GAZOLE
RATUA-II
MANIK-CHAK
OLD-MALDA
HABIBPUR
ENGLISH-BAZAR
KALIA-CHAK-II
KALIA-CHAK-I
Very Low
Low
Medium
High
Very High
REGION WISE:
'93-94 to 96-97
N
5 0 5 10 miles
Tal
Barind
Diara
Very Low
Low
Medium
High
Very High
REGION WISE:
'97-98 to '00-01
N
5 0 5 10 miles
Tal
Barind
Diara
Very Low
Low
Medium
High
Very High

Map No: 7.12

CROP PRODUCTIVITY INDEX: MANGO

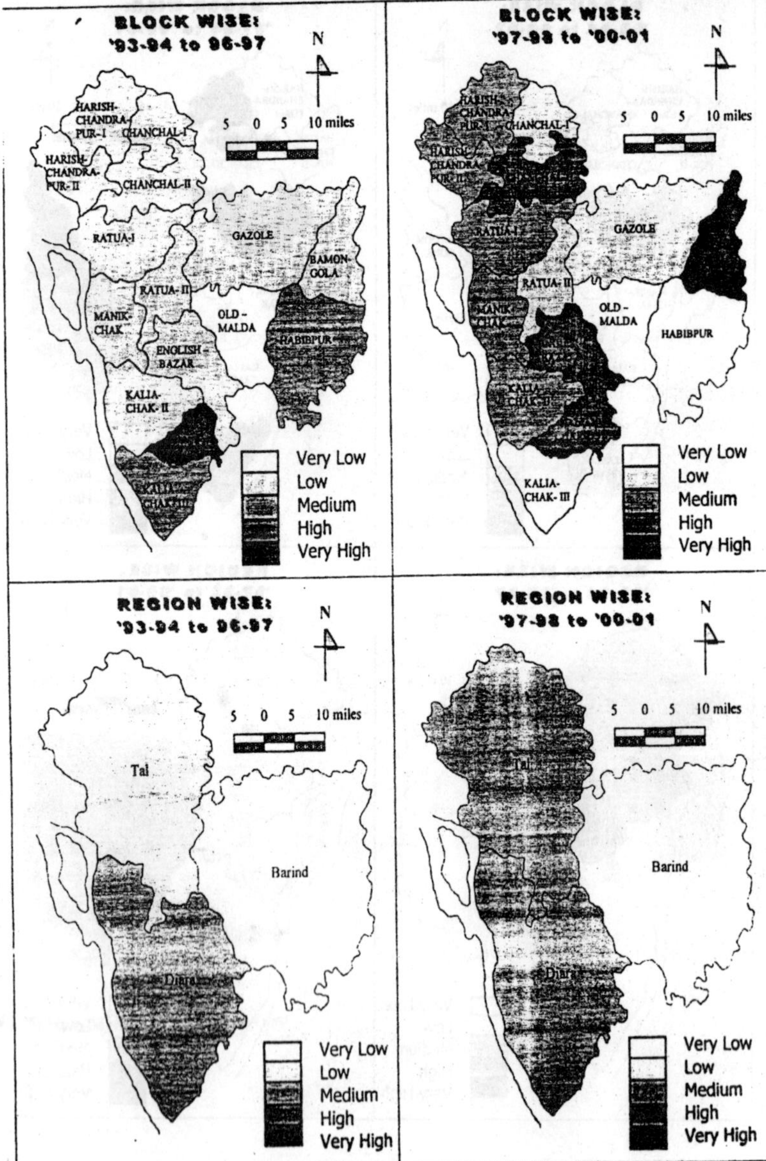

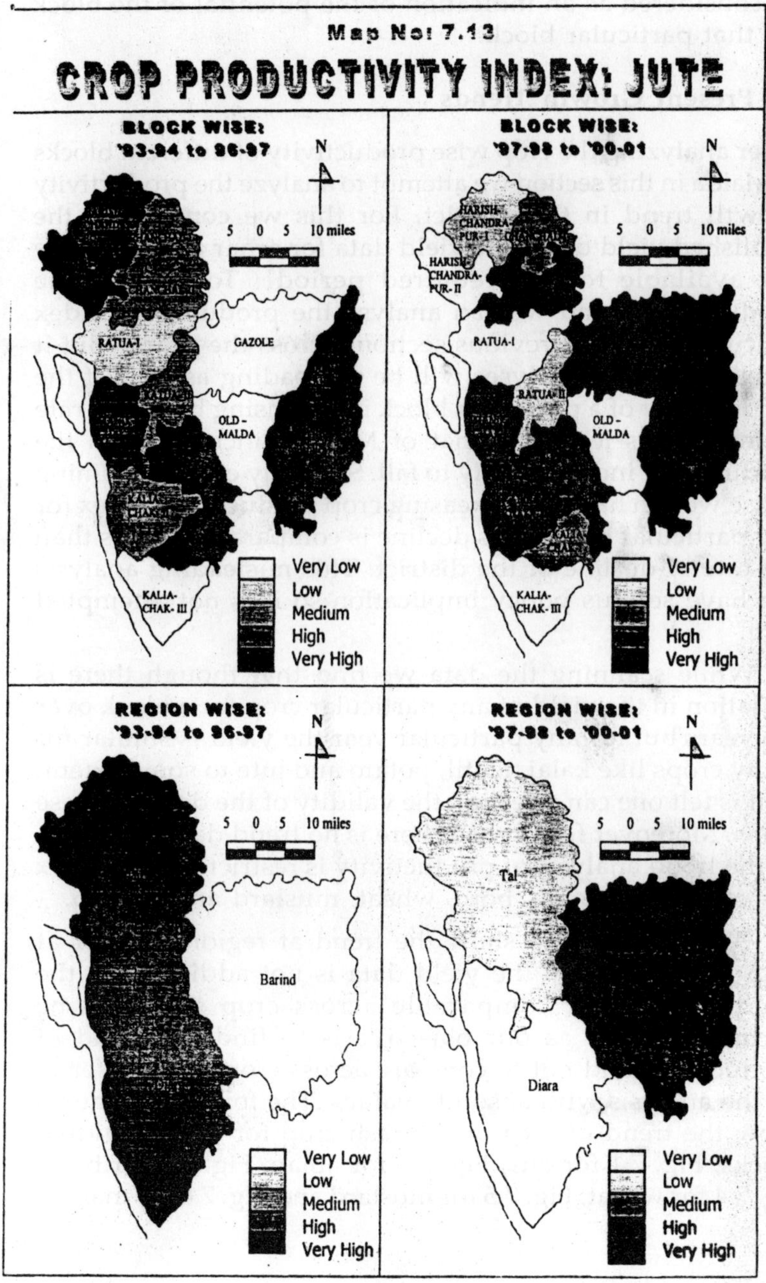
Map No: 7.13
CROP PRODUCTIVITY INDEX: JUTE
BLOCK WISE: '93-94 to 96-97
BLOCK WISE: '97-98 to '00-01
REGION WISE: '93-94 to 96-97
REGION WISE: '97-98 to '00-01
N
5 0 5 10 miles
RATUA-I
GAZOLE
OLD-MALDA
KALIA-CHAK-III
HARISH-CHANDRA-PUR-I
HARISH-CHANDRA-PUR-II
Barind
Tal
Diara
Very Low
Low
Medium
High
Very High

for any particular block shows dramatic change. This is to be considered as an indication of the potential of the block for that particular block.

7.c Present Growth Trends

After analyzing the crop wise productivity of different blocks in Malda in this section we attempt to analyze the productivity growth trend in the district. For this we considered the published yield data. The yield data for arhar and gram are not available for the required period. To analyse the productivity trend we can analyse the productivity index (calculated in the previous section) across the years. But it is felt that these analyses will be misleading as even if the productivity of a particular block is increasing but if the rate of increase is less than that of Malda's increase then the productivity index is likely to fall. Similarly on the declining phase we can have an increasing crop productivity index for any particular block if its decline is comparatively less than the rate of decline of the district. This misleading analysis can have serious policy implication so it is not attempted here.

While scanning the data we find that though there is variation in the yield of any particular crop for a block over the years but for any particular year the yield is similar for many crops like kalai, lentil, potato and jute to some extent. So it is felt one can question the validity of the data for these crops. Moreover for linseed there is no trend data available. So the trend analysis of productivity is restricted to only six crops viz. aus, aman, boro, wheat, mustard and mango.

We are unable to show the trend at region level or at crop group level as the yield data is not additive. As the yield data is not comparable across crop so it can be normalized. But as our objective is to find the trend of productivity and not to compare across crops, we prefer to do the analysis with absolute values. The following figures show the trend of area under cash crop for the individual blocks, Fig. 7.1 for aus, Fig. 7.2 for aman, Fig. 7.3 for boro, Fig. 7.4 for wheat, Fig. 7.5 for mustard and Fig. 7.6 for mango.

Fig 7.1 Block Wise Trend of Yield : Aus (1993-94 to 2000-01)

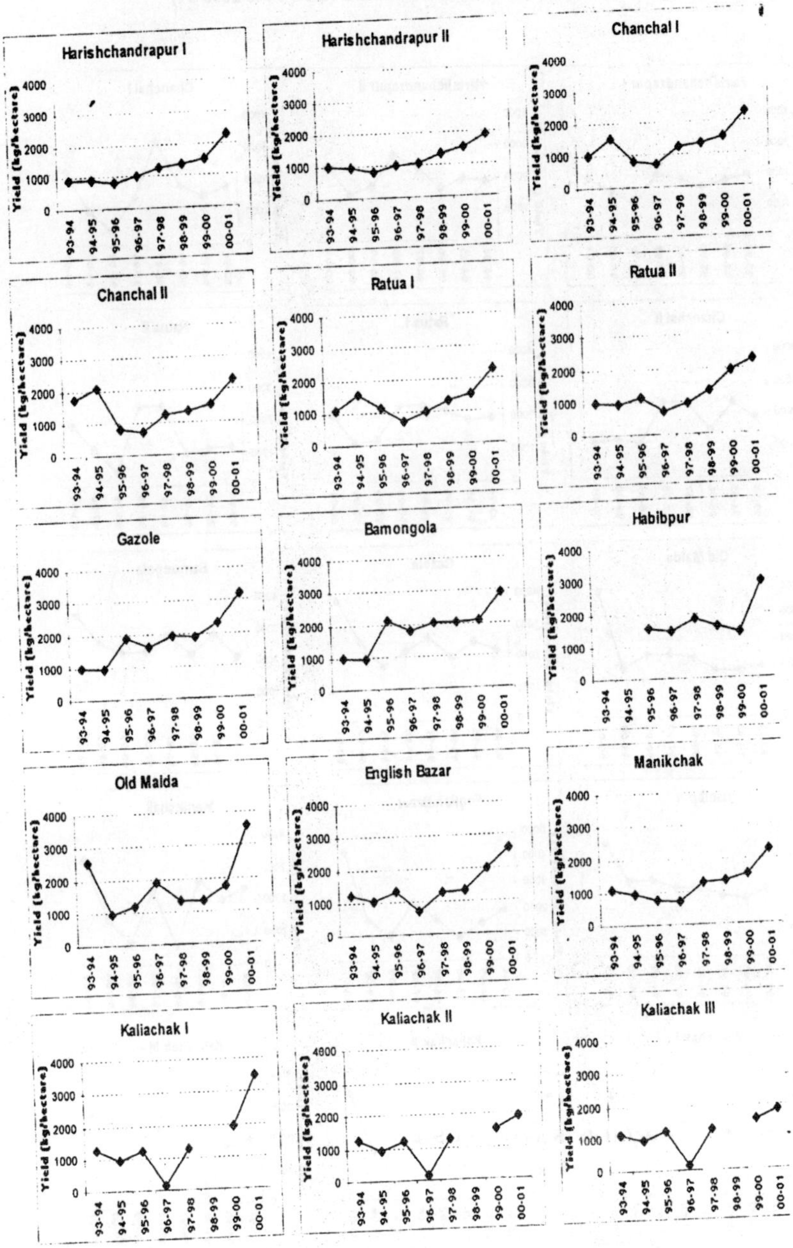

Fig 7.2 Block Wise Trend of Yield : Aman (1993-94 to 2000-01)

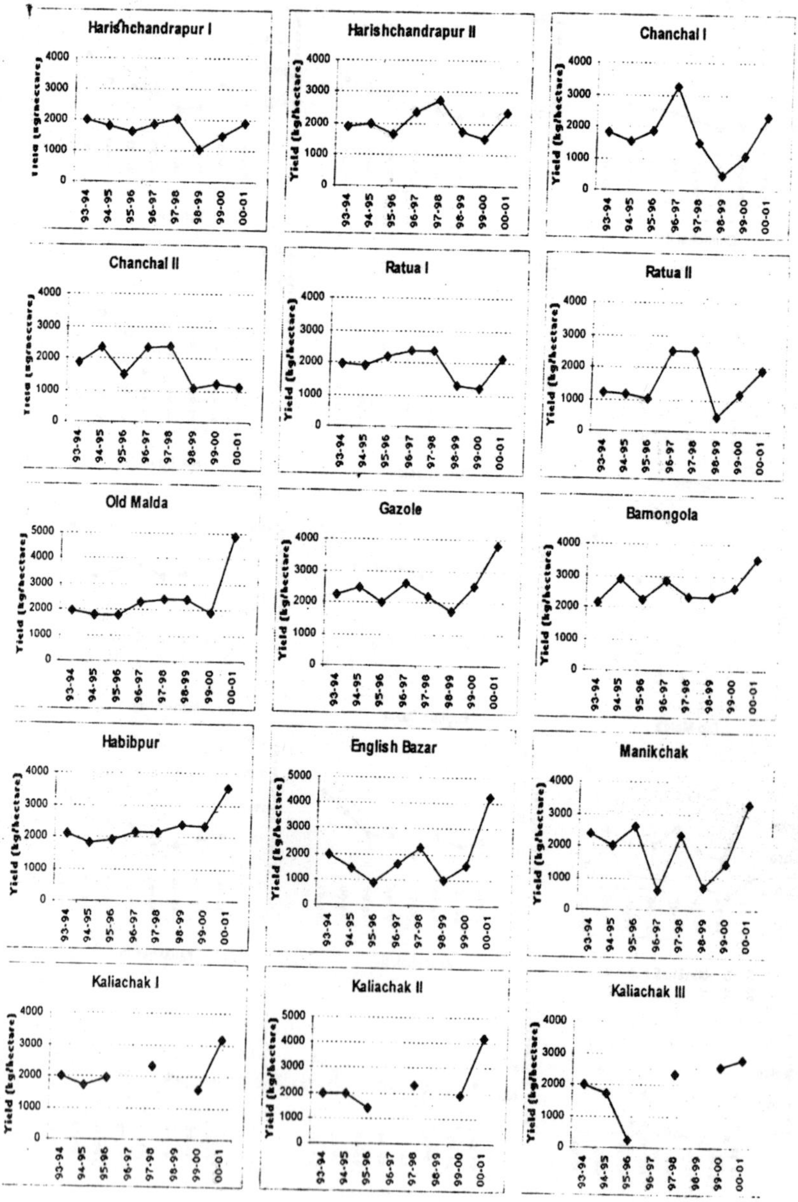

Fig 7.3 Block Wise Trend of Yield : Boro (1993-94 to 2000-01)

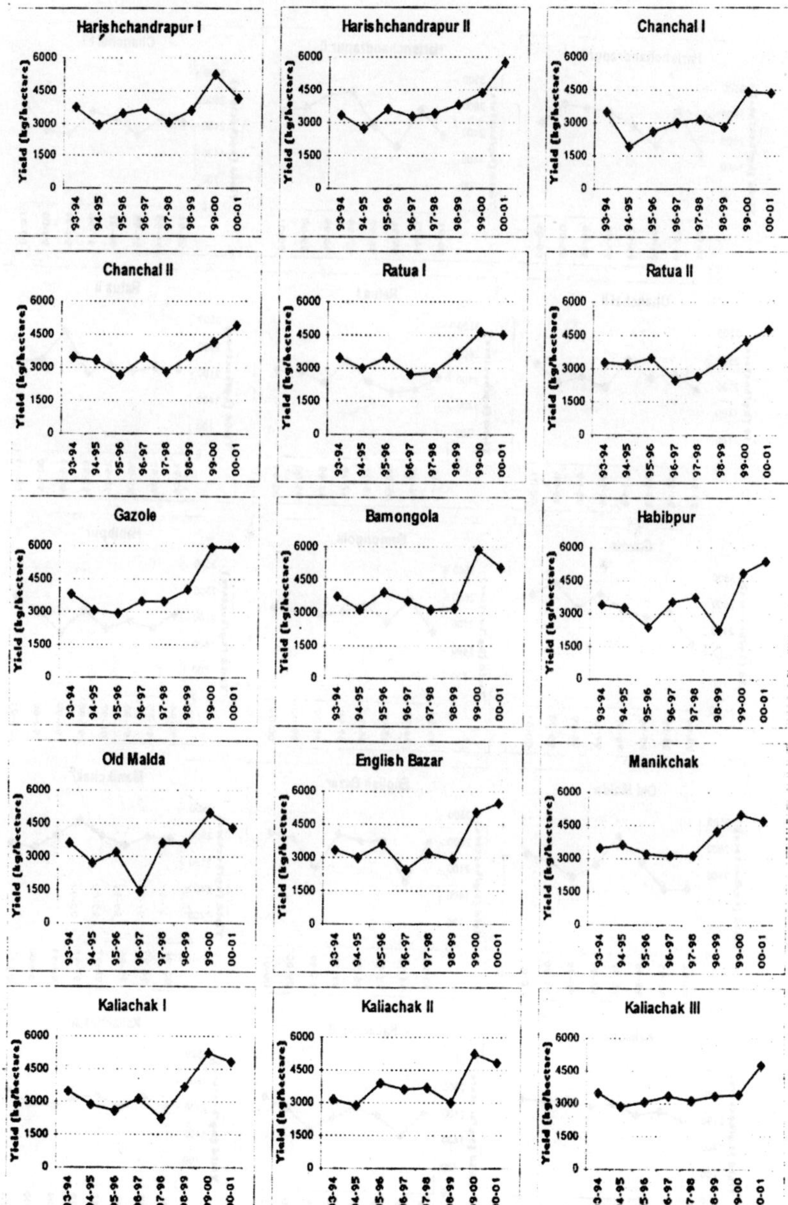

Fig 7.4 Block Wise Trend of Yield : Wheat (1993-94 to 2000-01)

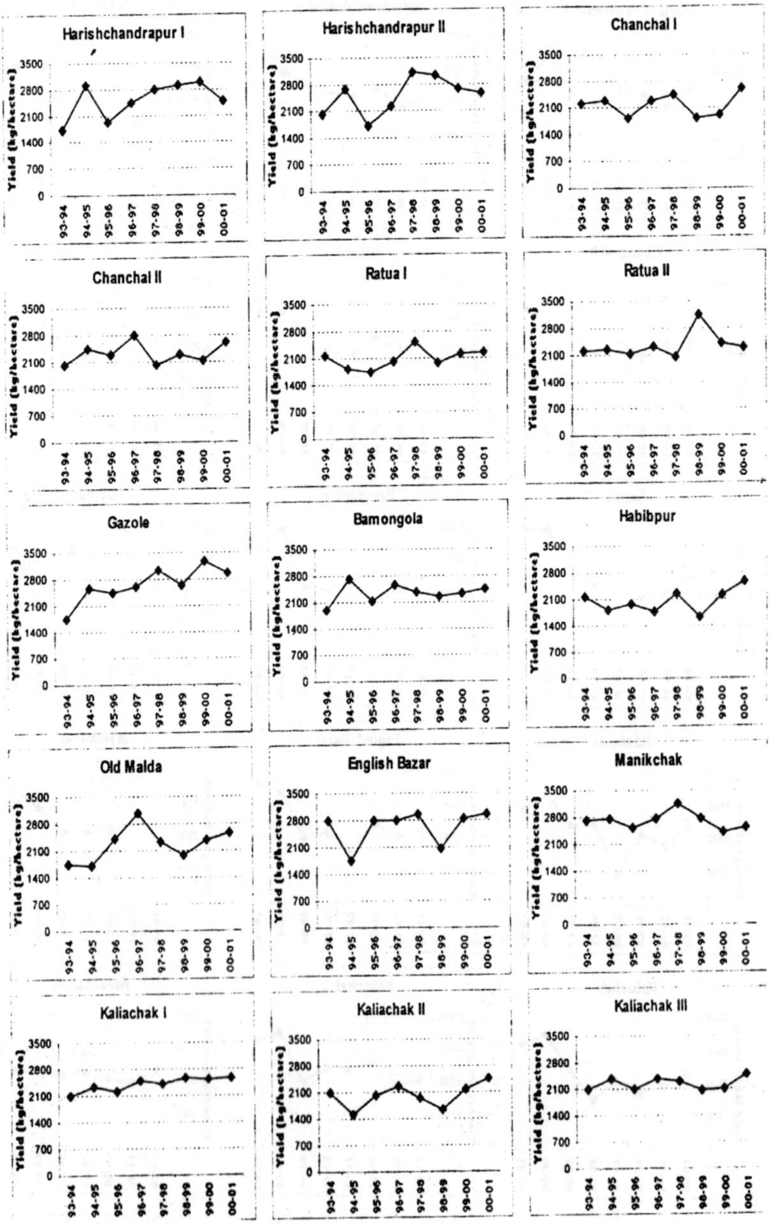

Fig 7.5 Block Wise Trend of Yield : Mustard (1993-94 to 2000-01)

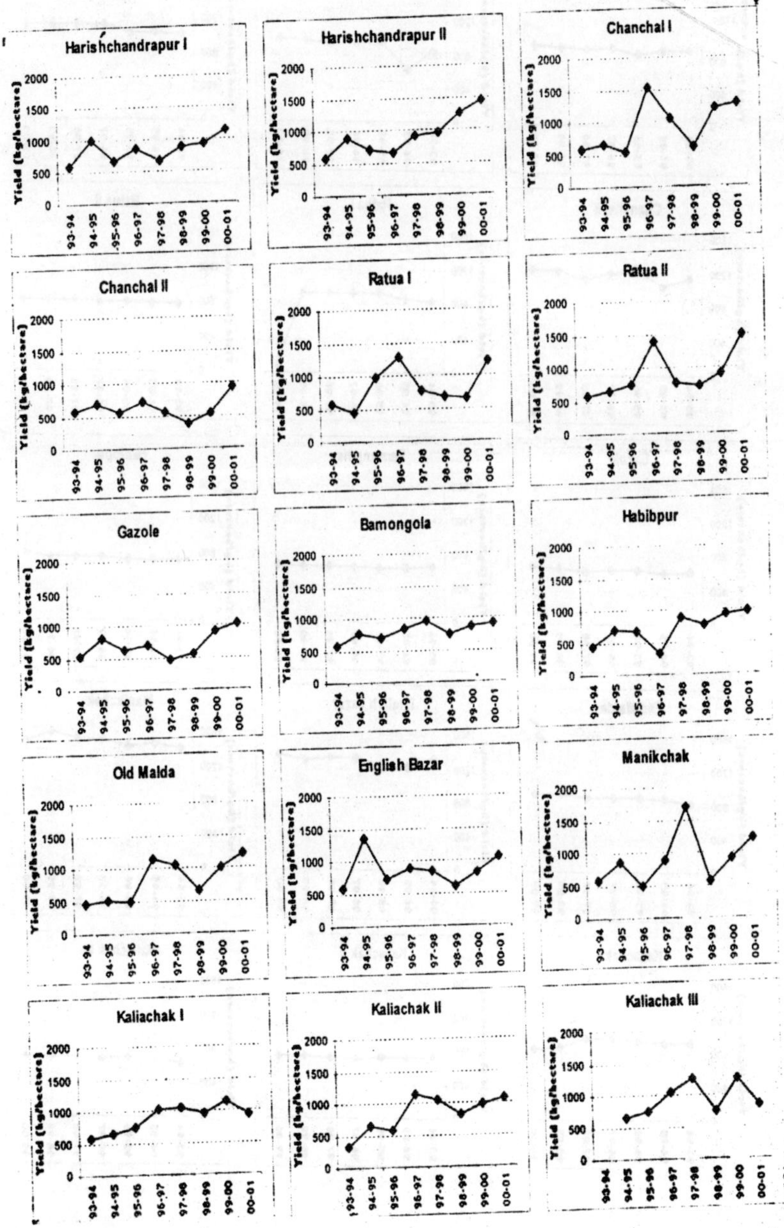

Fig 7.6 Block Wise Trend of Yield : Mango (1993-94 to 1999-00)

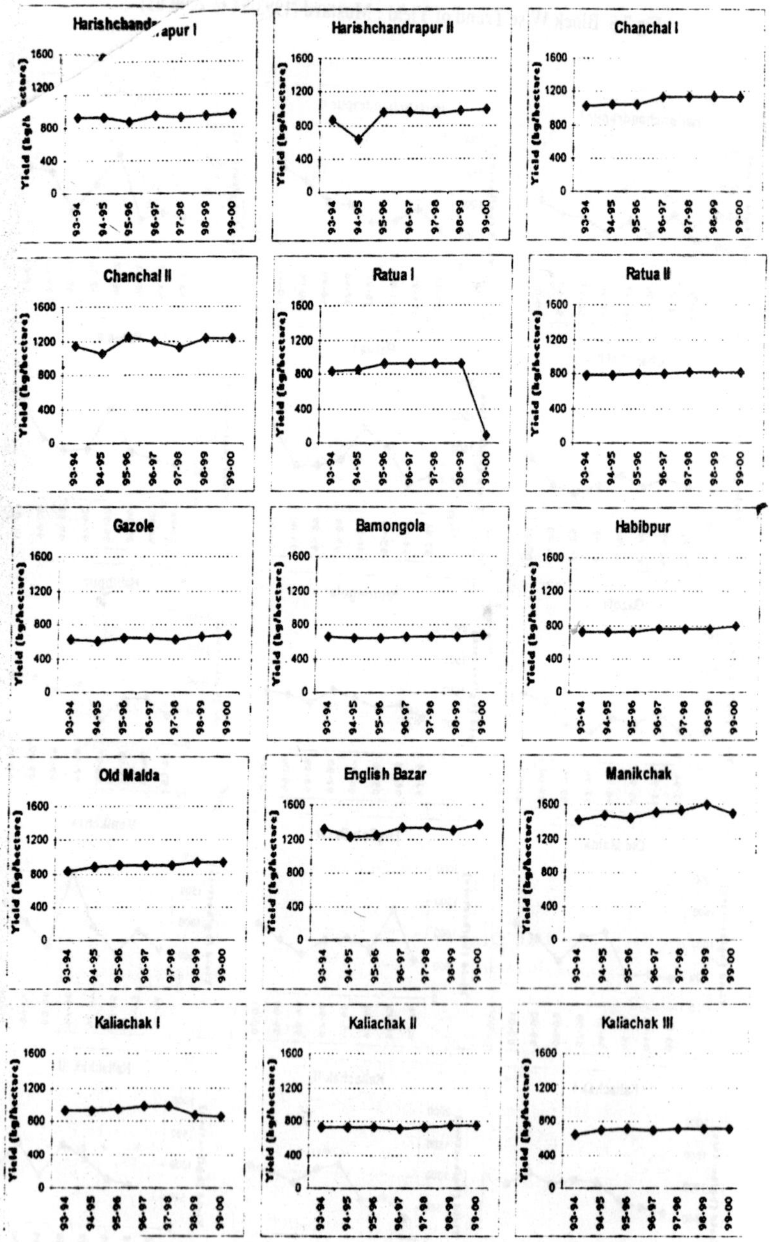

From the Fig 7.1 we find that the yield has increased for aus the most. Continuous growth is observed in some of the blocks but in majority of the blocks the growth rate is fluctuating.

In case of aman wide fluctuation is observed (Fig 7.2) but the over all change does not look significant. In the year 2000-01 all the blocks except Chanchal-II show considerable rise in yield.

There is a moderate rise in yield of boro in the district (Fig 7.3); but overall growth rate do not vary much amongst the blocks. The pattern of the trend lines looks similar for the blocks.

Yield of wheat have increased over the years marginally but annual fluctuation is observed across the blocks (Fig 7.4).

For mustard yield growth is significantly different across the blocks as in some we find CARG of 10 percent plus where in others below 5 percent (Fig 7.5). Here too annual fluctuation of yield is observed.

For mango the yield trend line for all the blocks are flat with minor exceptions (Fig 7.6).

Thus we find for major crops cultivated in Malda, there is an overall increase in yield over the years. But, this analysis do not provide the complete picture of yield growth as we are unable to comment on the level of significance of these growth rates and thereby we are not in a position to comment on the future prospect of these crops at individual block level.

For the purpose of analysing the significance of yield trend of six crops identified we have used the time series data for 8 years (1993-94 to 2000-01) of these crops of Malda viz. aus, aman, boro, wheat, mustard, and mango.

The exponential function $Y=AB^t$ was fitted to the data to compute the compound growth rates. Compound growth rate (r) =(Antilog b) 1* 100. The compound growth rates were tested for their significance by the students 't' test.

The co-efficient (e.g. 0.126) given in the table to explain trend growth can be interpreted as 12.6 compounded annual growth. The t-stat provides the idea of the significance of the individual coefficients.

Result and Discussion: The regression was performed for individual blocks and the results are provided here.

Table 7.2 provides the growth rate and the significance level for the individual crops under cereals.

Table 7.2: Growth Trend of Cereals: Block wise (1993-94 to 2000-01)

	Aus		*Aman*		*Boro*		*Wheat*	
	co-efficient	*t-stat*	*co-efficient*	*t-stat*	*co-efficient*	*t-stat*	*co-efficient*	*t-stat*
Harishchandrapur I	0.126	5.3	-0.031	-0.9	0.044	1.7	0.049	1.7
Harishchandrapur II	0.101	4.2	0.006	0.2	0.075	3.6	0.045	1.5
Chanchal I	0.091	1.8	-0.061	-0.6	0.071	2.0	0.004	0.2
Chanchal II	0.026	0.4	-0.093	-2.2	0.050	1.9	0.009	0.5
Ratua I	0.068	1.4	-0.038	-1.0	0.050	1.9	0.021	1.1
Ratua II	0.119	2.9	0.008	0.1	0.048	1.5	0.020	1.0
Gazole	0.152	5.5	0.039	1.1	0.087	3.1	0.063	3.4
Bamongola	0.136	3.9	0.035	1.5	0.053	1.6	0.012	0.7
Habibpur	0.086	1.4	0.066	3.1	0.059	1.3	0.020	0.9
Old Malda	0.066	1.0	0.092	2.3	0.064	1.1	0.042	1.5
English Bazar	0.108	2.3	0.079	1.0	0.067	1.8	0.023	0.7
Manikchak	0.117	2.9	-0.022	-0.2	0.053	2.5	-0.009	-0.7
Kaliachak I	0.159	0.9	0.040	1.0	0.071	1.8	0.026	4.4
Kaliachak II	0.089	0.6	0.083	1.7	0.062	2.4	0.027	1.1
Kaliachak III	0.094	0.6	0.136	0.9	0.037	1.8	0.006	0.5

PS: shaded co-efficients are significant at 5% level of confidence.

Aus

The trend in general for the productivity of aus is that of an increase. Over the years 1993-94 to 2000-01 the yield of aus have increased in all blocks but with varying intensity. The maximum growth has been attained by Kaliachak I of 15.9 percent but using t-stat value we find that this growth is not significant. Significant growth is achieved in

Harishchandrapur I (12.6 percent), Harishchandrapur II (10.1 percent), Ratua II (11.9 percent), Gazole (15.2 percent), Bamongola (13.6 percent), English Bazar (10.8 percent) and Manikchak (11.7 percent). Thus we find significant growth in seven blocks of Malda. This significant growth may look impressive but on further probe it is found that aus is not a major crop other than English Bazar, Manikchak and Kaliachak II.

Aman

The yield growth rate of aman, the principal crop of the district is likely to determine the effectiveness of various policies of the Govt. implemented in the district. The trend of aman yield varies within the district . The blocks of Tal region in general show a declining trend while the blocks of Barind and Diara clock moderate growth. But of the 15 blocks the CARG is significant for only 3 blocks: Chanchal II, Habibpur and Old Malda. While Chanchal II registers a decline of 9.3 percent the significant growth of 6.6 percent in Habibpur and 9.2 percent in Old Malda have policy implications. These two blocks of Barind have 70.7 percent and 39.3 percent of gross cropped area under aman cultivation and are mono cropped and three cropped region respectively. So yield increase of the principal crop is the only way for these blocks to prosper, without any support for crop diversification.

Boro

In general the district shows growth in boro yield. This variety of paddy which is totally dependent on irrigation facility, registering a yield growth implies that the district in general responds to the irrigation support. Harishchandrapur II (7.5 percent), Chanchal I (7.1 percent), Gazole (8.7 percent), Manikchak (percent 5.3), Kaliachak II (6.2 percent) are the blocks which registered significant growth during the period of analysis. Other than Gazole boro is a major crop in all the above-mentioned blocks. So an increase in the yield of boro is likely to have grater impact on overall prosperity.

Wheat

The yield growth of wheat in the blocks of Malda is quite low. Gazole and Kaliachak I are the only two blocks to have registered significant growth. The cause of growth in these two blocks is different, as while in Gazole wheat is not a major crop, in Kaliachak I, wheat is most important. So the growth in the Gazole is basically because of an erratic growth pattern with 9.2 percentage of area under wheat cultivation while in Kaliachak-I better irrigation facility have brought about the marginal growth.

Mustard

There is a general increasing trend of yield of mustard in the blocks of Malda. The growth rate varies between 0.7 percent of Chanchal II to 13.3 percent of Kaliachak II but significant growth rates are observed in Harishchandrapur II (11.2 percent), Ratua-II (9.2 percent), Bamongola (4.8 percent), Habibpur (9.9 percent), Old Malda (13.0 percent), Kaliachak-I (8.2 percent) and Kaliachak-II (13.3 percent). But amongst the blocks where mustard occupies more than 10 percent share of gross cropped area insignificant growth in Chanchal-I, Gazole, English Bazar, Kaliachak-III is a cause of worry as though these blocks show growth but we can not comment with confidence that the growth is likely to follow in years to come as presently it follows an erratic growth path.

Mango

The yield of mango in the district is marginally increasing in all the major blocks. Among the blocks where mango's share is more than 10 percent of gross cropped area, Manikchak and Kaliachak II show significant growth of 1.3 percent and 0.7 percent respectively. For the other two blocks of English Bazar and Kaliachak I, the growth or decline is not significant. For Mango we do not expect dramatic change of yield, as these are orchard-based product with age of trees ranging from 4 to 30 years.

Table 7.3: Growth Trend of Mustard and Mango: Block wise (1993-94 to 2000-01)

	Mustard		*Mango**	
	co-efficient	*t-stat*	*co-efficient*	*t-stat*
Harishchandrapur I	0.058	1.9	0.007	1.3
Harishchandrapur II	*0.112*	4.2	0.043	1.7
Chanchal I	0.103	1.8	*0.019*	*4.8*
Chanchal II	0.007	0.2	0.015	1.5
Ratua I	0.065	1.2	*0.020*	*4.0*
Ratua II	*0.092*	*2.1*	*0.009*	*5.7*
Gazole	0.051	1.2	*0.014*	*3.1*
Bamongola	*0.048*	*2.7*	*0.006*	*3.4*
Habibpur	*0.099*	*2.0*	*0.015*	*5.9*
Old Malda	*0.130*	*2.9*	*0.018*	*4.1*
English Bazar	0.013	0.3	0.011	1.4
Manikchak	0.078	1.2	*0.013*	*2.6*
Kaliachak I	*0.082*	*3.5*	-0.011	-1.0
Kaliachak II	*0.133*	*3.0*	*0.007*	*3.2*
Kaliachak III	0.052	1.0	*0.016*	*3.2*

* for the period 1993-94 to 1999-00.

PS: italicised co-efficients are significant at 5% level of confidence.

To conclude this chapter we find that the agricultural productivity for the district is different among the blocks and is changing. In the early 90's the productivity differential among the blocks were less pronounced than the 2nd half. In the late 90's we find while some of the blocks have increased their productivity others slide. This is in conjunction with the specialization that is happening in the agricultural scenario of Malda district.

In general the yield trend of 5 major crops viz. aus, aman, boro, wheat and mustard are increasing while for mango is stable. Yield growth rate is minimum for aus and for the primary crop of the district, aman, a moderate growth is observed. This has a policy implication as for the betterment of the agricultural profile of the district, aman yield needs to be improved along with the improvement of yield of other crops.

8

Major Findings: Problems and Prospects

The study has revealed that the agricultural productivity within the district is varying for different crops across blocks; the crop combination too is not similar. The growth trend for the area cropped also differs among the blocks. Attempts to club blocks based on a pattern for the above parameters do not really provide any definite cluster, though for individual parameters the clusters formed are distinct. So, to analyze and present the findings of the diversity we consider a grouping which is more pronounced and are based on physiographic, socio-economic and agricultural parameters and we get Tal, Barind Diara as the regions. These demarcations coincide with the political demarcation. Herein we provide an idea regarding the problems faced by these regions and highlight the difference in the parameters across blocks.

The findings have been presented in terms of problems and prospects in this chapter. To get a composite overview the chapter has been divided into two sections viz. Physical and Non-Physical.

1. Problems and Prospects of Physical Determinants

This section has been further divided into individual determinants viz. structure and relief, flood, soil, water depth and climate.

1.a *Structure & relief:*

Structure and relief is considered to be a constant parameter in any agricultural productivity analysis. Improvement of productivity is addressed by changing the factors in accordance to the structure and relief. Our analyses highlight certain features of the structure and relief for the district.

The Tal region, which is a low-lying area, is subjected to inundation by floodwaters of Kalindri River. The region reveals a gradual slope towards south and west, so flooding of Kalindri effects Harishchandrapur-I, Harishchandrapur-II and Ratua-I. Moreover 15.6% of the area is low lying.

Barind region, which is relatively an upland tract locally referred as *danga* region is comparatively less affected by flood. But the flip side of this is the region is not suitable for multiple cropping. The analysis has shown that Barind region is characterized by bi-crop cropping pattern, while its counter parts Tal and Diara are six and eight-cropped region.

Diara region is mainly flat land and has the Ganges as its boundary towards the western side. This makes this region comparatively fertile but the shifting nature of the Ganges has affected the region. The impact of shifting rivers and flooding has been dealt in the following section.

As mentioned earlier in the process of enhancement of agricultural productivity, structure and relief is considered to be a constant parameter but latest studies have shown that with policy intervention and Government investment in building of dams, connecting rivers through canals, this constant parameter can be made conducive for increasing productivity.

1.b *Changing course of rivers and flood*

Malda district *is* infamous for its regular floods. Some parts or the other is affected by flood on annual basis. The major flood in 1998 had a devastating impact on agriculture in the district. Before delving into analysis of flood impact we highlight the problems arising due to changing course of rivers. The Kalindri, Mahananda and the Ganges happens to be the major rivers of the district. Ganges, which acts as the western boundary of the district, has Manikchak, Kaliachak-II and Kaliachak-III on its bank. The changing course of Ganges and drifting towards east is impacting the area of Manikchak severely. Due to this change of course Manikchak has lost 13,203.94 acre, of land to the river. In total 15 mouzas are affected out of which of which 5 mouzas have totally deluviated. Kaliachak-III is comparatively less affected due to the shift with 3857.2 acre of land deluviated in three mouzas. Kaliachak-II is the most impacted block as 18 mouzas amounting to 17,972.03 acre have been fully deluviated while in 8 mouzas 6,099.87 acre has deluviated. Thus we see that the Diara region is impacted to a great extent by the problem of deluviation and this has created a sense of fear amongst the farmer of this region situated even few KM. from the bank of the Ganges.

The severe flood of 1998, which impacted the whole district, had a direct impact on the agricultural produce for that year. But the crop failure for any particular year has it's cascading effects, even for the next two harvesting year. The non-availability of seeds for following year of flooding is a defined problem for the farmers. Moreover the non-repayment of loan aggravated with no income impacts the farmer's financial position. His following years cash flow is imbalanced. Thus we find that flood act as a trigger point of the viscous circle of poverty.

1.c Soil:

Soil type, soil tenure and soil nutrient status is considered to be important physical determinant to influence agricultural productivity. The analysis has shown that these determinants are not similar within the district, so certain crops are cultivated in particular region and the productivity level too varies across the regions. It has been seen that Barind region is dominated by older alluvium soil. As this red soil of old alluvium formation is composed of clay containing iron and lime which becomes extremely hard in the cold weather, Rabi crop cultivation in Barind region is not effective. So the productivity in this region for oil seed are low and a negligible amount of area is under pulse cultivation.

So we find Barind, which is dominated by clay and clay

loam doesn't support multiple cropping, is predominantly a paddy-cultivating region with bi-crop cropping pattern of Aman and Boro.

The Organic Carbon (O.C.) content of soil in Malda is predominantly in the low and medium-low range. This implies that fertility level in the district is comparatively low. If we consider the range of O.C., 0.2% to 0.82%, which reveals improper management of soils. Moreover, the phosphorous content is very low across the blocks while potash content varies from Very low to High. This provides an overall idea of the poor soil fertility status of the district.

The *ph* level, another important component of soil nutrient status shows that while Tal and Barind has slightly acidic to neutral *ph* values, Diara has normal to alkaline values. As most crops are suited to neutral to slightly alkaline soil, the low *ph* value of the soil in the district is suitable for only paddy cultivation. Thereby production of high return vegetables and oilseeds are low.

1.d Ground Water Depth:

We have seen that ground water depth plays a significant role in determining the feasibility and the type of irrigation. In the district ground water level varies significantly amongst the regions.

The water level in Diara and Tal region is found to be comparatively high while that in the Barind region comparatively low. Due to this differential water level investment required in Barind region is comparatively higher. Moreover, with the water depth of 100 to 200 metre in Barind makes D.T.W. as the only means of regular irrigation. As the set-up cost for D.T.W. is very high, state intervention is required or else it is only the well off farmers who can afford it. As in Barind region the average land holding is not impressive expectation of D.T.W. being set-up by a group of farmers looks distant. Tal and Diara region, which have comparatively better irrigation facility, can support multiple cropping.

In Barind region, if irrigation can be provided on a sustained basis the prospect of change in the cropping pattern and crop productivity is likely.

1.e Climate

Rainfall, humidity temperature etc. which are main components of climate do not vary much from region to region within the district. So to use climatic variations as the causal factor for productivity variation is not justified. However, the climate has a major role in determining the overall productivity of the district and in this direction the analysis of monthly rainfall data shows that below normal rainfall had impacted the productivity of Aman in 1996 and 1998.

2. Problem and Prospect of Non-Physical Determinants.

This section as the name suggests tries to explore the problem in availability and accessibility of various non-physical determinants viz. size of land holding, irrigation, seed, fertiliser, pesticide, labour, transportation, market etc.

2.a Size of Land holding:

Average operational land holding of Malda district equaled the average operational land holding of West Bengal. In 1995-96 (the last time point for which the data is available) average holding of the district was at 0.86 hectare and in these eight years with the population rise the operational holding is expected to come down to around 0.7 hectare. This figure itself gives an idea that the farmers of Malda are subsistence farmers. With land reforms introduced in West Bengal and land ceiling act enforced the disparity has been minimized to a great extent but this in turn has created a low level equilibrium. Herein the farmers own land but the size of the holding is not economical.

As per the Agricultural census, West Bengal, though operational holdings of 10 hectare and above is considered to be large holdings; only 173 such owners are found in 1995-96. This gives an idea that the introduction of mechanized farming is not an economically viable proposition. Moreover, the tracts of land are being divided with 'ails' to enable water logging. This further reduces the effective operational land holding. During the field visits it is found the farmers hold land in different parts of the mouza i.e. a continuous stretch o land is not available. Thus proposition of mechanized farming is considered to be a theoretical proposition for the district with no practicability.

Analysing the land holdings based on the ownership pattern it is found that the average land holding of SC is 0.85 hectare while for the ST it is 0.99 hectare. With the average operational holding of 0.86 hectare for the district as a whole in 1995-96, these figures imply that the average land holding for the General Caste is below the district average. Muslims who are considered in the General Caste brings this figure down. It is basically because of he bigger sized family of the Muslims.

To bring about a change in the operational holdings it is suggested that community farming be tested in certain mouzas on a trial basis. Depending on the success of such community farming the results can be demonstrated to others. The problem that is foreseen is the political polarity in the society.

2.b Irrigation:

The status report of irrigation for Malda district is not impressive, as only 43.7% of the net sown area of the district is irrigated. The situation is grim in Barind region with only 30.4 percent of the area as net irrigated area. This problem can be explained with the physiographic features and the historical developments. 'Tangra', a tributary of the Mahananda, is the main river, which passes through the Barind region. This river being a seasonal river R.L.I. is not effective in the region. Moreover, the region being a high-land ('Danga and Arkandar') the natural flow of the water is away from the region. As previously explained the water depth in the region is comparatively low which makes D.T.W. as the only means of irrigation through ground water. The high investment involved in the set-up of D.T.W. is a barrier for setting up of this type of irrigation in Barind region. State owned D.T.W. faces the problems of maintenance and regular monitoring. Irregular power supply magnifies the problem.

The development over the decades wherein tanks, the major source of irrigation in Barind, are being converted to farmland augmented the problem. "There is a tendency towards the gradual diminution of the water-supply from these tanks in the Barind. Some of them have silted up, and there is no one in the locality with the initiative or energy to have them re-excavated. The banks of others have been encroched upon and ploughed up by the tenants. The landlords following a rather shortsighted policy have settled the banks in order to increase their rent rolls by a few rupees. In some cases the beds of tanks have been settled as well. Where the banks are brought under cultivation the inevitable result is that they become flattened out". *(Carter 1925)*

2.c Seed:

In Malda district with low literacy level and less penetration of technology, the usage of HYV seeds are limited. It has been found that though the farmers use HYV seeds but it is not a continuous process i.e they use these in alternate years or with lower frequency. Moreover the HYV seed usage is not complimented with proper irrigation, fertiliser or soil nutrient.

The farmers tend to use their own farm produces as seed in years when the cash flow is not adequate. The availability of these seeds is very poor which have a direct negative impact on the yield.

The farmers also tend to use 30 kg of seed per acre and thereby increase the number of seedlings. It is way off from the suggested 10 kg per acre to get good healthy seedlings.

Another problem observed during the field visit was that the farmers do not adopt proper seed treatment procedures.

State Seed Corporation (SSC) and National Seed Corporation,(NSC) which were formed with the objective of developing new improved variety of sees, do not support the farmers of interiors of Malda.

These imperfections make the seedlings of poor health. This has a direct impact on productivity. Proper intervention from the state and higher literacy level coupled with increased affordability can make a change in the agricultural scenario of Malda.

The availability of seeds is another problem identified. Seed outlets in the district are located in the urban centers. Thereby accessibility of these outlets by farmer of remote areas is not feasible. The seeds available in the local *hats* do not satisfy the storage requirements and also are charged with a premium. The combined effect is reluctance to the usage of HYV seeds.

The farmers who use their own farm produce, as seeds do not have proper storage facilities. So the yield of these seeds decline.

The farmers accept that rotation of seeds amongst themselves result in fresh seed for each farmland which can improve the yield. But it is found that in reality they do not practice this.

2.d Fertiliser:

The usage of fertiliser in Malda district is low and the ratio of N, P and K in the soil is not optimum. With low potash content and very low phosphorous content in the soil of Malda, it is expected that the farmers will be attending to management of phosphorous and potash. But it is found that the farmers use more urea, a nitrogenous fertiliser. Thus, proper soil management and soil nutrient management are not done in the district. Moreover usage of micronutrient specially zinc in the fertiliser schedule is absent. Thus we find fertiliser usage do not follow any specific pattern. The farmers are under the impression that usage of nitrogenous fertiliser brings growth in the plant. They are not aware of the concept of nutrient balance. Crop rotation is another means of maintaing the soil fertility effectively. The farmers are aware of the fact that crops need to be rotated, but they are more comfortable with traditional way of farming.

The other problem faced with fertiliser usage is accessibility to fertiliser selling outlets. These outlets are located in the urban centres. The makeshift outlets are found in the weekly local *hats*. The farmers are required to purchase their fertiliser requirements from these makeshift outlets. The consultation regarding the latest fertiliser and the most effective fertiliser is not available to them. It is the word of mouth that is being used to take such vital decision regarding the proportion of fertiliser usage and no scientific methodology is used. Usage of right fertiliser in correct proportion with suitable crop combination backed by proper analysis of soil content and nutrient level is likely to impact the productivity of crops in a positive manner.

2.e *Pesticide:*

The nature of problem faced regarding pesticide is similar to that of fertiliser. Here too the farmer uses pesticide based on the convention, tradition and word of mouth. It is found that they are also not aware of the effects of these pesticides on the crop health. They are also not aware of the safety measures that need to be adopted while applying these pesticides. It has been found that farmers' health is being affected and cases of skin diseases due to pesticides have been observed.

To cater the needs of small and marginal farmers pesticide manufacturing companies are now packaging pesticides in low volume SKUs (Stock Keeping Unit). But, the problem a farmer faces is the initial investment to purchase spraying machines. So this acts as a usage barrier. To tackle this, the farmer hires these machines.

The problem related to marketing distribution of pesticides is similar to that of fertiliser.

2.e *Labour:*

Labour that is considered to be a major factor of production and in less developed Malda should be found in abundance. This availability of labour had resisted introduction of capital-intensive farming technique. But, in the recent past it is found that labour supply is a problem during harvesting and sowing season. This problem can be related to the socio-economic change that the region is witnessing.

With low productivity and high pressure on land, members of the family are forced to migrate and with increased literacy, educated members are averse to consider farming as their occupation. The result is low supply of labour during the peak season.

Another problem noticed in the district, which is a reality

in this country, is that the women labourers are paid less than their male counterparts. This differential payment structure has forced women to take up other means of earning like *bidi* binding, housemaid etc. Thus we find that socio-economic changes have forced labour problem in the agricultural scenario too.

2.f Transport and Accessibility:

In modern day farming specialization of activities is the basic tenet and with more use of manufactured products selling of produce in predefined markets, transportation and accessibility assumes grater importance. In Malda district the problem of accessibility is acute as the villages are linked with unmetalled roads whose condition detoriates severely during the rainy seasons. This creates transportation of aman, boro, jute by motor vehicles impossible. Bullock carts and horse carts are the only resort of rural people for transport. Seasonal *nalas* and streams with no bridge across aggravate the situation. In such a situation farm produce are carried by human beings across these natural obstacles.

There is no proper mechanism for transporting the produce from the village to the market in a collective manner. As each individual farmer is expected to sell his own produce so transporting it in vehicles is not an economic proposition for him. So it is felt that if the farmer of a particular village forms a co-operative, and can transport the produce of the village, it would be economically rewarding.

In relation to transport of mango, the farmers face a major problem of non availability of truck during the peak seasons, The mango of Malda district which are generally sold in Kolkata, Siliguri and Agartala need to be transported on time as otherwise this perishable fruit do not command the right price. As demand for trucks rise during a particular part of the year, increase of fleet of vehicles is not justified to the private transporters.

Development of the rural roads and introduction of schemes for improvement of the traditional modes of transport are much felt necessity of the district for improving the socio-economic condition of the villages.

2.g Market:

The farmers' hard work of the year is rewarded at the market, so proper marketing facility facilitates farmers to sell their produce at right price. In Malda district marketing facility is still traditional wherein the farmers' produce are sold in the *hats* or local markets where from it changes hand in the hands of businessman. Thus the profit margin is not completely passed on to the primary producer.

The condition of these rural markets is poor, as minimum facility of shed, drinking water, drainage and public latrines are wanting. Some markets are extremely congested for the market users. Moreover private ownership of such *hats* and market is the main obstacle for the administration to effect desired improvements. Half hearted attention, of the Government, to improve the markets and marketing practices, in the rural areas of the district, is not sufficient to bring about the desired improvement in this field. All such private *hats* and markets in the district should be transferred and vested with public institution like Panchayats and regulated market committees.

The two regulated market in Samsi and Englisbazar are not sufficient to support the district's requirement. No such market in the Barind region is a problem in itself.

The role of middlemen in procuring the produce in small quantities and then able to sell at a higher price in bulk and at a time when the prices are high gives an indication of the imperfections in the market.

Another problem identified is marketing of mango, an important commercial crop of the district. There is no definitely earmarked place/market where the wholesale transactions of the fruit can take place. The growers usually sell the garden as early as in pre-flowering stage and there is series of changes in the ownership of fruits at the different stages till harvesting. After the harvest the fruit is packed in orchard and despatched to its destination at different terminal markets in the country by the traders. As a result of this the percentage share of the growers in the consumers price of the fruit is as low as 20 percent

2.h Storage Facility:

The cultivators sell their goods primarily jute to *farias* or village merchants immediately after harvest due to storage problem and due to urgent need for cash. Although eight purchase centres for jute (D.P.C.-4 numbers, Co-operative-3 numbers and C.A.D.P.-1 number) are functioning at Harischandrapur, Tulshihata, Old Malda, Nawbabganj and Bulbulchandi, it is observed that the actual benefit of the scheme is derived by the middlemen instead of farmers for whom the Government are so concerned.

The growers face a big storage and transport problem after the harvest of paddy and wheat and the middlemen and village traders take this opportunity to exploit the farmers and make big profit.

2.i Agricultural Credit:

The purpose of agricultural credit is defeated due to corrupt practices in both supply and demand sides. The farmers who avail agricultural credit are found to utilize the amount for personal consumption and are not in a position to repay. This makes them defaulters and they are unable to avail any further loan. It is also observed that government schemes of providing agricultural credit are spotted with corruption and political favouring.

The bank that provides the credit also indulges in corrupt practices of taking commissions for sanctioning loan amount. Thus we find that organized credit market is not effective.

2.k Other problems:

Other than the problems defined above the agricultural sector of Malda also faces the problem of land acquisition by Government, international boundary, political rivalry etc. Government had to acquire large tracts of land for development projects like Malda-Eklakhi rail route, widening of the National Highway, etc. Similar acquisition happened for setting up of B.S.F. camps in the district. These land accusations have made many farmers land-less and the compensation payment is delayed and in many cases not paid.

204 Km. of international boundary, with Bangladesh is a cause of another major problem for the district. It is complained that cattle theft and theft of crops and mangoes in the border areas is prevalent as Bangladeshis take the advantage of porous border. The fencing activity that had started some years back and presently complete gave birth to another problem. As per the understanding between the two countries the fencing happens to be 400 meters inside the Indian territory from the international border.

The farmers who owned the land between the fencing and the border are issued with passes to till their land. As there is no such fencing on the Bangladesh side the Bangladeshi take the advantage of crossing the border in the night and harvest the crops from the Indian farmers' land.

So to summarise, we find the present agricultural scenario in Malda is dotted with problems like:

- Low crop productivity
- Non-availability of good quality inputs – seeds, fertiliser and plant protection measure
- Cultivation practices traditional and in many cases counter productive. For example:
    - o Late raising of nursery and late planting of paddy, consequently late to very late sowing of wheat.
    - o Very high seed rate used in raising of paddy nursery, viz. 30 kg/acre
    - o Local and own produce used as seed
- Imbalance use of fertilisers: Nitrogenous fertilizers applied in much excess, use of phosphatic and potashic fertilizers almost negligible, zinc hardly applied
- Plant protection measures either absent or defective for lack of knowledge
- Farmers too vulnerable to existing market forces.

9

Corrective Measures Suggested

Towards increasing agriculture productivity in low productivity areas of Malda an important step recommended is to increase agricultural productivity in Barind, which is presently about half of the level existing in the regions of Tal and Diara. This increase in productivity in Barind is the key to the agricultural development in the district.

The recommendations are prepared on the basis of preliminary background work undertaken (Benchmark survey, site visit & discussions with the local people) with the objective of: **'Overall improvement of the agricultural productivity in the less developed regions'.**

For achieving this, the approach needs to be:

- Identification of farmer's constraint on the agriculture as a whole and productivity up-liftment in particular through Participatory Resource Appraisal (PRA) with farmers along with field visits.
- Understanding of the existing management practices of different crops
- Proper documentation of the base line data
- Determination of soil health status
- Frame action plan in consultation with the farmers without making drastic changes in their existing practices

- Extensive training cum demonstration to the farmers before cultivation of each crop
- Proper follow up of each step of management practices
- To arrange for visit of progressive farmers of the district to reputed agriculture institutes and farmers' field so that they can get an idea how other progressive farmers are farming.
- Arrangement of good quality and right variety of seed for the farmers from research centres and other areas on cost to cost basis

Technology: The technologies, which need to be followed in the district, should be farmer friendly and inexpensive. No modern technologies like Biotechnology, Genetically engineered crop are suggested now as these will not suit them now. In a nut shell the technology should be a combination of the following efforts:

- Selection of right kind of variety of a particular crop synchronising with the climate, market potential, soil test value etc.
- Advancement of nursery raising of Paddy synchronising with monsoon arrival which will help in advancement of sowing of Wheat.
- Taking plant protection matters and
- Farmers should be trained for cultivation of vegetables using modern technology.

Agricultural Marketing: The following suggestions are provided for the improvement of the marketing system in the district.

- More market link roads should be constructed on an annual basis
- Agricultural Marketing credit should be arranged immediately.
- Establishment of Agriculture Regulated Market in Barind region is urgently required. This centre is suggested to be at Gazole in Barind region so that it can easily accessed by the farmers of the blocks of the region.

- For effective National grid for Rural Godown, number of godowns in the district needs to increased from the present number of two (Samsi and Chanchal) to four immediately. The preferred centres are English Bazar and Gazole.
- For better dissemination of price information, more market intelligence centers should be opened at different hats / markets with a view to extending them up to the Block level. The present level of three MI centers for the whole district is extremely low.
- Along with the proliferation of the market intelligence centers the effectiveness of these centers needs to be reviewed. The farmers need to be informed of the grading system and the prevailing price of their products. For this educating the farmers about the scheme of Market Intelligence is required.
- Linking up of Agricultural Marketing officials with the weights and measures office, JCI and Agricultural Co-operative marketing societies. This will bring about an overall synchronized effort in ensuring the required change.
- Provision for distribution of Jute, wheat, Mustard and pulses seed among the trained up growers by the Directorate of Agricultural Marketing.
- The market level workers should be trained up so that they can analyse the collected data and forecast the market behaviour.
- Mango market should be produced in the producing area.

Transportation and accessibility: Roads linking the interior of the district with the market centres is of utmost necessity. Priority should be given in developing the road networking in Manikchak, Bamongola, Habibpur and Kaliachak-III blocks.

- Annual maintenance of *pucca* roads can be leased. The roads need to be constructed with long-term perspective, as many of the roads are not pliable in the rainy season.

- Bridge construction across the seasonal *nalas* and streams is to be considered.

Irrigation: Sincere efforts towards improvement of irrigation facilities in the district are required as the over all irrigated area is poor. The efforts need to be concentrated mainly in the blocks of Barind region and Kaliachak III.

- The viable mode of irrigation in the Barind region is D.T.W. that requires heavy investment. State intervention in the initial phase is required. State can built D.T.W. and lease to the farmers who in turn, over a period of five years need to repay.
- Maintenance of D.T.W. and regular monitoring of them also needs to be monitored.
- The villagers should be empowered with the monitoring and maintenance activities.
- Power supply should be made regular for D.T.W. functioning.
- State Electricity Board should consider power supply for D.T.W. as priority.
- Proper irrigation at right time(s)

Soil: For enhancement of productivity the right crop combination is necessary. To bring about right crop combination the farmer should be aware of the properties of the soil of his farmland.

- For this regular soil testing is necessary.
- The present modus of collecting soil sample needs to change by the introduction of mobile laboratories. Initially each region is to be provided with a mobile van and within next two years each block should be having a van.
- Suitable doses of lime should be used in the slightly acidic soil of Tal region and Habibpur and Old Malda

blocks for better plant growth and higher productivity.

Fertiliser and Pesticide

- The farmer should be educated regarding the right composition of NPK for individual crops.
- It should be demonstrated to the farmers.
- The number of fertiliser and pesticide outlets in the district needs to be enhanced. The concentration of such outlets in the towns is a hindrance.
- Effective monitoring of distribution of mini kit containing fertiliser and pesticide is required as these are being resold in the open market.
- Agricultural Directorate needs to monitor the effective price charged by the fertiliser and pesticide outlet and also the quality of the product being sold.
- The blocks where the organic content (OC) level are low serious attention must be paid in improving the organic matter content of soil.
- Attention needs to be paid to the management of phosphorous, as the average Phosphorous content in the district is poor. Since the farmers are using mainly Urea and DAP, this is possible.
- Management of potash should be given priority in low potash region.
- Addition of balanced doses of fertliser, introduction of micronutrient specially *Zn* (Zinc) in the fertiliser schedule.
- Depending on the nutrient content of the soil the fertiliser should be used scientifically.

Seed:

- Reduction of seed rate in nursery from 30 kg per acre to 10 kg per acre in order to get good healthy seedlings.
- ***Improved seed supply:*** As farmers of these areas are

used to use their own farm produce as seeds for both paddy and wheat year after year, the viability of these seed are very poor, which has direct negative impact on the yield. Good quality seed materials of different crops need to be arranged from IARI and should be provided to farmers on cost-to-cost basis. This approach is expected to contribute a lot in increasing the productivity of crops.

- *Seed Grower's Co-operative:* The system of arranging of seeds from outside may not continue for long. Hence inbuilt mechanism is to be developed for producing good quality seeds in the district itself. Seed Grower Co-operative needs to be formed whose members need to be trained at IARI, on seed production technology.

Agricultural Credit: Mechanisation of agriculture, usage of HYV seeds, fertiliser and pesticide is capital intensive. Agricultural credit can play a major role in enhancing the productivity by enabling the availability of these ingredients. For this

- The measures taken by Agricultural Rural development Bank to provide agricultural inputs in kind and thereby curb the misuse of loan amount is in the right direction
- Documentation required for availing the loan need to simplified
- Monitoring the loan disbursement process is to be implemented in the stricter sense, as corruptions are prevalent.

Revolving Fund: To have sustainability in the system without assistance from outside, a revolving fund concept has to be introduced. Neighbouring villages should form groups and develop this fund. Initially for three years input material cost is to be funded by the state. These input materials need to be sold to farmers on cost-to-cost basis and with the money on realisation from farmers, revolving fund is to be created. The farmers will use this revolving fund in revolving manner for variety of developmental needs including purchase of input materials from outside as and when required without further assistance from the state.

Storage Structure: Low cost seed storage structure needs to be built in the villages. *'Kothar'* built with unbaked brick with polythene lining as designed be IARI, Pusa is suggested. This structure saves the stored grains from insects and environmental hazards. Farmers need to be given training on construction of such *'kothars'*.

Institutional Training: Periodical trainings need to be given to farmers on different traits at different institutes. The traits need to be vegetable cultivation technology, maintenance of agro-machinery, seed production technology etc.

Educational Tour of Progressive Farmers: In order to provide an exposure to farmers on improved crop cultivation and farm management practices, progressive farmers in batches are to be sent on educational tour to visit IARI, Agricultural universities etc.

Women Empowerment Activity: An initiative needs to be undertaken towards empowering rural women. Under this programme, two lady workers from each village can be trained on formation of Self Help Group (SHG). These SHGs may take up different entreprenuership development activity themselves. They can be advised to take up agriculture related activities like compost making, raising of seedlings, etc.

Bibliography

1. Acharya, S.S., 1988, *Agricultural Production, Marketing and Price Policy in India (A Study of Pulses)*, Mittal Publication, Delhi.
2. Agricultural Census West Bengal: Operational Holdings and Operated Area, 1995-96, Land and Land Reforms Department, Government of West Bengal.
3. *Agricultural Marketing in Malda*, Government of West- Bengal 1999.
4. Ahmad, A. and Shamim, S.K., "Regional Imbalances of Agricultural Productivity: A Study of Upper Ganga-Yamuna, Doab, U.P.", *Indian Journal of Regional Science*, Vol. XXXII, No. 2, 2000, pp. 109-116.
5. Potato Crop Cutting Experiment, Evaluation Branch, West Bengal.
6. Anderson, T.W., 1958, *An Introduction to Multivariate Statistical Analysis of Multiple Series*, John Wiley and Sons, London.
7. Anderson, T.W., 1963, The Use of Factor Analysis in the Statistical Analysis of Multiple Time Series, *Psychometrika*.
8. Arora, K.C., 1976, *Development Agricultural and Allied Sectors: An Irrigated Area Approach*, S. Chand and Co. Private Ltd.
9. Bagchi, K.K., 2003, *Land Tenures and Agricultural Development*, Abhijeet Publications, Delhi.
10. Bansil,P.C., 1984, *Agricultural Statistics in India*, Oxford IBH Publishing Co.
11. Basavraja, H. and Dabali, S.D., "Land Use Dynamics in India-An Agricultural Perspective", *Agricultural Situation in India*, July-1999, pp. 199-201.

12. Bastine, C.L. and Palanisami, K., "An Analysis of Growth Trends of Principal Crops in Kerala", *Agricultural Situation in India,* March-1994, pp. 885-891.

13. Basu, E., (ed.) 1981, *Agrarian Question,* Oxford University Press, Delhi.

14. Bhakulabharnam, Vamsi, "Agricultural Growth and Irrigation in Telangana-A Review of Evidence", *Economic and Political Weekly,* Volume XXXIX, No. 13, March 27, 2004, pp-1424-1426.

15. Bhalla and Singh, "Recent Development in Indian Agriculture: A State Level Analysis", *Economic and Political Weekly,* March 29, 1997, pp. A.8-A.12.

16. Bhalla, G.S. and Alagh, Y.K., 1979, *Performance of Indian Agriculture: A District Wise Study,* Sterling Publishers, New Delhi.

17. Bhalla, G. S. and Singh, G., 2001, *Indian Agricultural-Four Decades of Development,* Sage Publication, New Delhi.

18. Bhalla, G. S. and Tyagi, D.S., 1989, Patterns in Indian Agricultural Development – A District Level Study, Institute for Studies in Indian Agricultural Development, New Delhi.

19. Bhatia, M.S., "Rural Infrastructure And Growth in Agriculture", *Economic and Political Weekly,* March 27, 1999, pp 43-48.

20. Bhatt, S.C. 1998: *Encyclopedic District Gazetteers of India,* Gyan Publishing House, New Delhi.

21. Borthakur, S. and Bhattacharyya, B.K., "Trend Analysis of Area, Production and Productivity of Rice in Assam: 1951-1993", *Agricultural Situation in India,* July-1999, pp. 203-205.

22. Boyce, J.K., 1987, *Agrarian Impasses in Bengal: Agricultural Growth in Bangladesh and West-Bengal 1949-1980,* Oxford University Press.

23. Chand M. And Puri, V.K., 1983: *Regional Planning in India,* Allied Publishers Limited, New Delhi.

24. Chandrashekaran, M. and Krishnamoorthy, S., "A Study Pattern of Growth of Fertoiliser Use in Tamilnadu-A Spatial Temporal Analysis", *Agricultural Situation in India,* February-1999, pp. 665-670.

25. Chang, J.H., 1968, *Climate and Agriculture: An Ecological Survey,* Aldine Publishing Company, Chicago.

26. Chisolem, M., 1962, *Rural Settlement and Land Use: An Essay in Location,* London.

27. Chorley, R.J. and Hagget, P., 1967: *Models in Geography*, Methuen, London
28. Cooper, M. R., G. T. Barton, and A. P. Brodell. "Progress of Farm Mechanization." USDA Misc. Publ. 630, 1947.
29. Crop Loss: Due to Flood-Malda, 1998-1999, Principal Agricultural Office, Malda, West Bengal.
30. Dasgupta, R., 1951, *Indian Agricultural Economy an Analysis*, Concept Publishing Company, New Delhi.
31. Dhawan, B.D., 1993, *Trends and New Tendencies in Indian Irrigated Agriculture*, Commonwealth Publishers, New Delhi.
32. Dixit, R.S., 1988, *Spatial Organisation of Market Centres*, Pointer Publisher, Jaipur.
33. Dixit,R.S., "Analysis of Spatial Distribution of Regulated Agricultural Markets, *Geographical Review of India*." Vol. 63, No. 2, June-2001, pp. 141-152.
34. Eneritt, B.S., 1974, *Cluster Analysis for Application*, Academic Presss, New York.
35. Fabricant, S. "Basic Facts on Productivity Change." National Bureau of Economic Research, Occasional Paper No. 63, 1959.
36. Gangwar, B., "Technological Advances for Increasing Crop Productivity in Diara Areas", *Agricultural Situation in India*, January-1999, pp. 615-622.
37. Goswami, S.N and Hazarika, U.K and Sharma U.C, "Regional Imbalances in Agricultural Production and Productivity in in North- East India", *Agricultural Situation in India*, December 1997, pp. 585-590.
38. Goswami, S.N., Chatterji, S., Singh, U.K. and Hala,O., "Crop Concentration and Divercification in India- A spatio Temporal Analysis", *Geographical Review of India*,Vol.66, No. 1,March 2004, pp. 50-63.
39. Government of West Bengal, "Agricultural Scenario, Malda", 1998.
40. Grigg, D.B., 1974, *The Agricultural System of the World- An Evolutionary Approach*, Cambridge University Press.
41. Griliches, Z. "The Sources of Measured Productivity Growth, U.S. Agriculture, 1940-60," *J. Polit. Econ*. 71 (1963):331-46.
42. Gulati, S.C., "District Level Development Indices: A Factor Analytical Approach", *Indian Journal of Regional Science*, 1990 Vol. 28, No. 1, pp. 57-64.

43. Haggett, P., 1965, *Locational Analysis in Human Geography.*
44. Hansra, B.S. and Perumal, G., 2001, *Modernizing Indian Agriculture in 21st Century, Challenges, Opportunities and Strategies,* Concept Publishing Company, New Delhi.
45. Harman, H.H., 1967, *Modern Factor Analysis,* The University of Chicago Press,Chicago.
46. Harvey, D., 1966, Theoretical Concept and Analysis in Geography, *Annals of The Association of American Geographers.*
47. Hill, R.D., 1982: *Agriculture in the Malaysian Region,* Akademiai Kiado, Budapest.
48. Howard, N., Barnem, and Squire, L.. 1979, *A Model of An Agricultural House Hold and Evidence,* The Johns Hopkins University Press, Baltimore and London.
49. Hunter, G., 1970, *The Administration of Agricultural Development Lessons From India,* Oxford University Press.
50. Hurakadli, S.M. and Patil,S.R., "Regional Imbalances in The Level of Food Productivity in Karnataka", *Indian Journal of Regional Science,* Volume. XXXI, No. 1, 1999, pp-123-130.
51. Husain Majid, 1979: *Agricultural Geography,* Inter India Publication New- Delhi
52. Hussain, Majid, 1996: *Systamatic Agricultural Geography,* Rawat Publication Jaipur And New Delhi.
53. Jairath, M.S., "Agricultural Marketing Infrastructure in Arid Market", *Agricultural Situation in India,* June-2000, pp-127-136.
54. Jalan, M., 1987, *Marketing of Agricultural Inputs,* Delhi.
55. Jensen, R.G., 1967, *The Soviet Concept of Agricultural Rationalization and its Development,* Karch.
56. Jones, C.L. and Darkenwald, G.G., 1966, *Economic Geography,* New-York, Macmillan.
57. Jorgenson, D. W., and Z. Griliches. "Divisia Index Numbers and Productivity Measurement." *Rev. Income et Wealth* 17 (1971):227-29.
58. Khusro, A.M. 1968: *Reading in Agricultural Development,* Allied Publishers, Bombay, Calcutta, New Delhi, Madras, New York, London.
59. Kishore, Avinash., "Understanding Agrarian Impasse in Bihar", Volume-XXXIX, No-27, July 31, 2004, pp. 3484-3491.
60. Kumar, S., Asrey, R. and Singh, R., "Fertigation: Need of Modern Agriculture", *Yojana,* July-2000, pp-31-32 & 37-39.

61. Leonard, M.C., Oliver and Byod, 1967, *A World Geography of Irrigation*, Edinburg.
62. Leslie, S. 1972, *Russian Agriculture- A Geographic Survey*, G. Bell & Sons Ltd. London.
63. Lokhande, T.N. and Powar, C.T., "Comparative Analysis of Service Areas of Market Centres in Kolahapur District ,Maharashtra", *Geographical Review of India*,Vol-66, No-1, March 2004, pp. 40-50.
64. Loomis, R. A., and G. T. Barton. "Productivity of Agriculture, United States, 1870-1958", USDA Tech. Bull. No. 1238, 1961.
65. Lumbourn G.E. 1918: *Bengal District Gazetteer*, Malda.
66. Malda District Annual Plan, 1998-99, 1999-2000, 2000-2001 Principal Agricultural Office, Malda, West Bengal.
67. *Malda District Census Hand Book 1971, 1981.*
68. *Malda District Gazetteer, Carter, 1925-1938.*
69. *Malda District Statistical Hand Book, 1994-2001*, Malda, Bureau of Applied Economics and Statistics, Government of West Bengal.
70. Mandal, G.C., 1989, *Technology, Growth and Welfare in Indian Agriculture*, Agricole Publishing Academy, New Delhi.
71. Mishra, Prativa, 1984: *Soil Productivity and Crop Potentials*, Concept Publishing Company, New Delhi.
72. Mishra, R.P, Sunadaram, K.V. and Rao, V.S.S.S. Prakash, 1947: *Regional Development Planning in India*, Vikash Publishing House Pvt. Limited. New Delhi, Bombay, Bangalore, Kanpur.
73. Mohammad, Noor, 1981: *Perspective in Agricultural Geography- Regional Dimension in Agriculture*, Volume-4, Concept Publishing Company, New Delhi.
74. Morgan, W.B. and Munton, R.J.C., 1971, *Agricultural Geography*, Methuen & Co.Ltd, Great Britain (London).
75. Munir, A., Khan, F. and Ahmad, Q., "Agricultural Productivity in Azamgarh District, Uttar Pradesh", *Geographical Review of India*, Vol. 51, No. 1, 1995, pp. 78-89.
76. Murty, C.S., "Large Farmers in Lease Market- Are Marginal Farmers Affected?", *Economic and Political Weekly*, Volume XXXIX, No. 29, July 17, 2004, pp. 3270-3279.
77. Naidu, M.R., Swamy, K.R. and Rao, T.K.V.V.M., "Trends in Area, Production and Productivity of Major Crops in North Coastal District of Andhra Pradesh", *Agricultural Situation in India*, November 1994, pp. 571-574.

78. Narasaiah, L. and Suresh, K., 1999, *Agricultural Production,* Discovery Publishing House, New Delhi.

79. Phule, S. and Bagade,A., "A Geographical Study of Land use Changes in Maharashtra Region, Maharashtra." *Geographical Review of India,* Vol. 41, No. 2, December 2003, pp. 41-47.

80. Prasad, Y.E. and Rao, M.M. and Reddy, V.N. "Analysis for growth and causes for yield disparities in Rice Karimnagar District of Andhrapradesh", *Agricultural Situation in India,* May 1996, pp. 69-72.

81. Prasad, A.S., 1985, *Agricultural Marketing in India,* Mittal Publication, Delhi.

82. Pretty, J.N., 1995, *Regenerating Agriculture,* Vikas Publishing House Pvt. Ltd.

83. Radha, Y. and Prasad, Y. E., "Variability and Instability Analysis of Area, Production and Productivity of Rice and Maize in Northern Telangana Zone of Andhra Pradesh", *Agricultural Situation in India,* January-1999, pp. 623-626.

84. Randhawa, M.S., 1974, *Green Revolution: A Case Study of Punjab,* Vikash Publishing House Pvt. Ltd., Delhi.

85. Robinson, H., Bamford C.G., 1978: *Geography of Transport,* Macdonald and Evans, Plymouth.

86. Sarker, P.C. 1995, Regional Disparities in India issues and Measurement, (Unpublished Thesis) Mumbai University.

87. Sengupta, J.C. 1969: *West Bengal District Gazetteers,* Malda.

88. Sharma,S.K., "Agricultural Innovation and Their Impact on Agricultural Productivity in Madhya Pradesh." *Geographical Review of India,* Vol. 41, No. 2, December-2003, pp. 49-64.

89. Sigemochi, H., 1978, The Structure of Disparity in Developing Agriculture, A Case Study of Pakistan Punjab, Institute of Developing Economics, Tokyo.

90. Singh Jasbir And Dhillion S.S, 1984: *Agricultural Geography,* Tata McGraw Hill Publishing Company Limited, New Delhi.

91. Singh, G.B., 1979, *Transformation of Agriculture: A Case study of Punjab,* Vishal Publication, Delhi.

92. Singh, J., 1976: *An Agricultural Geography of Hariana,* Vishal Publication, Haryana.

93. Singh, P. and Singh A., "An Analysis of Factors Responsible for Imbalances in Agricultural Development: A Comparative

Study of Punjab and Bihar", *Agricultural Situation in India,* December-1999, pp-527-533.

94. Singh, P. and Singh, I., "Ground Water Depletion in Haryana and Punjab: A Threat to sustainability in Agriculture", *Agricultural Situation in India,* October-1996, pp. 485-489.

95. Singh, R. and Maithlesh, K., "Tractor Use in Agriculture-A Study in Agra Division of Uttar Pradesh", *Agricultural Situation in India,* February-2000, pp. 687-697.

96. Singh, S.P. and Baleka, J.B., " Factors Affecting Fertiliser Consumption in The Western Maharashtra", *Agricultural Situation in India,* September-1999, pp. 361-367.

97. Suhag, K.S., Grover, R.K. and Goyal S.K., "A Study on Regional Varitions in Hariana Agriculture", *Agricultural Situation in India,* June-1999, pp. 121-128.

98. Taufique, M., Ahamed, M. and Munir, A., "Spatial Analysis of Agricultural Productivity in Western Uttarpradesh", Vol. 63, No. 2, June-2001, pp. 129-140.

99. U.S. Department of Agriculture. "Agricultural Production and Efficiency." Major Statistical Series of the USDA, vol. 2, *Agr. Handb.* No. 365, 1970.

100. Vaidyanathan, A. and Sivasubramaniyan, K., "Efficiency of Water Use in Agriculture", *Economic and Political Weekly,* Volume XXXIX, No. 27, July 3, 2004, pp. 2989-2996.

101. Vyas, V.S., "Diversification in Agriculture: Concept Rationale and Approaches", *Indian Journal of Agricultural Economics,* Vol. 51, No. 4, Oct.-Dec., 1996, pp. 636-643.

102. White, G.F., 1960, *The Changing Role of Water in Arid Land,* Tuscon.

103. William, J. C., "Cropping Pattern in the Canadian Prairies: Thirty Years of Change", Vol. 168, Part-II, 2002, pp. 97-115.

■■■■